Car Sharks and Closers

GARY SWANSON

DEDICATION

This book is dedicated to my wife, Wendy, who gave me the moral
support to hang in there during all the ups and downs of striving to be the
absolute best.

Other books by the author:

Close It Or Lose It
The Art Of The Car Deal
Hire-Education For Job Seekers
Hiking Sasquatch Country

CONTENTS

PREFACE

I wrote this book to fill a huge void. There are libraries full of books on selling theories; polite and pretty words that flow so beautifully from others but failed to bounce to the front of my memory when needed. There were no specific books on how to *close* car deals! Now there is!

What makes me the expert? I'm glad you asked. My bona fides; I have personally closed over seventeen thousand car sales! Add to that, probably five thousand that got away, and that adds up to a lot of experience to draw from. Couple that with over 30 years of sixty to eighty hour work weeks, and when you invest this much time and effort in a career as difficult as this one can be, you get damned good! I will freely admit to being damned good!

My time when not actually involved in closing a sale was spent on my feet and motivating salespeople (some of my people saw it as riding their asses); I saw it like herding cats, and making sure to force my people to be successful so they were rewarded for the hard work.

I tell it as I've lived it, and despite your concept of today's car business, don't kid yourself; the car business has not evolved any more than the crocodile. They still both exist in their ancient forms and are just as scary as ever!

Our business has certainly been tamed from what it once was, but this manuscript contains all of the techniques, both good and bad, because to leave out the rough and dishonest parts would be like denying that our mentors ever existed. After all, we car people didn't just inherit our reputation, we earned it!

INTRODUCTION

This book is for the 20 percent of salespeople and managers who earn 80 percent of all the money! If you are not in that prestigious top 20 percent, then I'll get you there! If you already feel that you're on the top rung of the ladder then hang on, because I'm adding another extension on it. No brag, just fact! Consider this as your textbook to earn a master's degree in closing car deals!

This training is not some researcher's concept of the ideal world; it is the hard and cold real world! I do not mince words, nor do I pull punches. The language used is that as spoken in the trenches.

The beginning section is a guide for someone to decide if they should even attempt this business, and a primer for selecting your first car job. I take the new salesperson through the entire process of selecting the right dealership (disregarding whether or not they have any job openings), and the actual steps to pick the store you want to work at. Then I instruct the applicant on how to obtain an interview, the right questions to ask, and correct answers to use during this phase; including physical and mental preparation as well as personal appearance and proper attire.

The beginner's instruction continues with what the new person should be prepared for, such as the hazing and mind games that are all a part of the initiation and proper break-in for the F.N.G. (Fine New Guy?). The newbie is guided through the roadblocks and trials that sometimes take months and even years to learn. This is a welcome shortcut that explains the proper way to conduct oneself, the avoidance of the pitfalls, the psychological tactics others may test you with, and how to comfortably handle yourself.

The majority of this book is devoted to making the professional closer into a *master closer*. The closes herein are not theoretical! They contain the exact verbiage that I have found works best, and each close in accompanied by the proper body language to use in its' implementation. There are millions of dollars' worth of actual closing scenarios, along with the proper time and place to use each particular one!

The professional salesperson and closer are well aware of the value of just one new idea used over a lifetime of selling! I offer you a book-full with my congratulations on your having the desire to be better.

I wrote this manual because the automobile industry has never put this information in writing. Up until now, it has always been a slow and tortuous learning by success and failure, and trial and error. The closing gurus at the top have always jealously guarded the *secrets of the close*. This hand me down training philosophy forces a salesperson to endure a lengthy and arduous rite of passage.

To further compound the problem is the fact that many closers do not keep their salesperson with them during the negotiating process, thus the salesperson doesn't receive any closing skills, and it keeps their proficiency in selling to a minimum. Many closers purposely do not want their salespeople to be with them — for different reasons; some are scared to look weak or by making errors in front of their subordinates, and many just want to keep a good producer selling cars for them, because they don't want to lose a good salesperson due to a promotion. Therefore, in these situations, the closer meets the buyer and sends the salesperson back on the floor. In these cases, if a good closer leaves for a better opportunity there is a void, because there may be no one trained to take their place! I instruct the proper procedures, in great detail, and believe strongly in training ever salesperson in every way possible.

I was fortunate to begin my career as a closer and was trained by one of the best, so I had a head start that saved me years; then I added 30 years of learning and experimentation to it! What I teach here works, and it works exceptionally well!

I would like to caution the reader on the use of this book — a good close used at the wrong time can ruin the entire sale, and for this reason, a general knowledge of the various techniques is really helpful to the salesperson, but they should not attempt the majority of them if a closer will be doing the negotiations. Let the closer do it!

Closers should not attempt some of these techniques unless they are very experienced and fast on their feet, because if they are not professionally delivered, they can backfire. I would suggest some role-play with your sales manager before you actually attempt to use them with a buyer. Your manager can be a sounding board for your sincerity and timing.

The closes herein are some of my favorites, and I know you must put them into your own words, but I implore you to be careful, as they work best exactly the way I have written them. Believe me when I say this, because I have experimented with each one of them *thousands* of times, and if the wording sounds too plain or unsophisticated, that's because I have found that it works best from the buyer's perception. *Be Smart, Act Dumb!*

This manual is not just theories or suggestions. I wrote it to do only one thing — To teach salespeople, closers, and sales managers how to sell! Period!

1 WHAT TYPE OF PERSON SUCCEEDS IN THE CAR BUSINESS?

This is important to anyone interested in the profession to analyze whether or not it is a good fit. The retail automobile business is not for everybody! To succeed in this type of selling, one must be prepared for the most intensive type of selling that ever existed, but yet what I feel is the easiest way to make a living in the sales business.

Let me qualify that: I have sold door to door, and had the door slammed in my face in the miserably cold Minnesota winter. I've sold insurance, I've sold people (as an employment counselor), and I have sold and associated with salespeople in all types of selling tangibles and intangibles. Nothing compares with selling automobiles!

The car business is by far the easiest of all selling! When I said the car business is the most intensive, I need to qualify that statement by adding; if you wish to succeed! By success, I mean to be in the *top 20 percent*. I always figured I could tie a note around a German shepherd's neck, and send it out on the lot and it would sell cars for me. So basically, it's almost too easy to get a job selling cars. It's almost, if you can fog a mirror, you're in! Why do you suppose that is? It's because there is such a high turnover in the car business, generally due to poor interviewing procedures and terribly inadequate training. It's like, "Go out there and see how you do, and if you survive your first month, I may invest some time training you." Part of the reason for this analogy is that we never know how the individual will react once they see the reality, therefore many managers want a newbie to get their feet wet before investing time in them!

As I already said; the car business is not for everybody. Sure, you can sell cars, and make somewhat of a living, but unless you have the inner strength that I am going to explain; don't bother. Go get a clerical job in a department store where you won't experience the giant ups and downs of car sales.

So, on one hand I say it's an easy and rewarding business and then I warn you against it. What gives? Well, by easy, I mean where else can you just sit there and have customers come to you? They come with restrained but obvious excitement! No other product creates such positive feelings and desires in people as a new car! You will be selling the most important and biggest expense item that the American people ever buy. You will soon realize that the average consumer spends more money on cars in their lifetime, and gets less value out of it than from buying a home.

This will be a very rewarding career if you can survive! At the onset, I warned that it won't be easy. It's not! Buying a car is a huge expenditure for people, and they have a lot riding on it, so even though they come to you with open arms, they can make you hate them! The car buyer won't trust you, they don't respect you, they despise what you represent, and they will put you through untold abuse and torture! So, you ask; "Why would I even want to get into such a business?" Because, for all they will put you through, if you can handle it; these people will pay very highly for the privilege of torturing you!

Yes, you have to study like crazy, put up with what most people would consider abuse; from customers, your bosses, and fellow salespeople, and it seems sometimes that even the weather hates you.

The bottom line though, is that if you learn this business, and learn it well, you will most likely earn more money than 80% of all of your customers! Funny thing about this crazy business; the better you get, the more money you will make, and the less abuse you will take, and the easier it gets!

Eventually, you will never even be able to imagine any other profession where you could earn so much money with no formal education required, and no investment other than your time!

Now, let's get back to the not for everybody statement. This job will be demanding – the car business demands a total commitment, like anything worthwhile! Kiss your weekend's goodbye, as well as set schedules of any kind for the most part.

The car business must cater to the buyer, and since most buyers work normal hours, *we* must be here when it is convenient to *them!* Your paychecks will vary a lot, especially in the beginning. Naturally, you will have minimum wage as your guarantee, but don't count on that lasting long, because neither you, nor your employer are going to be satisfied with that for any length of time.

If you feel that you are going to be different than the kind of people that seem to be the norm in the car business, and you will be a kinder and gentler person; get it out of your system! Forget your creative notions until you are in the top 20%. Then, you can work on creating your own persona. Only after you have proven to your employer and to yourself that you can do the job can you afford to deviate dramatically.

I've met a lot of new salespeople who entered the business despite *their* hatred of the process. They came into the business declaring early on that they would be different! They never lasted long! Ever!

If you think that the car business is a dirty business, and you disrespect it going in, and plan to start out being different, please just find something else to do for a living. You ask; "Why can't I be different? I don't like the way the car business works, and I won't feel respected!" To begin with, if you are concerned with the reputation that car people have, *you* won't change it. Sure, you can be different *after* you first learn to do everything exactly like you will be taught!

The public perception of your new profession is lower than whale crap, just like politicians, so accept it and analyze why — Because the public will never have a great deal of respect for anyone who can have such an effect on their lives; they have to *negotiate* with *you* in order to buy something they really want. They will always feel they paid too much, and you won't convince them otherwise. Therefore, accept how you are looked on and give them a good buying experience, and make them happy they bought from you instead of some poor slob who couldn't care less about them! That way the buyer goes home happy, and you go happily to the bank. They will also come back to you for their next car if you just stay in touch! People hate meeting new salespeople!

I've worked for some pretty questionable operators over the years, but I've always maintained my integrity and never had to be ashamed of my profession. I think you get the impression now; so, I'm advising you to go with the flow, and learn everything you are taught, and learn it well. One more word of caution I would have for anyone considering this business: if you are the shy, retiring type, or have fear of being outgoing or aggressive, you either need to just figure on working to overcome it or you will fail! Yes, you *can* change your personality. When you go to the airport, you get on board all the way! If you go into the car business, get on board, or stay away!

I have known men and women both who changed so much since the day they got into the business, that six months later, you'd never know it was the same person. The self-confidence they exuded after only a few months was awesome!

If you are prepared to earn above–average wages, and devote the time to become a professional, then let's go for it!

2 PRELIMINARY STEPS IN PREPARING FOR A SALES CAREER

I f you're still reading this book it means you are probably in that 20 percent; the *great* 20 percent of salespeople who earn 80 percent of all the money — Congratulations! Now, let's quit worrying as to whether or not you will succeed. You will!

At this point, I want you to form a mindset that you *will* be successful, and *never* question yourself again. I am a complete believer in positive thinking, and I would like you to look back on ancient history for a moment: Early in my career, I read a story of the great Carthaginian general Hannibal Borca. They said that after unloading his army, elephants, and supplies, and setting off to cross the Alps in his journey to destroy Rome, that his men turned and saw their ships afire! Hannibal had ordered them burned, so that there could be, no more talk of defeat, or of retreat. The only options were to win or die. I never researched this story further, because to me it paints the perfect picture of my personal work ethic; whenever I began a new job, I thought of Hannibal, and I would not allow myself to even let the thought of not succeeding to even enter my mind!

Because this book is written for your success, I will categorically state here that 90 percent of your success will be due to a positive mental attitude!

Another example that I had early in my career and prior to my ever getting into the car business that I never forgot, and urge you to save deep in your memory, because it will be more important than any amount of knowledge you can imagine; I was managing a credit life insurance department for a Portland, Oregon based insurance company. One of our larger accounts had indicated that they had been offered a higher commission on the policies they sold by one of our competitors, and unless we could match the offer, this longtime account was canceling! I reported this to our vice president, and this marvelous old gentleman said, "I'm going out there with you, let me know when the appointment is!" I scheduled the appointment with the partners, and we jumped in my VP's car and headed out. As he was driving, I stated aloud, "I sure hope we can keep this account, they are really important to us!"

In a moment, my boss had pulled the car over to the curb, threw it into park, and turned to face me and delivered a message that changed my future; he said, "Gary, this is a very important account, and we cannot afford any negative thinking! If you have negative thoughts, either keep them to yourself, or get out and take a cab back to the office!" He went on to say, "I *must* keep a positive mental attitude, and I cannot allow negative thoughts to *even enter* my mind!" Well, we arrived for the appointment, shook hands all around, and settled in the lavish office of the president.

The next lesson I learned just blew me away! Instead of starting the conversation in a plea to stay with us, my VP leaned back in the plush leather chair, and looking directly at the president, he said, "I want you to call your wife and tell her you're having guests for dinner." The president leaned forward and asked, "What do you mean?" My boss answered, "Because we came here to keep your business, and until you agree to stay with us, were staying in your guest bedrooms, and living with you!" Two hours later we returned to our office with a renewal contract in hand, and at the exact same percentage we had always paid!

That day I learned why this man was still vice president at an age way past retirement. This happened over 40 years ago and was life – changing for me! Thank you Dean!

I hope there is a lesson for *you* here; if you think you *may* fail, you *will!* You must develop the attitude that when it comes to your sales career, you *cannot* fail. Sure, you'll have small failures, but we all fail more times than we succeed when we start in a new position, but the successes will soon outnumber the failures. What your goal should always be is to *not think* failure. *If you keep your thinking from stinking, and keep your mind out of your behind, you will succeed!*

Once you develop this positive attitude, your entire bearing will change. Act as though you cannot even imagine failure, and you will become a different person.

In the car business, you may be called cocky, or smartass, and all kinds of superlatives, but when people watch you perform, they will respect you. There's nothing like walking into a large assembly room, and pausing to look around, when people start coming up to you and asking if you're the speaker? People can sense a successful person, and they can smell a failure. Your entire bearing will be one that projects success.

Okay, so now you ask; "You suggest I develop a positive attitude, but how do I succeed in the car business with just a great attitude?" You can't! But it's 50 percent of your sales success. The remaining 50 percent is half product knowledge and half practice. You've likely heard what happens when you assume? You make an *ASS* out of *U*, and *ME*. So never ASSUME!

I however, have made the assumption that the reader already is a cut above the rest of the crowd, or you wouldn't be reading this book. Trying to make an advanced judgment as to who will succeed, and who will make it in this industry comes down to a SWAG (**s**cientific **w**ild **a**ssed **g**uess) estimate. I have seen people succeed where I had reservations against even hiring them in the first place. Conversely, I have seen some of the most positive appearing people, fail miserably.

This brings back memories of a salesman referred to me by a call from another sales manager; he said his personal friend was looking to change to a different franchise from his and asked if I'd give him a shot. Of course, I agreed, as he came with a great recommendation! When this man showed up, I was immediately impressed! He was well-dressed, well spoken, and so positive, I thought I'd hit a home run!

Every day for the next three weeks, when he arrived promptly for his shift, I had the same greeting! He would come into the showroom with the announcement, "Today's the day, this is the place, and I'm the man!" For those three weeks, he proceeded to sit on his ass and never sold a car! But he was such a nice guy, even when I terminated his employment, that I also told him to use me for reference. This was the most glaring reminder that the positive attitude I say is mandatory; but that it must be accompanied by the ability and effort to do the job!

There are many wonderful trainers out there who make millions of dollars specifically teaching the art of selling automobiles. I highly recommend every bit of this type of training. They give you the scenarios, the words to use in each circumstance, and are so enjoyable to watch on videos, that I'm sure you can get a lot out of this type of training.

Over the years, I have sent hundreds of salespeople to these courses and appearances on everything from positive thinking, to body language, to psychology classes. What I got back out of all this was the same people I sent, but with a somewhat better all-around persona. They came back pumped, but soon after, they settled back down to themselves, only a little more rounded. People generally do better in grasping a new idea and then just using their own delivery and their own wording.

Early in my sales career, I remember buying several books on body language. I studied hard, and then after a while, the signals began to get confusing. I had trouble remembering what it meant after a trial close if the customer looked up and to the right, or if down and to the left, they were negative, or did a furled brow mean curiosity, or refusal, or on and on until I gave it up!

I learned body language through experience and acquired a sense of how to act and react just from a gut level! Once I gave up trying to analyze every action and reaction from the customer and interpret their every gesture and convert that to what my response should be and drive myself totally nuts — I found that we learn to automatically respond. Trying to analyze the situation when you're in the middle of negotiations is foolish and stilted. You just have to learn to feel the force, and your natural ability will take it from there! The human mind will implant memories of body language responses automatically, and we act more natural when staying completely relaxed and open.

Fortunately, in our business, study in actual selling situations can come from practice scenarios, but since we are in a people business, we really learn better by repeatedly trying. We fail, we succeed, and since you will have a track to run on, you will be guided to success, and even as a new trainee, you will sell cars! This track is simple for both us and the customer. The KISS (keep it simple stupid) formula is best for all of us.

To close this chapter, let me again say that *all* study about the world of selling will be beneficial. For the car business however, don't try to do too much advanced study. I qualify this by explanation that your new employer will tell you what they want you to study. You will have plenty of work to do, and I recommend that any other studies you do on your own all be done *after* your assignments.

Whenever I hire a new person, I want things done *my* way, and until this is accomplished, a new person will have all they can do to keep up. The training I am going to get into is unlike what others teach, and will delve into *advanced* closing techniques. My methods *are not basic* selling strategies; your dealer or sales manager will do that training.

Let the dealer work on the *basics*, like building the car. This book is like *turbocharging* the engine to maximize your performance!

3 HOW TO SELECT YOUR EMPLOYER

A lot of people get into the automobile business because they have a *friend in the business*. Others just decide to give it a try to see if they might like it. I can't think of how many applicants used to tell me in response to my; "Why do you want to sell cars" question, with; "I love cars, and I love people." These are not good answers to me, and I seldom hire these people. You know what makes me want to hire you? Your answer of, "I want to let make lots of money!" will get you a lot further!

The people we sell to like cars. I like money, and I want to hire people who like money. It stands to reason if you want lots of money, you will make me lots of money! Shake hands, you're hired!

I certainly hope that no one will get into this business to be around cars. I wouldn't give two hoots in hell about being around cars. If one wants that, I suggest a career in auto mechanics. The love of cars is what makes your customers spend way too much money on their ego satisfying toys.

Now let's look at where to begin your career. All too often, when one decides to try the car business, they think that a slow entry into the field may be the best. They pick a small, laid-back dealership with a quiet appearance. Their thinking being, to start out slow, and once they have learned, they can move to a larger, higher-volume store.

The problem with this thinking is that most of these people become quickly disillusioned with the car business. They may receive little training, and with no real chance to earn enough money to make the business appealing, some very good potential is lost forever. Why? Because the manager of the laid-back, slow moving dealership may have an owner who is very low-key and laid-back! In addition to that, a lot of the small stores have managers who may have very limited knowledge, poor training programs, smaller inventories, and less advertising. On the other hand, the little guy may be sharper than one may think, and actually be filled with advantages. You don't know until you actually meet, but be aware that you need to check into all possibilities and keep an open mind. Ask about training, inventory, and advantages they feel they have. The time to explore the smaller operations may be *after* you have been trained by the most aggressive dealer who will hire you!

First, let's take a look at the area or city where you live. Who are the most aggressive dealers? Where are the biggest advertisers, the nicest looking dealerships? You don't need to worry so much about the make of the vehicles they carry, but do try to stay with franchises that manufacture cars and pickups, and SUVs. Most makes such as Chevrolet, Ford, Toyota, Chrysler, Dodge, Nissan, Honda and so forth have multiple lines. Avoid single-line stores such as Lexus, BMW, Infinity or Mercedes; as when you are just starting out, you want a broad range of products that will have a broad range of appeal. Besides, in most of these type franchises, you will need a good track record to get hired, and they are not likely to even begin to teach you what I will in this book, as they hire seasoned professionals more often than not.

Since most multi-line manufacturers are pretty much the same in quality, warranty coverage, etc., most buyers will consider looking at many similar products to compare, before they make a purchase. The key to this is to pick the dealer with the most aggressive advertising, the largest inventory, and a clean and well lit building and lot. The dealership facility is not always critical *if* they sell a lot of vehicles, but you want the best you can get.

Again, don't worry a lot about making everything perfect, because it seldom is, however, put yourself in a customer's shoes. Would you feel comfortable in visiting this dealership if you were in the market to buy a car? Speaking of shopping, unless you have bad feelings about the place, that's your next step.

Drive-in, and pretend to be a possible car buyer. See how they treat you. Consider how soon you are greeted; the overall experience that you are having will give you an idea of what it's all about and if you feel like you'd like to work for this company, let's get ready to apply. Take your time; look at several stores, check newspapers, even though car dealers advertise less than ever in the print media. Go online, see if the dealer has an online presence, a working website, and gather enough information to see if you would like to work for them. *Don't* be intimidated by lots of activity, aggressive sales people running around, or if you are poorly treated by your salesperson. Get an overall impression of the business itself.

When you find a place you like, let's prepare for an interview. Don't bother to ask about job openings, because that makes little difference to you at this point. What we're going to do is prepare you enough that the dealer will make an opening for you. When one finds a place they wish to work, the saying is true that, "You never get a second chance to make a good first impression!" Your first interview may lead to another one if you have a lot of competition. If you blow it, there won't be another. If the job is important to you, then act like it! Develop the proper mental attitude. The first thing a customer sees is the *product*. That's you! The interviewer is the *customer*.

Look in the mirror. If you were buying a salesperson, would you buy you? When you were in the dealership scouting things out, were the men wearing ties? Were the women wearing dresses, slacks, or suits? You've heard the saying, "dress for success." If you're a man, and all the salesmen were wearing Hawaiian shirts, should you arrive for your interview in a Hawaiian shirt? No! Absolutely not! *They* already *have* the job! Once you are hired, assimilate however you wish, but do not mirror what you see at this point. Dress in a suit if possible; white shirt, tie and shined shoes. Sport-coats are fine, if you don't have a suit. Okay, if you don't own a sport jacket, try to borrow one. Under no conditions, ever walk in the door without a tie! When you are hired, you may never again wear dress clothes, but you *damn well better for a job interview!*

Let's look at an example on a different scale: you work for a company with a warehouse for sale, and you are meeting with the board of directors of a manufacturing firm to propose selling the warehouse to them. Would you appear before the board dressed as a warehouse employee, with your name tag on your uniform shirt? No, you would dress in a suit and tie wouldn't you?

What are you selling to the car dealer? You're selling you! So aren't you as important as some stupid building? You'd better feel you are! Remember I mentioned shined shoes? I *always* notice the applicant's shoes, and I always make certain that my salespeople have shined shoes! That goes for men and women. Shoes and belts must also match. Brown with brown, black with black! You don't wear a brown suit and black shoes. You *will* find that all car dealerships will have shoeshine materials. It's just that important! Customers are even more critical!

Women should wear a suit, dress, or dress slacks and comfortable shoes on an interview. A short skirt with four-inch heels, and a low-cut top won't get you anything but stares! What your interviewer is looking for is how you will look to their customers! Ladies, be neat, clean, and look as close to an executive as you can.

After you are hired, you will soon find out that if you're attractive, vibrant, and sexy, the male customers will like it and their wives will absolutely kill any possible chance you have of making a sale! You will quickly learn to dress down!

Now, another crucial factor in getting hired; I once made my living as an employment counselor, so I made my living selling people to companies. You can directly deposit what I tell you in your bank! I know what I'm talking about, so don't just take my advice with a grain of salt! Learn it well, because your future income will depend on it!

Look now in the mirror. When you're through blowing kisses at yourself, see yourself as others will see you. You have to be objective here, because you may feel you look great among *your* friends, but you have to be able to see yourself through the eyes of *my* friends.

If you are a twenty-something male and shaving is something that comes periodically, and your last haircut was far enough back that you can't remember the month; how will you be perceived by a 60-year-old bank president? If you are a woman who is a single mom, with tons of housework, and two children who are so demanding of your time, that you don't have the luxury of having your nails done; are they trimmed, are they clean? Does your shirt have a last-minute talcum powder dusting on it? We all need a full-length mirror, for final checks before leaving for work. Speaking of fingernails; guys, even if your hobby is working on cars, you better come to work with clean fingernails, clean clothes, and shined shoes.

Next, let's discuss hair. Hair length and facial hair have always been a taboo! This is a subject that needs to be addressed at length, because it may have an effect on your earnings. If it does, we need to examine why. I remember when I left Chicago to move West, I was a finance manager for a multimillionaire, and he asked me to find my replacement before I left. I ran the ads, and conducted the interviews. When I had my top candidates, I set appointments with the dealer so he could get involved. One candidate stood out from all of the others, and I felt he was perfect. The only problem the dealer had with him was that he had a mustache! The dealer said, "Hire him! But, tell him he must shave off the mustache, I won't hire a manager with facial hair!" I attempted to dissuade him from this requirement, because back in those days, I always would ask an applicant if they would shave the facial hair if it was necessary to be hired, and this applicant had reservations. Sure enough, neither side gave in, so I hired our second choice. Now that was in 1970, but there are large number of people in the sales business today, and many business owners in all types of professions, that still have prejudices against mustaches, beards and long hair. The reason for this is that it is a psychological *fact* that people act differently when they hide behind facial hair. When have you seen a male psychologist without a beard or moustache?

Car dealers are for the most part, more lenient these days, but this thinking all stems from the fact that it is to the dealers advantage to have all of his employees appeal to all of his customers. Look at it from his standpoint; if one out of twenty of his customers are mistrustful of the salesman with facial hair, and this salesman waits on only sixty customers in a month, he loses *three* of them, just because of the customer objecting to his looks! If the dealer earns an average profit on each customer, from sales, service, and parts and accessories of only four thousand dollars over their term of relationship, this amounts to a monthly cost to him of $12,000.00, or a potential of $144,000.00 a year in lost revenue. This maybe an exaggeration, but the numbers are not out of line! Now you can see why the Chicago dealer had this analysis etched in his subconscious!

Look at it now from your personal standpoint. Can you afford to lose *any* customers because you are unkempt, unshaven, or you smell bad? Before you start going nuts over that remark, think back to your personal experiences. Have you ever met a retail salesperson whose breath was so bad you were quickly turned off? Of course you have; we all have. From people who stink, customers shrink, and they don't get the ink (signature). Yeah, I made it up.

The sales business draws a different type of person for the most part;

more aggressive, more outgoing, and more high-strung. If the salesman you run into has just come back to work after a two-day drunk and the booze smell is still reeking through his pores, does it turn you off? Maybe there was a reason; death of a relative or a friend, celebration of a major event? Whatever the *reason* he stinks, he still *stinks*, and you do not have to be subjected to discomfort.

Is your salesperson a smoker, or just have dragon breath enough to singe your eyebrows? If the salesperson who first greets the dealer's customer is offensive, then both the salesperson and the dealer lose! You can see why this is all so important to someone making the hiring decision; whose own income will be affected by you!

Now, let's talk about hair length. This is a sensitive issue for people, as are all of the things we're discussing. So what about hair? Maybe the crowd you hang around with all have long hair. Yes, I'm addressing the male gender here. If long hair is important to you, and you like it on your shoulders, stay home. Don't even waste your time. I always figure that a person can always ask permission to let their hair grow and grow a moustache or beard *after* they have the job, and *after* they have proven themselves! Once a salesperson has the job, and is making a good income, they may find that their new look isn't all that bad! You must try to appeal to the most people you can.

The ideal example, if there is such a thing, of a look for salesmen is dark slacks, white shirt, tie and shined shoes. What you need to strive for is to be innocuous. You need to dress so as to not stand out. You are not there to have more flash than what you're selling. A peacock cannot sell a crow, but a crow can sell a peacock.

If you have a doubt as to what you should wear, stop in at a high-end clothing store. I say high-end, because these salespeople are used to dealing with professional salespeople. I'm sure the salespeople in Nordstrom or similar stores will know how you should dress for an interview. You don't have to buy from them if the prices don't fit your budget, but just remember *who* helped you when you start making the big bucks!

Again, remember I said high-end. Don't ask fashion opinions from a clerk wearing a three dollar shirt. Don't be afraid to ask and *invite* a critique of your personal appearance. It's necessary to do so with a stranger, because your friends won't be honest with you. Now, do you feel ready? Let's get to it.

4 DEVELOP THE PROPER MINDSET

When I suggest you look around your area for where you may want to work and then visit that store, is what you should do, don't worry about openings! Who wants a job that's open to everyone?

Keep in mind that when you are looking at dealerships don't be intimidated if there are salespeople standing all over the place and who greet you as soon as you get out of your car. Over-aggressive dealerships, while not seemingly friendly, could be the very best place to get the training you need. A lot of times, these large dealerships may have what seems like an overabundance of salespeople, but they also may get an overabundance of customers! As with all car stores, you need enough people on duty to cover the sudden rushes of traffic. Another thing to consider is that with all of these salespeople available, they must be making money, or they wouldn't just stand around where they were starving!

Ready? Let's go get a job! First of all, park somewhere so as to not take up a choice parking spot. Preferably park in the service parking area, and enter the showroom from the back so you can walk directly to the receptionist.

You want to ask for the new car manager, or in large stores, the sales manager. Don't ask for the used car manager, as he likely will be busy and seldom does the hiring. In larger stores where they have assistant managers (closers) or team managers (closers), you may be directed to one of them.

If the receptionist asks what you would like to see them about, just respond with, "I want to see them about a sales position." She may just hand you an application and ask you to fill it out. Go ahead and do it, and when you're through, again ask to speak with the person who does the hiring.

If the receptionist tells you someone will call, don't accept this. Anytime you are told by any employee, other than the person who actually does the hiring, that you must leave the application and, "We'll call you," just stand your ground; politely but firmly ask again to see the actual person. Aggressiveness *when polite* is respected in our business.

If you are met by a manager who informs you "there are no openings," before they even talk with you, ask more forcefully. You may say something like, "You haven't even interviewed me, how can you be certain?" Any statement like that will grab their attention. The manager may say, "You might try another dealership." Your response needs to be, "I appreciate the suggestion, but I want to work here!" You *will* get their attention. Car people love politely aggressive people.

Once, when I went into a dealership applying for a closer's job, the owner told me there were no openings, and I asked how many sales crews he had. He responded with "four," and I said, "Well then, *fire the weakest closer, and I'll take his job!* I know I can make you more money!" He did, and I did!

Car people cannot resist this kind of genuine self-confidence. Of course you won't have this bearing until you've accomplished, but the old rule of, *fake it 'til you make it* applies here. Sometimes you just have to get crazy!

I remember once before I got into the car business, I was working in a finance company and wanted to move up to a bank job. A friend told me about an opening he heard about in this large bank in their loan department. Instead of calling ahead, I drove right to the bank and entering the loan department, I asked for the vice president who had the opening. His secretary told me she was sure the job was filled, and I asked if I could see him anyway. Reluctantly she rang his desk, and upon shaking hands and taking the proffered seat, he informed me of what I already knew. His statement was, "I have a man ninety percent hired we're just waiting for his papers to clear." I proceeded to briefly discuss my background and my ability, and why I came in. Remember, no application, no resume, just conversation; and the more we talked, the more we both felt I was a perfect fit, and he said he wanted to stay in touch for the next opening. At that point, I took a big chance; I leaned over his desk and slammed my fist right in the middle of it, and said, "Mr. Childers, I want this job!" I said it loud! His pen set actually jumped in the air, and he stood up (I thought he was going to hit me), he held out his hand, and said just as loudly; "You've got it!" He said, "Anyone that aggressive is who I want, I'll find a different job for the other guy!" This happened in the prestigious loan department of a major bank! When people have a job that needs filling, they will want a person who shows an interest in having that job.

A good friend of mine went into a dealership and asked to see the owner. The secretary asked why, and he said he wanted to apply for a manager's job. Without letting him know, she instead summoned the general sales manager, and when he came up my friend asked, "Are you the owner?" The man said, "No, I'm the general sales manager, and I do the hiring." My friend replied, "You don't understand, it's your job I'm applying for." This was an uncomfortable situation and my friend should have explained to the secretary exactly why he wanted the owner, but it made for an interesting meeting. There was no opening, and he didn't get the position, but it was gutsy!

As long as you are polite, aggressiveness will be respected. Sometimes aggressiveness and rudeness are close together, especially when you are dealing with a self-important receptionist or secretary who thinks they own the place, but be tolerant and act humble no matter how you feel inside.

You must get to the person who actually makes the hiring decisions. Leaving an application is distasteful to me, but do what you have to do to get your foot in the door.

Once, I decided I wanted a job at an insurance company in a management position. I called ahead for an interview and was told there were no openings; I persisted and said, "You haven't even seen my resume!" The assistant VP was polite, but said, "Frankly, I don't care to see it because I have *no* openings!" I responded with, "Okay, then humor me — give me your mailing address so I can mail it to you." He responded with, "Okay, since you don't listen, here it is!" I sent it, and he called me a week later! I met with him and the senior vice president and was hired on the spot! It's not that I'm that good. I just feel that if I want a job, and I feel I can do it, then I know I can do it better than anyone, because I will work that hard to accomplish it! *You* need this mindset!

Coming in second for a job isn't an option! Once you have the interview, sell yourself! Make eye contact with the interviewer *at all times*. A few dos' and don'ts:

- Do *not* ask about benefits! Why, because in the sales business we are looking for confident people. Benefits signal security conscious people.
- Don't ask about hours; they *will* be long.
- Don't ask if they furnish cars for salespeople (demos). Some do, most do not. It used to be, before insurance costs became outrageous that salespeople had demos. A lot of people wanted to sell cars, because they had a nice demonstrator as a perk.

The only questions you should be asking are those questions that *the interviewer wants to hear*! That's right, you already know you want to learn the business, you already know the hours are bad, the weather demanding and the rewards are very good. What else can you ask? If you want to impress me:

- Ask me about training.
- Ask me about computer follow-up systems so you can stay in touch with customers.
- The only important question you had better ask me is, "How soon can I start?" Then, "Where do I park?" "What should I wear?" "Are there any other rules?"

What's the most important question? "HOW SOON CAN I START?" And do it with some excitement! You'd be amazed at how many people fail to ask for a job they truly want!

Once, when I was an employment counselor, after sending an applicant for his fifth interview with the same employer, I called the personnel manager at the company. I said, "Bob, I've sent this guy in five times, at your request. Are you going to hire him or not?" He said, "You know Gary, I just love this person, he's my ideal choice, and I wanted him the first time he came in, so I kept having you send him back all these times because I was looking for just one thing — The S.O.B. never once asked me for the job, and I won't have anyone working for me that doesn't want the job bad enough to ask for it! Today was his last chance! Find me someone else!"

Remember this! If you want the job, you'd damned well better ask for it. If you get a negative response or a "We'll let you know," don't accept it. Ask what you have to do to get hired. Just lean forward in your chair and call the interviewer by name; Ms., Mr. Jones, "I want this job! What do I have to do to get it?"

Should the answer be "We'll let you know," and you have no choice, take the person's card, and go immediately out, pick up a thank you card, send a quick thank you for your time note, sign it, and mail it as soon as possible.

Next, show up the next day dressed for work. Ask for the manager; reintroduce yourself by, "Hi, remember me? Gary Swanson. I just wondered if you were ready for me to start work?" *Be prepared* for them to say, "Okay, let's go ahead." The last thing you want is to get the job, and not really be ready. If they say now, shake hands and thank the person.

I most always made it difficult for new hires to get a job with me. Not out of arrogance, but because I wanted the best. To begin with, I would never interview a salesman without a tie, or a woman sloppily dressed in jeans or shorts.

A dear friend now, but new then, applied for a sales position with me. He came in without a tie, and I told him I'd talk to him *only* if he came in with a tie. The next day he came in with a tie. We talked; I had him fill out an application, and took his resume. During our visit, I asked him if his beard (he had a neat one) was important to him, or if I requested, would he be willing to shave it?

The following day, he showed up again *without* the beard, and really impressed me, saying he felt that if I asked, it must mean I preferred that he not have one. I told him I'd let him know the next day. The next day he showed up, but *without* a tie. He aggressively came in and said, "Well, can I have the job?" I answered, "Everett, I told you I don't talk to applicants without a tie." He looked incredulous, when he said, "I thought we'd already done all the interviewing?" I just smiled *without* answering. He went home, put on a tie, came back and I hired him. He turned out to be a great friend, and an excellent salesman.

You may think that these methods are extreme and unnecessary, but salespeople are by nature more aggressive than other people. The good ones will try your patience and test the waters continuously. Parameters must be established, and rules must be rigid. Ev and I understood our relationship from that day forward, and I never again had to say something twice.

When you become a new salesperson for a car dealer, you are an important part of the organization. Look on the sales force as a large bird nest, and you are one of the chicks. It's tough to give everyone attention when all the mouths are open. That's why we have rules. Following the rules makes it possible for all the chicks to get fed when they need it. Not following the rules and established guidelines means that you must have unnecessary, individual attention. You will be given certain instructions and guidelines which you will be expected to follow. Do not try to improvise and reinvent the wheel.

Certainly, different dealers will have different methods, and varying systems which they use to sell cars. Maybe you worked for another dealer, and when you hire on, you are anxious to tout your knowledge and better ways to do it. Forget it! You'll only cause yourself grief! You'll embarrass your manager by showing his way is wrong, or you'll find that they've already *been there, done that*, and changed.

There are no new ways of selling cars. Do the job the way your dealer teaches, work within the system they have, and until you're running the place, keep your ideas to yourself unless asked.

Now let's examine what you can expect to happen when you hire on as a new salesperson.

5 HOW TO SURVIVE YOUR TRAINING PERIOD

This chapter carries an alarming message on purpose. You *will* be tested! This chapter will give you the whys and the wherefores of testing, bullying and hazing. You may not experience any problems, and again, you may have some times when you have second thoughts about your new profession.

I will cover many possible challenges you may face, so you will be forewarned and be able to easily handle anything that happens.

First of all, understand that you may have to earn acceptance. Just because you get the job, you cannot expect to be accepted as an equal by the other salespeople. This is to be expected.

A while back, I said that 20 percent of the sales force will likely earn 80 percent of the commissions. Your goal is to be among that 20 percent.

Before we work on succeeding, let's take a quick look at the majority of any sales force, who may well be making decent money, but that are not super achievers! These people may be earning to the limits of their abilities, and may be great people, but do they wish you the best? Unlikely to be sure, but that's human nature!

A sales force is a highly competitive group. Let's take a quick look at that human nature I mentioned. If a salesperson is having a tough month and everything seems to be going wrong for them, do you think they will be super glad to see you come in and do better than them? No, they will be embarrassed. It's only natural. Just like someone you've known or worked with, working alongside someone else for years, when suddenly the other person receives a promotion. The "Why not me?" question pops up. Self-pity sets in; the person who was not promoted may not have any idea as to why they were not the one who went up the ladder. This situation can be devastating, and unless the person in charge uses some finesse, the person left behind may soon leave the company or their production will worsen. It may be a promotion based on personal friendship rather than merit, but that hurts worse.

The car business can be referred to as a dog-eat-dog business, but it works the same. Those who sell cars create a natural acceptance from those at the top of the totem pole, and resentment from those on the bottom. When someone who has been selling in the store for a long time is having a bad month, and a new person hires on and lucks into a great sale, and makes a big commission, they will resent you for it. There is a natural jealousy among sales professionals, where each person wishes the sale was theirs.

That's human nature! Every one of us desires to be the best. That's what creates a competitive business. The conquering armies returned to Rome with the heroes and their trophies up front of the columns, and the further back one was, the lower they ranked. Every salesperson wants to lead the column, and be the hero with the most sales and the highest commissions. Don't be too thin skinned and just understand why you must earn your wings, and if someone makes a sarcastic comment while you're running around in excitement, accept that they're not bad people, just good people wishing it was them and not you.

Keep in mind that the ones wanting to see you succeed can be counted on one hand; you, the dealer, the sales manager, your immediate superior (closer) and anyone else who stands to participate in a percentage of the sale profit. Everyone else may or may not care a bit whether you stay or go.

Even though you belong to a sales team, the group is made up of individuals all competing for their own piece of the pie. It is a team only as the sales force may be broken into competitive groups within the dealer's own company, but the only rewards for group achievement may be bonuses shared for being the top performers as a sales team or crew.

Your individual performance is how *you* are graded, paid and rewarded. The no I in team does really not apply here, as it is *all about the I!* In the sales business, the only person you need to worry about is the one who greets you in the mirror! If you are having a bad day, then you need to get an *exam.* Set an appointment with Doctor YU and get a checkup from the neck up.

For the most part, you are on your own. Certainly your peers may be of help, as well as the person in charge of your training, but when it comes right down to it, you're totally on your own when it comes to success or failure. This does not mean that the camaraderie won't be there. You'll have lots of friends!

During your training period, learn all you can about the procedures, product, rules and the way the dealer wants things done.

6 AFTER BASIC TRAINING — YOUR NEW TRIALS BEGIN

When I speak of your training period, this will be the necessary training and instructions you will be given before you are ever allowed to approach a customer. No intelligent organization will allow a new and untrained salesperson to have customer contact before they have *some* training. For this reason, I suggested you consider the more aggressive dealerships, as they are more likely to have a structured training program.

I'm not saying the smaller dealer won't, but a lot of the really small stores may not have the time or desire to even attempt training. They likely, for this reason, will have little interest in hiring an inexperienced salesperson. They may pay a higher commission to get the pre-trained salesperson. There is a danger even here, as sometimes they may hire about anyone just to have bodies, because they don't get quality applicants. Don't worry about the commission paid, as there are too many variables, but they are all comparable.

I highly suggest that you do a lot of self-study. When I hired new people, I told them right up front that, I would expect them to thoroughly learn the product knowledge on their own. The biggest reason for that is the simple fact that I had very little product knowledge myself, and I had no desire to learn it! My sales team however, was expected to know it completely! I didn't have a huge bank of product knowledge because *they* were expected to answer *all* of those questions.

When I got into the retail car business, my first experience was as a finance manager, and thereafter other managerial positions with other firms. My next experience was starting out as a general sales manager. This job was above my experience level as far as I was concerned, but I gave it a shot. Then I was offered the opportunity to become a closer. This is the person who runs a sales crew, trains the salespeople and personally does all of the negotiating with the customer.

Later on in my career, I had a couple of occasions where I went in to a couple of dealerships on the line (sales force) as the dealers had *promote from within* policies. To stay within their rules, and be able to replace certain managers; I went on the line, proved myself in front of the other salespeople, sold cars, made good money and when I was promoted, it was accepted that I earned the management position! I still didn't do much product study, but paid lip service to the manager who had no idea that I was only there to replace him! Fortunately, these were always very quick promotions!

The thing that stood out most was that my temporary managers kept pleading with me to learn something about the product. I wasn't really motivated to learn this phase, because the dealer and I both knew I'd never again need it! For you, as a new salesperson, trust me; you *need* it! This why I say that you *must* study and learn everything about the products you are selling.

The manufacturers today have such wonderful training videos, that you will be so much better trained than people were when I began in this business. Over the years, I actually watched the training and took the tests myself alongside my people. Knowledge of your product is essential. Your customers *expect* you to be knowledgeable, and believe me; a customer will be much easier to close when they are in love with the product.

How can you compare the car you're selling to your competition if you don't know what you're selling? Like I said, Your customers expect and demand that you know — but, they sure as hell don't want too long a spiel! Know your product so you are able to answer intelligently when asked. *Use a small percentage* of what you know. Selling is all about hitting key features and being able to elaborate *when* you are asked! I have seen countless salespeople talk themselves out of sales by never knowing how to shut up!

Now that I have explained more about how cool I am, let's get back to why I advise you to learn product on your own. As I mentioned, I had my people learn that part, and the part I specialized in was how to sell.

During your basic training period, you are taught the rules. Now you need to learn to fly. For product training; come early, stay late, borrow videos if they permit, and do all of that on your own whenever you are able. You need above all, to learn to *sell!* Learn how to approach people, what to say, how to say it, and always keep in mind that you have two ears and one mouth — remind yourself that this is so you can listen twice as much as you talk!

When you first meet a customer, you need to know how to greet them, the words to use, and the body language that is key to the situation; both theirs and yours!

Now let's discuss why this chapter refers to your new trials! As we previously discussed, when you do well, some of your fellow salespeople may resent it. When you fail, some of your associates will find inner satisfaction. Like the saying, *misery loves company.* You will generally find new friends when you lose a sale, but don't get used to them, you'll soon move up again.

If an associate is having a tough month, and *you* lose a sale, *they* mentally gain. It's strange for one to understand, but as long as you do, you can accept this important failing in mental preparedness. You must be able to forgive the occasional sarcastic comments if you make a good sale, and to understand the fact that someone who is failing wants your company. I say here; don't become a SNIOP! A SNIOP is one who is **S**usceptible to the **N**egative **I**nfluences of **O**ther **P**eople! Remember, your success is dependent on keeping a positive mental attitude.

You *will not* and *cannot* sell everybody! Let's say that on the average, you will sell one out of every five customers you meet. So let's say that you meet 30 customers in a month; you sell six. You will find later in this book that it won't deviate much at all once you have established your personal percentage of closing. This means an average. You won't sell customer number 5, then number 10, and so forth. You may not sell the first 25 and the 26th through 30th customers will <u>all</u> buy!

What I will teach you in this book, is how not to become a SNIOP and have the patience to persevere. You will learn to ignore those that would like to see you join their miserable ranks and to hang with those who are successful.

Eagles don't hang around with turkeys. Peacocks are seldom pals with crows. Learn right off to associate only with successful people. You can be cordial to those failures that wish you to join their suicide pact, but don't spend much time in their company.

Will Rogers is known for his famous quote, "I never met a man I didn't like." I find that hard to believe, and would imagine that he probably meant that he could find something he *could* like about everybody if he tried hard enough. When I'm around negative people, I don't generally spend a whole lot of time digging around too hard in search of something to like. I just try to politely avoid people who are on downers. Unless they work on my team, and then I pat 'em on the back or kick their ass; to do whatever is necessary to eliminate their stinkin' thinkin'!

Stay out of the *circle jerks*. Do not get caught up in standing around with the group while waiting for a customer.

Once you are given the all clear to hit the line, your only job is to get an up. Up, as in *up to bat*! Yes, you're up whenever you are awaiting an opportunity to greet a customer. Most likely you will hear that term as soon as you start. Just like baseball, nothing can happen until someone picks up a bat and steps up to the plate. Different dealerships operate in various ways, and you need to find out the rules from your *manager*, not from your fellow salespeople! *Know the rules* of waiting on customers, so no one can fool you.

Your chosen store may operate on a common system which is open floor. This means that an incoming customer belongs to the first person to get to them. This is the dog-eat-dog method of selling, because it creates a very competitive environment; which turns off a lot of customers. There are ways to temper the animal house appearance of this system; which I'll go into in greater detail later on. I liked it, because I always trained my salespeople to be the most aggressive! I had highly paid individuals who thrived on this type of competition.

Another method used is the rotating up system. This method is more polite, but has its pitfalls. Salespeople take customers in a prearranged order. Selections are based on many methods, but basically you take turns, and when your turn comes up you wait on the customer, when sold or exhausted you go back in line. I will also go more into detail later, but the downfalls in this system are obvious. This luck of the draw method, although more polite, rewards the weaker salespeople. As I said; I'll go into more later on, on the whys and how to make it work for the stronger people.

Once you know the ground rules, you are not subject to the cons pulled by the experienced salespeople; which is part of the breaking in the new guy hazing you are to experience.

You need to know what to do if you hit a blank wall and need help. Do you introduce your customer to your manager, to another salesperson or what? Most dealerships will have you turn your customer to a team mate. You politely introduce the customer and go away. I'll go into great detail before we're through.

Once you turn your up, you are dependent on the salesperson you turned to, to sell a vehicle. If they do, at best you will split the sales commission. I say at best, as there may be complications. If the procedure they teach you is to turn to your manager, then he or she may give you the guidance to allow you to complete the sale. In which case, the commission should be all yours! The manager's pay plan is normally separate, and does not include a part of yours, however rules vary per store, and that is also covered later.

Find out where you are to stand while awaiting your up. Also, find out what places you are *not* allowed to be; mainly because of the first impression given to a customer when they drive in. Learn the rules, and later on, I'll show you how the more aggressive and successful salespeople tweak the rules without breaking them. You will find that upper management respects people who think outside the box, and if you're producing sales and income for them, you can get by with a lot. No, the dealer will not be offended by me saying this, because they're not hiring saints, unless you're in Utah, and then only "Latter Day Saints." They make great salespeople too!

There is another very important part of your immediate training that you need to learn up front and carry it with you for the rest of your life! In fact, this is probably the *most important* lesson I can give: *Never be late!* This is what creates success more than you would believe.

Let me digress for a minute: Back in my early years, I was working for the Minnesota highway department; our office was currently working on Interstate Highway 35; which we began with the initial surveys, the testing and final completion by the contractors. The attitude was typical of what seems to be governmental type jobs, and I was allowed to be lax in my work habits. Although I worked only five miles from where I lived, I was normally late for work by five to 10 minutes every day. Since we usually hung around for a half hour before heading out to the freeway, no one really cared.

Then one day my direct supervisor took me aside, and changed my life for the best. He said, "Gary, I personally don't care, because I've been doing this for 22 years, and plan to retire here, but I notice you're late for work a lot." He continued, "This is just an observation based on a long career of watching people. I have noticed that people who are consistently late are not happy with their job." He patted me on the back and just said, "Think about it." You know, I did, and the next morning I walked in with a whole new attitude! I thanked him for the advice, told him I hadn't even realized it and gave him two weeks' notice! Without this man's caring, I may have spent my career being bored. Thanks Tuffy!

Therefore, my advice to you is *never be late*, because I'm certain you *will* love this car business. So, you're thinking, "How can I never be late?" I'll tell you — Of course things happen that can include dead batteries, flat tires, and any number of things. So, allow for these things. Leave early enough that without anything going wrong; you'll be a half hour to 45 minutes early. If something does go wrong, you will have the time to handle the situation and still make a timely appearance.

The alarm didn't go off, and power failure excuses don't cut it! Buy two alarms. Get an electric one with a battery backup and a separate battery only alarm. Set the battery only alarm to go off 10 minutes after the first one. I did this religiously, and I was *not ever late for anything for over 40 years*! People could always count on me, and they should be able to count on you! In the sales business, *you* are entirely dependent on *you* for your success or your failure.

Let me make just another quick note on being on time. Most dealerships expect their sales managers to have a meeting with their sales crew when they come on shift. If one person is late, the rest are inconvenienced, and it shows disrespect, not only to your manager but also to your peers.

In some places I worked, each time a person was late in a month; I would go to the sales board and erase one letter of their last name. If their name disappeared before the end of the month, they were no longer employed! The people with the shortest last names had a disadvantage, but my message was clear. I very seldom had any problems on a sales crew, also because I was always there waiting for them when my people came to work.

A lesson for you when you move up the ladder; I don't give a damn for a boss who comes in late! One of my biggest problems with any business is that the person who's in charge had certainly better be early. I most always beat my bosses to work, but I worked for some high powered people, and people who make the big bucks know the importance of *leading* a pack! *They* are not late! A pack runs at the speed of its leader!

7 PROSPECTING AND FOLLOWUP

Now we're ready to begin learning the car business. You should know the basic rules and regulations, and by now you know where to find your product training.

At this juncture is where a lot of people begin to cut corners and take the entirely wrong attitude of; "Well, I think I'll try selling for a while, and if I like it, then I'll learn the product." Stinkin' thinkin'! Don't you dare to begin failing already! Selling cars is going to be the greatest job you've ever had! Prepare properly and tell yourself, "You are going to succeed!"

Set aside so much time for product study every week, even if you're not certain that you will stay with one franchise or not. You may be at a Chevy dealership because the Toyota manager advised you to get some car experience and then come back and see him, because they only hire experienced people. You would naturally have a reluctance to learn all about Chevy's when your goal is to sell Toyotas. I can understand this, but today's automobiles are manufactured so much alike, and I don't mean to over simplify it, but if you learn one, you generally learn 'em all.

Besides, you may start making so much money selling where you're at, that you may decide to stay where you are! I've seen this happen so often, because I have had a lot of salespeople come to me over the years who were sent to get some real experience by a sales manager, who either didn't wish to bother with training, or just felt he only wanted successful salespeople, and would let me do the training and then try to steal my best people.

Once I trained a person in my ways, they were for the most part, too experienced to care about that other place. I always felt that if a salesperson worked for me for six months to a year, they were qualified to be an assistant sales manager (closer) in another store. Fact! When I began what I like to refer to as the hard core car business, I was extremely fortunate to be trained by the best! Then, I became the best!

As I previously mentioned, I did not start on the line (selling). I began my career at a point that takes many people many years to achieve. Talk about being in the right place at the right time!

I bumped into a general sales manager who had been in the audience when I held a meeting as a factory rep years before at an auto dealer group in Seattle. He offered me a closers job. When I told him I wasn't qualified, because I'd never even sold a car, he countered me with, "I don't want you to sell cars. I want you to close sales, and I'll tell you what to say!" He did. When the salesperson came in with an offer, the manager sent me out to meet the customer. He gave me directions on what to ask, how to ask, when to ask and to write down what they said. I'd come back to him, tell him what they said, he'd load my lips with more and send me back out. I didn't even have to think. He gave me the lines; I'd recite them and come back for more. I learned so fast from this expert, and it worked so well, in six months I was so cocky, I bought my own car dealership! But that's another story. Thanks Larry!

I digress like this for a reason. I want you to learn enough from this book to be the best! There is no reason whatsoever, that you can't be. What I'm going to go through will be like loading your lips and loading your mind.

If you have any lingering doubts, clean 'em out now, let's get at changing your life, and don't even allow yourself to think negatively! I can say that because if you're still reading, you are special! All good salespeople are special. By now, if you've never heard this old saying, then I'll lay it on you, because I've heard it forever; "Nothing happens until somebody sells something!" I'll leave the analysis up to you, but when you really think about it, selling is the basis of our entire economy! Our world could not survive without salespeople, so why not sell the things people love!

We're now going to get into the subject of this chapter; *Follow up*. Today's follow-up systems are wonderful! Back in the day, we kept records on 3 x 5 file cards in an alphabetical index. Computers today can make things so great for staying in touch with customers, but you must make this a priority. *Most* automobile sales people do a *terrible* job in follow-up! The reasons behind this are laziness and being spoiled by easy money.

Begin immediately to dig in to the dealership's preferred follow-up system. Manufacturers have systems available, and a lot of dealers have spent small fortunes on their own in-house programs.

Setting up your follow-up system is *critical* to your future. It's even more important than product knowledge in the beginning. Why? Because the first day you start work, you are now a car salesman! Say you stop in the grocery store on your way home on your first day, and when you say Hi to the checkout clerk and the conversation leads them to ask, "What kind of work do you do?" Whatcha' gonna say? "I sell cars for XYZ Carco!" Hopefully you will have business cards. Many stores won't order imprinted business cards for you until you prove you can survive the training, but they all have blank business cards with everything on them but a name. You need a supply of these cards. Print your name on a bunch of them, and begin handing them out to everyone you meet. People always love to talk about cars, and they love dealing with new salespeople that have not yet grown the customary dorsal fin.

This grocery clerk is your first contact. You definitely hand them your card and say, "If I can ever help you, or answer any questions, please call me." It really helps if they give you *their* name and number. Oh, don't think it won't happen! If you're friendly and easy going, people may suddenly have a jillion questions.

Think about this for a moment — If I am in a crowded elevator or a room full of people, I will guarantee you I can start an instant conversation. All I have to do is loudly say, "Is there anyone here who would like to buy a car?" Guess what I will hear; "What kind do you sell?" Try it — it works! I know most people would be flat-out embarrassed to do something like this, but I truly believe that the car business is the only product that you could do this with, and draw a positive response! America's love affair with the automobile is still strong! Now chisel this into your subconscious; unless you want every year to be the same as in the movie *Groundhog Day*, and if you have desire to retire with money, keep a good follow-up system!

That's the fun thing about our profession; you can get an enthusiastic response from most everybody when you start talking about cars! Can you see how important it is to begin prospecting from day one? Everyone you know needs to know you're in the car business! Everyone you meet from now on needs to have your card, and you need all the information you can get from them! Please believe me when I say to begin your follow-up program immediately!

I have personally closed over 17,000 car sales in my career. Since I closed these sales for other salespeople, I did not keep them as my personal customers, but instead the salespeople entered them into their individual records. Many people leave follow up on the back burner until they really are certain that the car business is for them. Sometimes, they procrastinate for years.

Let's look at it from a different angle. Say you spend a year in the car business and have five hundred or a thousand contacts. What value do you suppose they would have to you if you decided to start your own business? What if you went to another dealership? Naturally, the dealer will have rules against your stealing his customers, but I've never seen too many dealers push this issue. When someone leaves a dealership, their leads are given to other salespeople, but as lousy jobs as most sales forces do, it is unlikely that anyone will ever call them anyway.

It's funny when you consider how much follow up an insurance agent will do to renew a policy that makes him a hundred dollars, but a car salesman doesn't bother staying in touch with a customer who made him $2,000.00! Remember what I said about this being a lazy business, you can make an excellent income by being an effectual, lazy bum! You can also make an extremely high income, consistently, by doing things right. Another reason you need to keep accurate and thorough records, is to make your future years easier and more profitable!

You already know that customers hate the car buying process. They are aware that they must go through meeting someone new each time they want a new vehicle (because salespeople rarely follow up), so they must repeat the process all over. Those salespeople, who regularly follow-up, are a godsend to the client, and their employers.

Allow me to make another journey into the past, to further exemplify the importance of follow-up. I worked with a salesman a few years back that was on another sales crew. This gentleman was in his sixties, and had been selling cars for about 30 years. Every month he sold about thirty cars. He did this very consistently. His method was to set his sales goal at the beginning of each month, which was 30 sales. If he fell behind, he worked more hours. The dealership allowed salespeople to come in on their days off if they desired, and he did this often. The sad part of this was that this gentleman would not have had to work so hard, especially at his age, but he had one huge failing. He *never* did follow up!

This dealership had what they called a birthday list. The first of each month, they handed each salesperson a list of their customers who had birthdays coming up during the following 30 days. This list contained name, address, phone number and the vehicle they had purchased. If the salesman wanted, the dealer would pay for the birthday cards and the postage to send them. The salesman I've been speaking of *never did anything* with this birthday list. The insanity of it all was he had an average number on his monthly list of over ninety people! People that had already purchased from him and were loyal to the dealership!

Even though he didn't work for me, I asked him one day why he didn't ever do any follow up, and his answer astounded me! He just said, "It's too much work. I'd rather just get a new up when I feel like it, and I won't have to worry about being here for appointments." During our conversation, he pointed out two different customers with two of our salesmen who he had previously sold cars to. I just shook my head and walked away trying to comprehend how anyone would want to start over every month, when they had over 1,100 loyal customers on file, and adding thirty a month.

I'll give you a positive example next. When I bought my dealership, I experimented with different follow-up systems. This was 1979, and they were all by hand; no computerized systems in those days. One of my salesmen that began our selected system started on it then, and by 1981, he was consistently selling at least five repeat customers every month, and a high of 11. He achieved this after only two years; and in a small town dealership. Every single month, repeat and referral business gave him from 5 to 20 buyers that he would sell without any fresh business! Add that to his new sales, and he couldn't fail!

I also know of many successful people that *will not* take fresh customers. They have all they can do with their customer base and referrals! This is the goal one needs to achieve.

When I was a factory district manager, I was visiting a dealership during a promotion, and there were customers all over the place. I approached a salesman sitting in his office doing paperwork and questioned why he wasn't out getting ups. He said, "I don't have time. I have so many customers, that I only work with repeat clients and their referrals."

That was after nine years of selling. Soon thereafter, this man purchased his own used car dealership. Can you imagine how many letters he mailed to his customer base from his new store? Do you think he remained successful and never missed a beat? He had it made!

The secret to a successful career is to treat your customers right and stay in contact so they know they can depend on you to take care of their future needs. They may not always stay brand loyal, but make sure they know you can get anything they want! Besides, everyone likes to be able to refer their friends to their friend in the car business!

Many salespeople go so far as to have their customers call them when they need a *service* appointment. The salesperson arranges the appointment, and meets them when they come in. Many of them drop the customer off at work also. One of my salesmen in Chicago even purchased several used cars which he himself loaned out to his customers at no charge when they dropped off cars for service.

Proper follow up is a shortcut to success in the car business. The sooner you begin the follow-up program, the sooner people can send you their friends and relatives, and in a very short time you will create your business inside a business.

Salespeople who do a lousy job of follow up, and just grab ups as fast as they can with no concern for their longevity are what we call floor whores. Much of this comes from the fact I keep mentioning, "This is a great business, but a lazy business!" Many of these people have been selling cars for years but still haven't made the mental commitment to take it serious.

I always have said I still didn't know what I wanted to be when I grow up, and that seems to be prevalent in sales!

Learn the follow-up system, learn it well, and get on it *immediately* when you start work.

One last word on this subject; remember my salesman who started with me in 1979? Well, a few years later the economy tanked, and I closed up, but to show you the value of follow up; every dealer in town tried to hire this man, but he was heading to San Francisco to become a highly successful accountant. When they couldn't hire him, two of the dealers tried to *purchase* his follow-up system because they heard how well it worked for him. Great work Paul!

8   MEET AND GREET

This is where your sale begins. Now we are going to get into the actual sales process.

Here is where I begin to go in depth in many things that you are unlikely to be taught by your trainers. Some of the things I will cover may be contrary to the way your dealership wants things done. In all cases, I want you to follow your present dealership policies.

Imagine that my teaching is so that if you had to learn the entire car business on your own, and by the time you were self-taught, you could go directly to work. My intention is to cover the basics, but then to transition to the sophisticated closes and techniques seldom taught, and less often learned, by most managers in the car business. You will find that even managers in this business do not continually learn or improve their skills!

Inquire up front as to whether your dealership uses name tags. If they don't, ask if they mind if you obtain one on your own. I believe in name tags. Your dealer may think it is silly, but look at it this way — you need to get on a first name basis with your customer. *A person's name is the most important thing they can hear*! When making an introduction, *repeat* their names, write them down and *repeat* their names often! This is your *key* to rapport. Now, do you suppose your customer would appreciate the same courtesy? You bet they would! You will be trained to remember and repeat their names, but *you* are the professional. How about extending the same courtesy to your customer by allowing them to reciprocate by calling you by name! Wear a nametag!

Where? Glad you asked! A nametag needs to be on your *right* side and on the upper chest. Why the right? Because there is only right and wrong! People (85%) will notice a nametag on your right side, because it will be on their left, and that is where most people will see and *retain* your name! Right is right, and the other choice is wrong!

I am a believer in also handing a business card to each customer immediately upon introduction, but I advise you to obtain permission to do so, as many dealerships do not like this practice. They will say that if the customer has to be T.O.'d (turned over) to another salesperson that that person should be the one to card them before they leave. This argument doesn't hold water as far as I'm concerned, because I feel it's a silly rationale. If that was the case, I'd just say, oh, let me trade cards with you, here's mine, and I'd get the first person's card back. Big deal if they're eventually leaving anyway!

Also, this carding up front prevents the customer from his easy out later on which many customers use, and that is, "Well thank you, we'll keep it in mind. Could I have your card?" You'll have already handled this up front, so they'll need a different exit line. I also find that by giving my card to each of them, they can be calling me by name when they can't see my nametag. I know from experience that customers appreciate it, so no one will ever convince me otherwise. I give one to each person in the party. Cards are a cheap investment!

Your first time on the line will be a nervous moment. Depending on the situation in your dealership, you may be in a group near the customer parking area. You may be in a rotation, there are many possibilities; that's why I said to know up front what the rules of the game are.

Other salespeople will do their best to interrupt and confuse your game plan. This is part of your indoctrination. Someone may say, "Those are my customers," when you're headed out. Your response should be, "Then I'm sure they'll ask for you," and continue to go greet them *without* hesitating!

If you're in a store that calls its ups, it works like this: A vehicle drives in and the first person to call it wins. Let's say a blue Chevrolet truck is coming in, the proper call may be "blue truck," or "up-truck." Often the make or model may not be apparent, and calls such as "red car," or "up red" may be heard. Anytime you are calling ups in this manner, it is important to know the rules. When one person feels they called it first, they will call out "late" to the other person. Clarification by someone else or a coin toss may be needed, but it's all quick, easy and friendly. An unknown up is just not important enough to argue about who won. There's always another one. Don't just accept it when someone calls, "late," it may be a trick. As I said, it's no big deal, but an older couple coming in with a four year old sedan is what we call a good up! The twenty year old in a newer Mazda may not be. You'll learn the common sense deductions from experience, but who do you guess is the best up? The older car is most likely paid for, and they want another one. The young person is more likely to have negative equity and finance problems. These may not be fair generalizations, but you learn over time what type of up you prefer.

In one large auto group I was with, we had some of our stores with one way glass enclosing the up room. Ups could only be called from inside. Some stores had bleachers behind the glass, so everyone could view the entrances to the parking areas. Disputes were settled out of sight and earshot of customers.

This was a very professional way of handling traffic, as only one salesperson approached the customer after they parked. In direct contrast with this were other stores where the only rules were no rules!

The first person to greet the customer won. There would be salesmen on each car door, and whoever came out first, driver or front seat passenger, the nearest salesperson won! I've seen customers keep driving further back in the lot before daring to stop, and with salesmen chasing them all the way. This is a horrible impression, but it was up to the winner to explain to, and calm the poor customer who felt like they had fallen into a pool of sharks!

Many years ago, I found myself between jobs after I walked out of a store after an argument over a commission shortage. A friend suggested I come to his store, as he felt it was just a matter of time before I would be offered a management position.

I hired on, and there I was, in my forties, running after ups with kids in their twenties, and winning my share. It was quite embarrassing on Saturday mornings, as our showroom was very close to the street, and at least twenty-five of us were out front by the entrance in a mob. When a car came in, there were generally from two to four salesmen surrounding it. I really didn't like this operation, but soon I was promoted, and since the money was great, I soon accepted it as necessary, but how horrible it would be for a new salesperson. Of course, we only hired experienced people because new people would be eaten alive.

Many stores will keep salespeople separated; some on phones, some split among different areas, some out front, and try to make it more customer friendly. Image and first impressions are important, but a dealer knows that too many restrictions may not retain the best salespeople. There is a fine line between a good image, and a good atmosphere for your sales force.

That's why there are a lot of rules that keep getting bent and broken; with your better salespeople constantly taking liberties by encroaching on other's areas and skating. Skating, is basically as it implies, if you picture customers walking up, and suddenly another salesperson appears between you and these people, as if they were on skates. He or she just skates up between you.

You may have been standing in the group of salespeople on the car lot, and won the call, and then you patiently wait for the customer to park; you feel there is no reason to run since it's your up. Now, you professionally walk toward the customer, and suddenly another salesperson is greeting them and shaking hands. This is definitely against the rules, but the other salesperson (skater) has the customer, and proper conduct dictates that you cannot interrupt. As I promised, this is how aggressive salespeople tweak the rules, while not breaking them.

The skater knows that you can't do anything about it, and if he or she sells a car, management is not likely to do anything about it, even if they knew. The other salesperson is pretty sure you'll get another up, and forget all about it, and even if you should feel compelled to report the incident, he can plead ignorance. They may say, "Oh, I thought I won it — I didn't hear you." Or, "I didn't see anyone heading for them. I thought they came in the back entrance." This will happen, and you soon learn that if you win the call, then you'd better be there when they land on a parking spot.

As you get better, you may very well find yourself trying-on a new salesperson. It's all part of the rite of passage. You learn your limits, and the best people are usually pushing those limits to see how far they stretch. The old saying, "I'd rather beg forgiveness than ask permission," seems to permeate the ranks of car selling. Aggressive people always try to bend and stretch their confines, often just to see if they can. This does not mean that it is always dog eat dog, because you'll soon find that what goes around comes around.

I remember an old time salesman in Madison, Wisconsin. I worked for the Bank of Madison, and we helped a car dealer buy a new dealership. I was there a lot handling financing, and I got to know their sales force. They had an up system where they more or less took turns. The showroom was long and narrow, with the main door to the street in the far corner from the sales offices. I kept seeing this one old timer, who had worked for the previous owner for 30 years, getting most of the customers. It seemed as if everyone who came in was his previous customer, which courtesy dictates were *always* his! I positioned myself close to the door when the next people came in, and he called out in his usual style from across the showroom, "Hi folks, good to see you again! It's been awhile." Then, in low tones as he shook hands, "Oh, I'm sorry; I thought you were someone else. How may I help you?" He pulled that stunt continually, and it even worked on his fellow salesman who had worked there for 28 years! How much do you suppose he unfairly took from the other salesmen over all those years? Did he steal? Not really. Was he dishonest? Not according to the rules of the business.

Just always be aware that selling is *not* fair. The strong survive, and that's why I caution you not to accept anything you are told by people who stand to gain and cause you to lose. Paying their dues costs new people a lot of money. I've seen so many new people back off from a customer when another person claims the up as theirs. That's why, when you've called an up, and someone says it's their customer, that you need to politely but firmly respond that when the customer asks for them, you'll call them over. Establish up front that you know the rules, and won't be tricked. You will receive instant respect, and establish yourself as one who won't be conned. This quick response should eliminate any more games.

Getting the right up is luck for the most part, but there are certainly ways to improve your odds. Say you're at a Toyota dealership, and a customer comes in driving a five year-old Camry. The odds are very good that they came to buy a new one. A five year-old trade translates to equity, product loyalty, nice trade with high value and a good commission. That's the up you want!

Now on the other hand, you probably won't have a lot of competition for the up who drives in with a one year-old Chrysler 600 and goes up to a Toyota Prius. Read this as buried (owes more on their car than it's worth), poor trade value even with tons of cash down, (Toyota dealers aren't ever going to be super excited over

Chryslers), and Prius has a low markup and sells very well. Need I say more — No product disparaging intended, you'll get the same reaction from any Chevy or Ford full-size passenger car. I know this kind of pre-qualifying is not right, but we all do it.

You'll soon notice that competition for ups will get more fierce if the vehicle driving in has a good resale value; it won't take you very long to see what constitutes a good up, and what generally makes a bad one.

Do not be fooled however, by forming too many preconceived notions. Especially don't listen to the opinion of other people, except management, who have your best interests at heart.

Going back to the beginning of this chapter, meet and greet properly. Repeat their names often. Make sure they know your name. I used to make sure they didn't forget it, by some statement using my name in a third party manner, such as, "My boss said to me just this morning, 'Gary this is probably the best value on the lot, and I'd like to see you sell it.' Well folks, I'm showing it to you now because Gary listens to what Gary is told." Anything so simple as to just repeat my name to them will work, especially if I'm calling them by name, and they're not reciprocating. Generally soon after my little digression, the customer will have a "Gary" question for me.

From the moment you begin work, you are establishing your place in the pecking order. By not being a pushover from day one, you eliminate the one to three month torture period often awaiting new hires. You're there to go to work.

Don't worry about flak you may get if you're the only one wearing a nametag, just never leave home without one. Yes, leave it on when you're shopping; you will find that people will ask questions such as, "How's business?" Always remember, no matter what, the answer is, "My business is great," or fantastic, or super, or any other superlative. People love to deal with winners, and they avoid losers. Your business will always be *great!* People *must* always perceive you to be doing *great!*

YOU'RE UP! Before we begin the next part — *turn off* your cell phone! Okay, so are you ready to rock? Of course you are!

Today, we take our first up. You're on stage and naturally nervous. Take a quick analysis as to what you have to worry about. The worst case scenario is that you won't make a sale. Best case scenario is that you will! Now in reality, what do you have to lose? It cost you nothing to get the up. You did not have to make any sacrifice other than your time. If you blow it terribly and make absolutely stupid mistakes, who's to know? You and the customer, and they won't run up to your boss and say, "This person is stupid." No, only you and the customer will know. It's like a play with no audience. If you flub a line, or get tongue-tied, who's to know? If you perform well, you're a Broadway hit!

This is how you learn. Everyone in the sales force makes dumb mistakes, says idiotic things, and gets lockjaw at the wrong time. It happens to everyone, and that's why dealers for the most part have turn policies. It's so that only one salesperson won't be the determining factor as to whether or not a sale is made.

Here now is your chance to experiment and you will get to experience firsthand how customers react to questions. Approach with a smile, and just go with the flow. There is no wrong way to say "Hi" to someone, as long as you smile!

Don't have your script too long, but definitely know how your dealer wants his customers treated, and if they have a script they want you to use, then do it! They have created it from experience, so trust them and use it.

You may be asked to carry a notebook or portfolio with which to reference material, and to make notes on. If your sales manager says carry it, then do so; don't cheat by not doing it correctly, regardless if your fellow salespeople are doing it! Your dealership may not give you any instruction as to your technique, and if they don't you'd better have a notebook, business cards and two pens on your person. If you are dressed casually without a jacket, then having a portfolio, clipboard or notebook really helps. Your dealership may not want you to carry anything in your hands, so you have both hands free. This is my personal favorite, because I like the freedom of movement, but I know of highly successful people who carry a portfolio, and excellent managers who insist on it. Good job Ken!

Buy a card-case! No one likes to have a business card handed to them that's been carried so long the corners are rounded! Even if you're not carrying a notebook, a card-case in the pocket is perfect. Once you hand a business card to each customer (they're the cheapest investment you can make), take out another card, turn it over on your card-case and you can use it for notes — works great! In many situations, I've made notes on an entire meeting or seminar on just a few business cards. You can also write all information, such as VIN, miles, license plates, etc. by using both sides of a business card.

At this point, we have what we need to begin. Now, go back to the first sentence in this chapter, and let's take a few minutes to discuss it again at length. Cell phones are such a part of our lives today, but they will absolutely cost you so much money in the sales business that you'd better change any habits you have on day one!

Put a message on your phone that says, if you don't answer, you are likely with clients and will be returning calls between 4:00 and 6:00 p.m. (you pick the times, but set specific times). This way, customers will not think you are rude, and friends will leave you alone!

When you are between customers, check you caller ID for work related calls, and *shut the damned thing off again*! I'm very serious about this. Younger people today are glued to their phones, but if you can take hours each day conversing with friends during work hours, then you are cheating not only your employers, but you are cheating yourself and your family! It's a strong statement, but analyze it! The most important thing a salesperson can have is a positive mental attitude; I'm sure we all agree with that.

So what happens if you are just about ready to take an up, and your phone rings? Supposing you pick up to say, "I'll call you back," and your friend quickly says, "I just wanted you to know my mom died!"

Tragic? Yes! Effect on your mental state; devastating! If you had not known the call came in, there would be a message, right? The news would have been just as sad, but before you got the bad news, you may have sold a car, made a thousand dollars, and later when your day got ruined, you would still have made an income!

You can justify the reason to leave your phone on, in case of emergencies, but your family should have your work number for such genuine emergencies. No matter even if a friend called just to say hi on your way to an up, it still messes up your mental preparedness!

Look at it this way: Let's say you're playing a stage role, and you have just made your entrance. Just before you deliver your first line, someone in the audience yells out, "your fly is open," or "your shirt is torn." What are the odds that you will flub a line, and maybe throw off your performance? Whenever you approach an up, you are *on stage*. Your customers see you approach; even before you speak, they are analyzing you. Your body language introduces you before a word is uttered!

Have I disparaged your phone use on the job enough? I certainly hope so. Don't let modern convenience destroy old-fashioned common sense and person-to-person selling. Don't put it on vibrate, *shut it off!*

You called the up and they're all yours. Be there promptly. If you are experiencing a lot of traffic, you should be prepared to wave to the incoming customer, and indicate a place they can comfortably park. Have a spot to direct them to, keeping in mind that people park a car easier with a left turn into the spot. You may need to direct them down a right turn aisle, but if you do, have a left hand spot in that aisle picked out for them. Don't worry about people thinking you're too aggressive, because you are the only person greeting them, and it's not like the group approach I previously covered. Trust me; customers will greatly appreciate your thoughtfulness! Even if they don't realize your courtesy, they will feel comfortable with their initial experience.

This is all part of making a customer feel at ease. Never put a person in a position of embarrassment such as they would feel if they had to see-saw back and forth into an uncomfortable right hand parking space. If it happens anyway, and you have no choice, they know you were watching; make your greeting something like, "I don't know how you got in there, I wouldn't have even dared. Good job." Now, go for your introduction. You'll notice that you can open your conversation with anything appropriate before you introduce yourself.

My personality keeps things light. I never really worry about what I plan to say because I stay loose to be able to quickly react to whatever someone says. I may not even go with a formal greeting. For example, if someone drives in with a classic car, I know they aren't likely to trade it, but they brought it for a reason! Think about it for a minute. Maybe they own a five year-old plain Jane car that's really not even something you would look twice at. They feel that they are not proud of this beater, but have enough pride to not want us to judge them by driving in with what they want to get rid of, so they bring their show piece.

I may approach this customer with some off the wall comment such as, "Okay, how many new cars do we have to give you for it?"

How's that for a greeting? Certainly they weren't expecting it! They were waiting for some tired and overused standard sales approach, weren't they? Did I get a positive reaction? Certainly! Did I give them a feel good moment — yes. I did exactly what needed to be done by complimenting them, and approaching with a friendly attitude.

My next step is to ask, "How may I help you today?" Yes, *before* a handshake. Who knows, they may be headed for the parts department, need a bathroom, or whatever. Therefore, I first greet them and ascertain whether or not they are a prospect. You don't want to embarrass yourself by holding out your hand and having it refused. No rush, go easy.

Once the customer identifies their interest, I now introduce myself and shake hands. Here again, I will elaborate on another very critical step in a proper approach!

We are going to discuss this in detail, as you are going to learn something that can often make or break a sale, and you'll never know why! A high percentage of car salespeople handle this moment wrong, and a lot of people never learn. *You* are going in armed with proper procedures!

When I grew up, my generation was for the most part I would say, for lack of better words, a more polite and formal generation. Men always shook hands, and most often a woman would receive a slight bow and a courteous hello. Certain parts of the United States will still follow the more formal introduction.

I remember the first time when I moved to the West, I met a lady who just thrust out her hand and pumped my paw; it surprised me greatly. Still, there is a procedure to follow. Be courteous, and give the lady a chance to indicate how she feels. *Don't ever* push the issue by forcing her to shake hands.

Shake hands with her husband, and watch her eyes. You will be able to tell quickly, as she may just nod and say hi. Don't automatically stick out your hand, as she may then shake so as not to embarrass you or her husband by refusing. She will however, resent your intrusiveness! You'll know when you've judged her wrong, but by then it's too late. A slight bow, and "How do you do?" is always acceptable, and is very much a sign of respect and courtesy.

Many, many people have arthritic hands, and I've seen older men and women wince in pain when Joe the wrestler shakes their hands like he's milking a cow, or loosening a fence post. I always bow slightly and greet the lady, and if she wants to shake hands, as is more popular these days, she will make the first move. Often a lady will make a pleasant smile, and you can tell that she is *surprised and pleased* with such respect that she seldom has experienced!

Don't forget this! It *will* affect your income! When you do shake a lady's hand, it is only necessary that you take it, you don't have to shake it. This may seem like a lot of preparation for the simple job of sales, but for most people in other professions to make the kind of income you will be capable of, it would take six years of formal education. You have entered a profession where we are extremely well paid for a very small investment of our time and money. Only in America!

Once your customers have identified their needs, our qualifying process begins.

9 QUALIFICATION AND SELECTION

We have met the customers, given them each a business card, and written down their names. We are ready for the next challenge.

What are they looking for, when will they buy it, can they afford it, and a hundred more questions need to be answered, but let's begin slowly.

"So what brought you to *XYZ Ford?*" That's a question that you need to ask early on. We need to find out; why us? Maybe they're previous customers, maybe they saw an ad on TV, maybe their relative in Amarillo just bought a new Mustang, and they just came in to see what it looks like and have no intention of buying a car. How good would it be to know this before a twenty minute test drive? I know of many occasions where my salespeople didn't ask and they didn't find out until the customer said goodbye!

You will find that qualifying the customer is the most difficult part of your job. Customers are not going to tell you the truth up front. They are coming in to look at what you have to offer, but they may have a different agenda. Maybe they just feel if they give you their basic needs to see if what you will recommend is what they secretly think they want. Maybe they have already picked out a Nissan Murano, and are just taking a last look at the Honda CRV because it's a lot less money, and they want to be sure.

It could be that one of them just changed jobs, and a company car is one of the perks of the new position. In this scenario, the company may be making a fleet purchase from somewhere else and having it delivered to the customer, and he's just here to take your time to see what he's getting.

People don't think a lot about how a salesperson is paid, as it's hard for a lot of people to conceive of a non-salaried position. Many people don't even care. This is all part of the job. Maybe if this customer is honest with you up front, and you treat them courteously, and give them some time, then they may buy a different vehicle from you in the future, or may refer friends to you. For this reason, we roll with the punches.

Let's take a look at a typical scenario that you will often encounter; customer drives in and parks farther away from the usual area, and by the time you catch up to them, they are already walking among the inventory.

As a side note here; be careful not to startle them! If people don't see you coming, and you suddenly shout out a greeting, and startle hell out of them, you might as well go get another person to help them! Make sure you let people know of your approach. You can cough or make some other sound, but I usually just pretend I'm calling out to someone, and I turn to my side, and call out, "Thanks folks, I'll see you later," or anything like that.

Now my new up turns to look at me, and they see me facing away, and waving to some non-existent person, but they will always focus on me. Then, as I turn back toward them, I can make my greeting. Even if they were startled by my approach, they *were not* embarrassed. This type of shopper sneaks in and quickly goes out in the inventory, hoping to remain unnoticed.

When I approach these types, I will not automatically hold out my hand and introduce myself. The typical scenario will be like; "Hi folks, welcome to ABC Motors, have you been helped?" Sure, I know they haven't, but I'd rather they didn't know I chased them down when they thought they came in without being spotted!

They react with, "Can we just look by ourselves, we'd really like to be allowed to take our time, and if we need help we'll come and find you?" Here's what they really mean; "We don't like car salesmen, we hate the process, we don't trust you, and we don't want you trying to influence us!" You can almost hear the theme from JAWS playing in the background.

So, how do you react? Your boss is watching, and you know you are expected to take control, but if you're smart, you will sense that if you don't back off that these people will leave, and you are correct! They will!

Here's how you handle it; "Why certainly you may. If I may, since we have so many vehicles in stock, I'd like to just point out where they all are, and then I'll get out of your way and let you look. Are you looking for new or used? (They answer.) Well, those are over there, and you may find a few more back there that just came in. Allow me to just point out how to read our stickers," and I'll give a quick guide so they can understand them. Then I'll say, "Okay folks, I'm going to give you my card, so if anyone else comes up, you won't have to go through any more questions, just tell them you've been helped. Fair enough? Oh yes, I'll just stand by over there just in case you have any questions, just wave me over."

By the time I'm through showing them how polite, and how informative I am willing to be, and how I have not even mentioned anything about buying, trading, or even asking their names, the chances are, I'm in! I almost always will have the customer ask me a question within a couple of minutes of my trying to depart.

Once you have been asked a question, answer it, and now the lines of communication have been opened. You may now begin to qualify these people as to their needs and wants. People like this have likely had bad experiences in the past, and have been burned before, and are determined to avoid another bad experience.

Stay loose and informative. Do not begin asking too soon about their timetable, trade-in, and the like. Just spend some time touring the inventory. Soon, you will likely have them apologizing to you for their initial standoffishness, and they'll spill out their past experience that created this distrust. These types of buyers are some of my favorites, because they are most often going to be your biggest profit sales of all!

Just don't push too fast! Earn their trust, and it may take a little more time, but trust the fact that once the barriers are down, you will be amazed at how easy they will buy!

Now, if this up turns out to be just an investment in time, you may indeed have earned enough respect that they will return to you. Once you have shown this customer around, and touched base with management if required, then get back on line. Just because you invested some of your time, you haven't made any money, so other than a quick break, you're still here to get a *live one*. Too many salespeople think that working with a customer for 30 minutes deserves a 40 minute break. Why? Other jobs aren't that way, and you need to focus on actually treating car sales as a real job! Just because it's a lazy business, we don't need to let ourselves be made lazier.

In this example, if you are on a rotating up system, they may accept this as a non-opportunity, and let you get back in rotation. If not, then accept it. It happens to all of us. Never get too excited about these things, as rules are there as rules and *not* as suggestions. Don't ever lose your temper, or vocalize your contempt for a decision that goes against you, as it may, if this no-chance up turned out to cost you your place in line. What goes around comes around, and next time may very well go in your favor. Besides, it generally works that your next up will be better anyway!

By the same token, if you realize that your customer is using your time without any intention of buying, it does you no good whatsoever to express anger and make rude comments. To appease your ego, you insult the customer and ruin any chance that he will ever come to you in the future. Feel better? You still wasted the time, so count it as an investment, and let it go at that. Chalk it up to experience.

I have seen customers use my salesperson's time, and hand them a twenty, fifty and even a hundred dollar bill on their way out! No matter what happens, always maintain a professional demeanor. Remember, you represent your dealer. How do you think he or she would treat this customer?

What I will do in qualifying customers may be different than you would be comfortable with. I hope so. As Will Rogers said, "Thank God you and I are different; otherwise one of us would be unnecessary."

Find out why the customer came in to your store. If he just came in because he's in the market for a new car, and he's just going to look at all different makes, why mine? You can ask, "Have you ever purchased a car from our dealership before?" Maybe he hasn't, but he has his service work done at your dealership because it's convenient.

If you work at an Acura store ask, "Have you ever owned an Acura?" If the answer is no; ask, "How did you hear about it?" There are many ways to find out the motivation that brought this person into your store.

Customers normally answer questions with "Just looking." Of course they are! "A shopper is a shopper until he meets a salesperson!" We don't want to barrage this customer with an endless stream of questions, but if we phrase them correctly, it's easy to break down the customer's resistance. Questions like:

1. Have you done business with us before?
2. Have you ever owned a (*your make*) before? (If so) How was your experience with it?
3. If they own one of your products now, did they buy it from your dealership? What experience have they had with it? Are they planning to replace it (trade) with another one like it? (Never use the word trade, because it is like asking if they're here to buy — too soon at this point.)

You see, the answer to one question will automatically lead to another one. Car buyers don't resent questioning if it enables you to help them.

Questions that create resistance and barriers are those that lead directly to whether or not they are buying now. It would be great if we could just ask one question up front; "If I show you cars, pick one your like, take you for a test drive, buy you coffee and sodas, treat you nice, make you a good deal, and respect you, will you buy a car from me today?" That's our ultimate goal isn't it? I've seen a lot of salespeople almost slap customers with a string like this. Don't talk buy until you earn the right!

Remember that your customer didn't wake up this morning and say, "I want to make a new friend. I'm going to a car lot." You as well; are not looking for a new friend. I hope my customer and I can do business and that a friendship will result, but it will be a business friendship based on trust and service performed.

Customers will even tell you, "I have a friend in the car business." My answer to that is, "Now you have another one, what may I show you?" Everybody has a friend in the business. The good thing about that is most people feel that they can't negotiate as well with a longtime friend. They may feel like their friend will expect them to pay more profit, and they may not even like the product their friend sells. Don't ever worry about losing a car deal to the friend — Customers will buy from the Devil himself for a better deal!

When qualifying your customer, be careful to ask enough questions as to their needs and wants to make certain they are picking something that will really fit their needs. Simple things to watch for are the uses they intend for the product.

The wife may be looking at a two-door Honda Accord, and she mentions that she takes her elderly parents on errands and doctors' appointments every week. Ever try to get in the back of a sporty two-door car? Who's going to pull Grandpa back out if he can get in it? I love Mustangs and Camaros, but I will not ride in the back! Because I'm claustrophobic! If they have children to drop off and pick up, who's going to get out and open the doors for them? What if you live in the Pacific Northwest where it rains all winter? Thanks anyway!

The customer may be looking at the Mack Daddy pickup with the monster engine to tow his boat. When going into detail on how often he does this, it may be twice a year. In the spring he tows it to the marina, in the fall it comes back to the house. Meanwhile, he drives Chevron's best friend sixty miles a day to and from work! Could he not have the boat towed twice a year by renting a pickup? Don't be afraid to ask questions, as if you are to be of actual service, a question like this will show you are genuinely trying to help.

Now I'm not saying you should talk against a customer's choice, but let's look at it another way. Suppose you go along with this program without ever asking a question, or bringing up the usage they are planning for the vehicle. You just go blindly along until you get down to the dealing. Now, the customer finds out their payments will be over $600.00 a month, and their insurance will go up horribly, gas costs may raise out of sight, and all the excitement in blowing up this balloon suddenly blows up in your face!

Don't think your customer will just say, "Hey, let's just pick something else." Wrong. It won't happen. They're going home. Will they return to you? No. You were their assistant buyer and you *failed them.* They were embarrassed right into the arms of the guy down the street. When they get to the next store, they already know what they don't want. They know their budget and their needs, and really are pretty much set up to buy from your competitor.

The next salesperson they meet will be telling everyone, "These folks just came in, picked a vehicle, and rolled right over and bought it. Easiest sale I ever made!"

Sure, you can't be expected to know what makes people tick, and you can't sell against your customer's desires, but you need to figure out what their budget constraints are during the selection process. Questioning how the vehicle will be used is a normal question, so let's ask the right questions to make certain we select the right vehicle up front. Select the right vehicle, present and demo properly, and guys like me may be unnecessary! It's really a pleasure for a closer when the salesperson comes in with a full bore deal, and all they have to do is shake hands!

If a customer comes in not knowing what they want, it's pretty easy to ask what vehicle they drive most often (they may not have brought it in). Ask what experiences they have with their present vehicle and what they would like their new one to do. Ask them if they have any needs besides the ones they've already mentioned. You will find that most buyers just want a new car! They may not even indicate any dissatisfaction with their present car, so be careful at this point, because you sure *don't* want to say aloud the obvious, "So what do you want a new car for? You don't need one."

Now, you bring them to the same model they currently own, and proceed to tell them about all of the new features and improvements over that nice, but obsolete car they have! There are always so many changes in cars that manufacturers create in order to stay fresh, that the current can't live without features make it easy to sell! You need to make certain to learn all the newest features for this situation, as even though they don't need a new vehicle, your buyer depends on you to create a need. They *want* a new car. They can't justify it simply on want. They can afford it, but caution dictates that they be conservative. You must convince them of the advantages of moving up now rather than later! Believe me, people love to change cars, but they need to be able to make that justification; your job!

Let's take a look at the older customers, and especially men! Men love cars. From the moment a man buys a new car, he thinks about his next one. He finally gets his wife to accompany him to look at the new models, and you can see the desire in his eyes. *He* needs your help! Help in using a logical, reasonable, and cautiously low-key presentation. He knows if *you* can convince his wife that they will benefit from the new ride, she will give her consent. *He* was sold before he drove in!

So, how do you become his representative without giving the appearance of the two of you ganging up on his wife? That's easy. Do you think she cares about the automatic transmission intercollator that reduces the electrostatic firmament before it reaches the nitronducing coil for the travelator?

She will be impressed by the ride! People usually see a difference in comfort. What she needs to hear is that they will have a safer and more comfortable trip when they go to visit their grandchildren. She needs to know about the side-curtain airbags that will protect her loved ones when they are in the car with them! She needs to know that Papa will get out of his recliner more often if he gets a chance to enjoy his new car.

You don't sell the majority of women on mechanics and engineering. If you say your product is better engineered than your competition, she will think you're a liar. Which you probably are! Don't make claims that are unproven. Let the manufacturers do that; then the recalls can fix them properly!

Another thing I need to mention about selecting a vehicle for your customer is, don't overwhelm and confuse the issue by showing them too much. The more vehicles your customer sees, the greater the confusion. If they come in to see a new RAV4, don't take them all over the lot, and look at Highlanders, 4Runners and Sequoias. Sounds silly, but a lot of people do it. I can't call them salespeople, because they're not.

If you're working for a Chevrolet-Cadillac store, and the customer comes in to see the new Impala and really likes it, but has some reservations, the secret is to get them to drive it. Oh sure, if your whole idea is to just get them to show you super excitement, then take them next door and show them a Cadillac CTS! You won't sell it, but at least they will really love it! Good job of switching! Now you don't have to work late. Remember, you must show the best product you can and stay within the customer's budget.

What I'm trying to point out is the foolishness that weak salespeople use to impress people right out the door! When you're going to the inventory, try to keep it as short and simple as you can. If three vehicles are on the row, the customer says, "I like this one," stop and begin discussing it. If the features on the vehicle are enough, then stop right there and sell it! I've observed salespeople say, "I have a lot more in back, shall we look at them?" What do you think the answer is? Stop as soon as you get a yes!

If a customer asks if you have any more, you need to find out what else they want on a vehicle that this one doesn't have. People, for the most part, like to feel that they have looked at everything. You need to make them feel that they have. Nobody likes to be told, "We have this one, and I hope you like the color, because what you see is what you get." If I'm in that position, and I only have one left, won't they wonder why it's the last man standing?

So my story may go as follows: "I'm sure I heard it from someone this morning in the sales meeting; we were all out, but this one just came in, and I am surprised that it's still here! I really didn't expect it to last, and I should caution you that if you like it, I'll have to check real quick to make sure it's still available!" Now, will your customer think it's a picked over car, or will they be thinking, "I'm lucky I came in now, as I know it won't be here tomorrow!" I am not advising you to lie. I'm sure that if you had been listening, someone did really say those words at the meeting, didn't they? The old saying of "Tell 'em what they want to hear" likely came from this type of situation. A little white lie can sometimes really make a person feel good and do no harm. The secret here is I'm sure that somewhere, sometime, someone used those exact words, so I don't lie!

When the customer with the trade-in painted the most butt ugly color you've ever seen starts to apologize for the color because their friends have continually tortured them about it, what do you do? Do you agree that it is terrible and have them feel that you will give them a lower trade value because of it? Of course not! I would pay them a compliment on their choice, "On the contrary folks, that was actually a very limited, special-order color, and my used car manager was excited when he saw it! He said, 'I know that car will sell fast!' " Did I lie? No. I'm certain my used car manager would say it exactly like that!

The color was limited because not that many customers would go for such an extreme color; the factories occasionally do this to draw stares, and they tone down the majority of the rest of the paint jobs. Will it sell fast? Yes, because the used car manager will give such a low appraisal, it will have to! I didn't tell them the appraisal would be high, did I? The customer is happy; they feel vindicated and can tell their friends they got top dollar for it! Everybody wins!

If a customer says to you, "I like this vehicle; can you get it in black?" Your first inclination is to say, wait just a minute, and I'll find out! So you run down a manager, do a vehicle locate, and come out to find your customer looking at something totally different. You say, "Yes, we can get a black one." Do they care? Probably not. Your correct response to that question should be "If I can get it for you in black, would you buy it?" I call that putting the turd in their pocket, or some more polite people call it giving them the gorilla.

Whenever possible, answer a question with a question. A customer asks me if I could get his payments under $400.00 a month. I ask; "If I could, would you own it right now?" He says, "Yes;" and I say "Follow me" and I head for the showroom. If he follows, I have a buyer! Keep it simple.

Your immediate supervisor will spend time with you on qualifying your buyers, and selection of the right vehicles for your customers. Always take care to listen to what the customer says, and listen also for what he means. Maybe someone says, "I want a sporty car." That's what you heard, but what did they really mean? A family with four kids and two dogs would *like* a sporty car, but they *need* a van. You can't just laugh and fold your arms and say, "What does it feel like to want?"

So what can you sell that's sporty? How about one of the crossover vehicles with fancy wheels and a bright paint job? They manufacture two-wheel drive sport utility vehicles just because they fill a niche. They make them for the older generations who detest station wagons and vans!

The kid carriers of my youth became almost sale proof! Even though they were really the most practical for carrying people and cargo, the image became jaded. The vestiges of the family station wagon and the traditional vans all but disappeared because buyers wanted a new image; that of the off-road adventurer and carefree, fun lifestyle. Practicality still rules, and thus the emergence of the all-wheel drive sport-ute; the roomy, yet stylish crossovers of today. Now when someone says I want XXX, give thought to their needs as well as their wants, and do your job as an assistant buyer. Notice I did not say assistant shopper, that's the other 80% of salespeople, not you!

A very high percentage of automobile buyers don't end up purchasing the right car! This is evidenced by the number of current, and one and two year old models of certain cars on used car lots. There are many cars out there that are such bad buys, that I nicknamed them W.T.'s. I even rounded up a bunch of these W.T.'s once when I was a used car manager at a big store. I had a company come in and create a special W.T. pinstripe package, and had them all custom striped. There were many similar cars by different manufacturers, and all were just bad cars in my opinion. Incidentally, later on, the stripers asked me what the W.T. stood for; wretched turd.

There are still many vehicles manufactured that qualify for this title. You'll see them. Cutesy little cheap cars that we mainly sold because of price alone! I mention this not to throw rocks at any type of car, but to point out to you that although a great many people *buy* cars and trucks, a greater number of people are *sold!* Being an assistant buyer is only good for so much. You need to be a salesperson. You need to *SELL!*

Concentrate less on asking buying and qualifying questions, and try to keep the conversation focused only on the customer's needs and wants. Invest time without guarding your outlay of service until you feel you have a buyer. Too many salespeople are so obvious about their questioning methods that it's almost like they have a sign on their forehead that asks; "If I spend time with you, is there a good chance you will buy from me, or can I just go back inside and continue texting my friends?" All kidding aside, this is the way a tremendous number of salespeople act. They make their customers uncomfortable and reluctant to ask too many questions if they aren't sure they're buying at the time. Believe me, when I say; if your method of qualifying customers is a steady stream of obvious buying now type questions; you will starve yourself out of this business! A lot of this type of over qualifying is not done only by inexperienced newbies. Oftentimes an otherwise successful salesperson will occasionally act out of desperation, and begin to take these short cuts and keep burning through ups looking for the definite buyers today. The major problem with this type of stinking thinking is that not only do they blow out a lot of potential buyers and cheat their dealer, but remember this; most buyers that walk in your door with the "I'm here to buy, and you'd better give me a good deal" attitude, a lot of times turn out to be a pain in the ass! The biggest profits come from the people who are just looking!

Salespeople may wait for hours before they get an up, and then because of trying too hard to find out if they are working with a real buyer, blow out a great opportunity so they can go back to sitting around waiting for another chance! This is stupid! Dance with the one who brung 'ya!

10 THE USED VEHICLE SALESPERSON

The used vehicle salesperson is generally a better salesman than their new car counterpart. Some dealerships allow their staff to sell both new and used, but many stores have separate lots, and separate staff, and they don't allow crossover. Now, let me clarify my opening statement when I say the used car people are better. By better, I mean more experienced and more skilled. The reason for this is that it takes a lot more skill to sell used cars and trucks, and in most dealerships, you must earn the right to sell on the used car lot.

Let's look at the differences. How much skill does it take to sell a car with a price label printed by the factory, has a full warranty, virtually no miles, no stains, no scratches, no dings and nothing at all to apologize for. Contrast this with the used car with mileage, dings, dents, tears, stains, tire wear and likely without any warranty. Maybe it smells, and even though polished and clean, it's used! The only advantage is that it costs less than a new one. You see where the skill comes in?

So, you ask, "Why would anyone care to sell used cars?" For one thing, it pays a lot better! Many stores even pay a higher percentage of commission on used vehicles. Markup will usually be a *lot* greater than the factory set profit margin on a new vehicle. There isn't a likelihood of finding one exactly like it on another lot across town, so when you find a buyer, it is easier to sell if they like it. Your selection will be more varied, as a good used car manager tries to stock a wide variety of makes and models, and so you will attract a lot more buyers.

Your new cars are limited by the factory selection and availability, where a used car manager will vary his inventory with a lot of trucks, 4 X 4's, sport utilities, sports cars and anything to appeal to a vast audience. Have you ever noticed how many dealerships of all franchises will usually have a Jeep Wrangler on display from the street? The Wrangler has always been a good draw card, as are the Mustangs, Camaro's, Z cars, high rider 4 x 4's and the list goes on.

Now let's examine used cars. Take a 2010 Dodge 4 x 4. Your first customer that looks at it points out a hard to see dent in the rocker panel as he's looking it over. Later on, another customer is looking at it and notices a small oil leak. The next time you show it, the customer tells you it feels like the transmission slips. Yet another shopper spots a ding in the tailgate, stained carpet and excessive tire wear. Still later, some other looker tells you there is a distinctive miss in the engine.

The next day, a customer stops to look at it, and asks, "Is there anything wrong with it that you know about?" You reply, "I don't think so, it just came in and it looks like a beauty doesn't it!" Congratulations; *you* are a used car salesperson! That's why, in a nutshell, that used car salespeople make bigger paychecks and are often the most experienced in the store. This goes back to sending out the German shepherd with a note around its neck to sell new vehicles. I've never met a Shepherd that could sell used cars!

You may not feel that used cars are for you. If you put yourself in the last scenario, and *you* would have just rattled off a list of what all of those previous customers told you, your up would have walked away. If this is what you feel would be proper, then you should stay away from used cars or change your outlook. If this type of selling goes against your sensibilities, then stay away from the sales business entirely! Yes, all fields! The reason that a used car salesman is always referred to as being one to watch out for, is a well-earned image! The used car salesman has always been personified as an example of the con man. This is a rather unfair label, but you cannot hand buyers a laundry list of problems, and still make a sale. It's like when your spouse found out all your faults, if he or she had the list upfront, would there have been a marriage?

Different people will see different things on vehicles. No dealership will fix everything on a used car. A good used car manager cuts every corner he can, because he's not paid to make old cars new. That's Aladdin's job! As long as the engine and transmission seem okay, the rest is cosmetic. Make it look good, smell good and make it go away. They will change the oil and filter, because customers have always pulled the dip sticks to check the cleanliness of the oil. It may have never been changed by its previous owner, but when your buyer sees it, they say, "Well, they must have taken good care of it; the oil's really clean!" Now if you can stand there nodding your head in agreement, you can make a good used car salesman. If you could stand in front of a dent while the customer looks at the flawless finish, you could be a used car salesman!

To learn to sell used cars, I don't want to make you feel it's all sleight of hand and dishonesty. That's not what it's all about at all! It's the ability to overlook faults in a product and sell its virtues! You need to find the *good* points, which will vastly outweigh any flaws. Another important fact to keep in mind in selling used cars; your customer will not normally be as picky as you are. They likely can't afford new, so they will still get a good, serviceable car, and save a lot of money! Besides that, they may not have concerns over appearance anyway. I've had a lot of buyers express to me that the reason they are buying a used vehicle is to save money by letting the previous owner(s) put the first ding on it, and suffer the depreciation!

In order to be a good used car salesperson, you need to learn a lot of product knowledge on your own. Studying the owner's manuals, that hopefully you will find in the vehicles, will give you a good knowledge of operating most general features of used cars, plus that, most vehicles have similar features if they are the same age, regardless of make.

Your store may have used vehicle price labels that list options and standard equipment. Since most cruise controls function alike, most transmissions have the same gearing selection, and so forth, you need to spend a lot of time in and out of your used cars to learn all you can!

Here's where you invest in yourself. Get a notebook, and if you do nothing more than write down the make, model, mileage and transmission type of each car and truck in your inventory, you will have a leg-up on your fellow salespeople. By the time you complete your initial run through the inventory, you will gain a confidence that will rival anyone else when it comes to availability and selection. *You will be the expert.*

Now when a customer comes in, you will be able to say, "Yes, we have one of those, and it is right over here." The customer will feel that if it's nice enough for you to be familiar with, it must be a good vehicle! A good used car manager will shuffle the inventory on a continuing basis, so you need to constantly walk the inventory.

As I said, do this on your own, and find out where your used car staging area is. By this, I mean every dealership has a place for fresh trade-ins where you tag them and park them when they come in on trade. Then, when the sale is final, they go to a staging area, are scheduled for a service check, and will likely be in various stages of get ready. Learn also where the receiving area is for vehicles the used car manager buys from the auto auction. Cruise these areas every time you come on shift!

If you are doing your job, you will be forming a *looking for* list where you will note cars and trucks you have customers looking to buy! Very often your used car manager may buy a rare and beautiful vehicle that will sell so well that people will be fighting over it.

By being on your game, you can have a first shot at it for one of your buyers. This is how you become a real success; by going the extra mile for your customers and your employer! Believe me when I say that you really will find it very easy to excel in this business, because most salespeople don't make this extra effort. They become satisfied with making a better than average income, but they don't strive harder to make all they can. I repeat again, this is a lazy business. You won't think so at first, because there is a lot to learn. Learn it well, and do what you must so that you are allowed to sell new and used; and set time aside every single work day for prospecting, follow-up and study. Just like an apple, when you're green you grow; when you're ripe you rot!

11 THE DEMO DRIVE

We have another saying in the car business; *"The feel of the wheel is half the deal!"* The demonstration drive is where you make or break your sale. This is the point where you find out if you've selected the right vehicle. The demo drive is critical to your sale, and I will not negotiate a deal before the buyer has driven it; not to say that there won't be a rare occasion, but when I say *never* will, it's like everything else in the car business, *nothing* is chiseled in stone. Naturally, there is a desire on the customers' part to hold off driving the vehicle and falling in love with it before knowing if he can afford it. Your job is to get them to drive it beforehand. You can qualify them as to whether they feel they can afford it, but you must demo them before you talk about buying! Also, you are fighting the customer's desire to avoid the feeling of obligation.

Get that ether in their nostrils! There is nothing like the new car smell to tranquilize your buyer. Again, we have a system in place for test drives. Some dealerships have a selected model of each line that is there for demonstration purposes only. The majority of stores however, will have you drive your customers in the *car they want to buy.*

So, you've selected a vehicle the customer likes and you excuse yourself to get the keys. You will also need to get a dealer plate if the car doesn't have current license plates, and you even may be required to make a copy of your customer's driver's license before you go on a drive. Whatever your stores' rules are for the test drive, follow them and don't take short cuts.

I've had cases over the years where my salespeople have had guns pulled on them, been pushed down, and all sorts of crazy things to steal a car! When one dealership started to require a driver's license copy before anyone could drive a car, I still had an incident. The customer came in and asked to look at a beautiful Nissan 300ZX I had just bought at the auction. My salesperson got the keys, opened the car, and made a presentation. She told the customer she would need to copy his license before he could drive it. He told her he didn't need to drive it, but he would like to hear the engine. Since he was sitting in the driver's seat and the door was open; and since she was standing there explaining the features, she handed him the keys. He started the car, knocked her to the ground and took off! By the time the police arrived and were taking my report, our state police were in pursuit going across the state line. The Z car thief outran them and by the time the car was recovered, I had lost seats, wheels, tires, T-top and had $15,000.00 in damage. My salesperson was fortunately just fine, but shook up! Just be careful, and follow the rules and use common sense.

A female salesperson needs to be especially cautious. If you have any uneasy feelings, turn the customer to a male. Your well-being and safety are top priority. If your dealership does not have a policy where they photocopy the driver's license, you may wish to do so anyway, tell the customer it's for insurance purposes, and leave the copy with the receptionist or the sales manager. If the customer objects, then tell them they can have the copy back when you get back. If they still object, turn them to a man.

For the men in the audience, a caveat for you to remember; many a dealership has handed the keys to a new car and the title for it to a lady customer who made a claim against a salesman for unwanted sexual advances! So when an attractive woman comes on to you on the test drive, and you think it's going to be the test drive you will never forget; quite likely it will be! Keep it in your pants guys!

Going back to the thieves, I've had a lot of salesmen call the store in need of being picked up because when they went to get out and switch drivers on the demo drive, the customer locked the door, slid behind the wheel, and sped off! I've seen them tell the salespeople to get out, "if they didn't want to get hurt." Also, if a thief is taking the risk of grand theft auto and assault, do you think they won't demand your money and your cell phone?

I am not intending to scare anyone, you will not likely experience anything like this, and the way to guard yourself against it is to use common sense. You need to be in command of the keys at all times! When you switch places behind the wheel, take the keys with you. Yes, shut it off, and walk around; the customer can start it again. I've even seen where, because of cold weather, the salesperson and customer both jumped out, but one of them accidentally hit the power locks, and there they were, standing there listening to the engine and wishing they were inside!

Now let's get into the selling, big time! The test drive is where the sale is cemented! Your customer is getting the new car smell (even the used car smells better than the beater they came in)!

Individual dealers have varying rules on test drives. I'll give you my preference, and you do what they instruct you to. If they don't have a preference, then do it this way! The salesperson should *always* drive first! Let's examine the reasons.

First of all, your customer is unfamiliar with the vehicle. You may be too, but you never want to put your buyer in an uncomfortable situation, and believe me, driving out in a strange vehicle, in a strange place, in front of a bunch of strangers, is a very uncomfortable position for you to put your customer in! If they kill the engine or have trouble seesawing out of the parking spot, you may have just embarrassed them.

Maybe your customer is very familiar with the car and just wants to go for it, and drive it out. You will get stuck sometimes where you need to just go ahead, but you should be able to stay in control if you take charge. The easiest way is simply, act! Say, "Okay folks, I'll drive it first because there are some features I'd like to point out!" Next, hold the doors for them! Forget that sloppy crap about slapping your butt behind the wheel and yelling, "Get in!"

Have some manners. Before we pull out, make sure your customers are comfortable. Help adjust the seats for everyone, lock the seatbelts and have the same politeness you would use for your grandparents, regardless of the age of your customers. It will be noticed and appreciated.

Start the car and start pointing out important features of the car, by using the *Feature/Benefit Presentation*. Think of the word SELL. The S means "show the feature." The E means, "explain the feature." The L means, "lead to the benefit." The other L means, "let the customer decide." This is an easy way to remember the feature/benefit way of selling. Let's go over it slowly, because it is the only true way you can sell a product. Remembering S E L L is just a reminder on how to present any product.

Let's take *cruise control* and use the SELL concept to explain it, and yes, there still are people out there who have never had cruise control, may have never used it and don't know how even though it's on their present car! I *show* the feature: Here is the cruise control on and off switch. Next I *explain* how it works, how to accelerate and decelerate with just the buttons. Now I *lead to the benefit*; better mileage, gas saving, more on the road comfort by not having to use the brake or gas pedal. The last L should be used as a closing question; *let the customer decide* is where you need to use a question like, "Isn't this something you'd like on your next car? Wouldn't that be of benefit to you?" Just remember, if you can't use this SELL method of presenting a feature, why bother? Pointing under the hood and telling your customer, "Look at that," does nothing!

I'm not going to go into a detailed sales presentation, because your dealership will do that. Also, there are so many sales training videos that will inundate you with questions, answers and things to say, that it is not necessary you hear it from me. There are fantastic trainers with the command of the English language, and the smoothness that the average salesman can only wish he or she had. As I previously mentioned, I love their words, actions, reactions and their butter-smooth delivery, but they're not me; nor will they be you.

You can practice your delivery and scripts until you become a master, but what I am giving you are the very foundations that you must learn in order to build your success on! Something as simple as a feature-benefit presentation can and does fill volumes.

Now, let's go back to the test drive. Our intention when we go on a demonstration drive has multiple facets. We are buying time to completely explain, and let the customer experience the vehicle he selected. We are away from the distractions of the dealership and the rest of the inventory. Also, in addition to privacy, keep in mind that if your test drive takes you fifteen minutes away from the dealership, then it's going to take you fifteen minutes to return isn't it? That gives you at least 30 minutes of privacy in order to sell the car and develop a relationship with your customer. How difficult would this be if you stayed on the lot? Your customers need to be isolated with you in order for you to develop rapport!

You will be taught how and where to *present* the car before the test drive. Most trainers will have you pull the vehicle out of line (isolate it), and do a presentation where you will have room to go over it thoroughly without blocking the drive. In many stores, this is not always easy due to crowding of inventories and little space for selling.

I taught my salespeople to go over enough of the vehicle on the lot, and then get on the test drive as quick as possible. Then I had them go to a favorite, quiet place to do a full presentation! Think about all the opportunities for a minute; a city or county park, a business parking lot on a weekend when they're closed, a church parking lot (most of the week), and many other places where you can open the doors, hood, trunk, and really give a great show, and without interruption. Find a place where the property owners won't object. Ask them ahead of time if you don't know.

Have your own place, and keep it to yourself. As soon as you brag about how well your magic place works, it'll be like telling your best friend about your lucky fishing hole. Next time you go there, you'll have a lot of company, and soon the property owner will kick you all out. Most companies, churches included, don't mind an occasional use, but don't share your secrets, or you'll lose.

Your demo route needs to be carefully planned to show off the product; and let it sell itself, which it soon will. Remember I said, "The feel of the wheel is half the deal?" Well, I didn't coin the phrase — the car biz' did, because it's the flat-out truth.

Your route needs to have a convenient place for you to switch drivers. During your turn, you should be selling features and benefits, and talking about the comfort, asking how they feel about this and that, their jobs, hobbies, and giving a good and thorough pitch on the attributes of this model. Now it's time to switch, so you let your customer know you are pulling over (never startle them), and your question needs to be, "Who's going to drive first?" You may get a reaction from the wife like, "Oh, let him drive it, I don't want to." We're not through asking yet, but switch with him first.

In most cases, the wife has started out sitting behind her husband who took the passenger seat up front. Your job now is to open the back door and the front door, and move her up front, with you then getting in back. In many cases, especially with older people, she will say, "I'm comfortable where I am, you go ahead and sit in front." It sounds reasonable and sensible; doesn't it? Not to me! I will say,

"Dixie, you aren't going to sit back there when you and Jerry are driving; and I want you to see how the front seat feels." This is important, and as your manager, I want to see you in the back seat and your customers up front when you return from your demo; every time! Without exception!

Well, during your turn, you talked, you sold, explained and you asked questions. Now that he's driving, quiet down! Don't completely shut up, but zip it. Make sure he's comfortable, they're both buckled in, seats adjusted, mirrors readjusted and controls explained. From here on, you should be saying things like, turn right at the next light Jerry, and we'll get a chance to go a little faster; mainly instructions on where to turn, and let them experience the type of quiet driving they are used to when they are alone.

During your turn, you should take the route that will allow your customers to make right turns only on the way back to the dealership. You never want to put your buyer in the position of having to turn across traffic unless it can't be avoided. A left turn on a green turn arrow is fine, but I always want everything to be easy and safe for my buyer.

Now, you need to have a *second* turnout planned. That's right; after he has driven for a while, now you say, "Jerry why don't you pull over up ahead, and let's give Dixie a chance to drive." She may very likely do it, especially if you've made the drive comfortable and safe for him. She may well refuse, but you must try your best to make it happen!

I'll give you an example. This is just one case, but I remember it so well, because the lady was spot on! I was trying to close a sale on a very expensive and beautiful GMC Suburban. The vehicle was for the wife, primarily for shuttling kids and dogs and soccer mom duties, and all family activities. It was not going well, and finally I asked her, "Sandy, it seems that this vehicle will be perfect for you, what is there about it that you're not comfortable with? The way it drives has to be better than the vehicle you're replacing!" Her comment was, "I really don't know! These jocks were too busy talking football; I never even got a chance to sit in the front seat!" Stupid! Ridiculous? Yes, and rude!

I had the husband sit at the table with me and told my salesman "Go ride with Sandy, let her drive anywhere she wants, and don't even talk unless she asks you a question!" I was mad and disgusted, but we all learned the basics that we already knew, but in a manner we would not forget, as it was the subject of my sales meeting the next day!

They returned from the test drive, walked up to the table, and Sandy said, "We'll take it! I absolutely love it!" Could we have made more profit by doing things properly the first time? You bet!

Put this in your memory, and never forget it — no matter who the vehicle is for, the husband or the wife, spend 60% of your presentation on the wife! Without her acceptance, he won't buy squat!

When I was in the motorhome business, we had a desk in front where the salesperson who was up sat. On this desk was a sign that read; *Gary's rule of 95*, it said, "In 95% of all cases, the wife will make the buying decision. In the other five percent, she *allows* her husband to do it!" That's a little tongue in cheek, but think about it for a minute. Who controls the money in the majority of American households today? Guys don't even bother to answer, just nod your heads.

If the wife drives it, you have definitely got the job done well! She, after all, is the key to the purchase, and it scores well for you if you get her to drive. If, when you first meet these people and find out the car is primarily for her, then she drives second, and her husband third; but that situation is a little more flexible, and I would never insist that he drive, just ask, and if he says no, don't even bother to try forcing the issue. If you should insist that he also drive, you risk insulting her. Conversely, you cannot insult him by insisting that she drive *his* car.

So let's recap. A car for the family or for the husband, we need to have the wife drive, and he will appreciate it because he needs her blessing. If the car is for her, she drives; don't worry if he doesn't drive, because the buying decision is hers anyway. The easy way to keep this in mind might be to compare people to pheasants. The male pheasant is pretty and in charge. The female human is pretty and in charge. So unless you are selling a car to a pheasant, give most of your sales pitch and attention to the lady!

Now you are returning to the dealership, and your customer should be making a right turn into the store. You can unbuckle your seat belt if you need, so you can lean forward and point out where she should park. Your dealer will show you where they want you to put it when you return from test drives. Make it easy; if it's crowded, have the customer stop anywhere, and *you* park it!

If you have an option, park it right outside the showroom window, and seat your customer where they can look out at it the whole time you're working out the details of the sale. Some scripts will teach you so say, "Park right there in the sold row," or some other way. So now, how do you get them inside to negotiate?

I always will use an assumption, as I firmly believe that if I must ask someone if they want to buy my car, then they may feel that I have some doubt that it's the best choice. I don't believe in ever creating a doubt as to whether or not my product is best for them, or that I could even comprehend them *not* buying it! My comment will generally be, "Okay Monica and Dante´, let's go inside and get the paperwork done so you can take it home!" I don't ask, I tell. After all, I have the right, don't I? We picked out a vehicle that I know they will be happy with. I know for a fact that there is no finer product, and cannot conceive that they would have any doubt! People will follow — trust me!

Now; instead of implying that I have any doubt, if they do, they have to tell me. If they say they want to think it over (number one objection), what do I do? — I respond with, "Oh really, what is it you wish to think about?" Then they have to answer the question; and most often they'll tell me what I need to do to sell them the car! Whatever answer they give me as to what it is they want to think about, I can respond to and win! I should be able to overcome any think it over objection, as people always feel they're rushing into a sale. They may tell themselves before they leave home that, "We're not going to buy anything today." Suddenly, they are at a point of going back on their commitment to not make a commitment! Neither person wants to be the first to go back on their agreement. Your job is to get a mutual agreement.

I can reiterate the fact that this car does everything they want it to, what else would they need that my car doesn't have, and what it all boils down to is that people always start out thinking that they are going to look at all the makes, and then pick the best one. Yet, here they are, close to buying the first one they looked at! I just need to make them happy they don't have to keep going through all the shopping, and can get it over now!

Let's digress for a minute, and assume that in this situation they told you upfront that they weren't buying anything today, and they even refused a test drive until you said, "I can appreciate that, but wouldn't it be a shame if out of all the cars you looked at, you liked this one best, then when it came time to drive it, you didn't like it? Why not take a few minutes right now and drive the car? Then you will see if it's even worth keeping on the list at all." So with that argument, you got them on the drive, and now suddenly they're coming out of the ether! They weren't prepared to buy today, and suddenly they're confronted with a total change of their game plan. Maybe they can be convinced that if they like the car, if it has everything on it they want, they like the color, the dealership and you; then why not just go ahead?

Whatever happens, we should end up inside. If I can't get them to change their minds, I still need to move them from the outside to the showroom, don't I? Since I likely already gave them my business card, I can't say, "Come on in and I'll give you my card." I can say, "I want to give you something," or why not just ask, "What is it you want to think about?" If they give me the same, "It's all happening so fast," or some other cop out, I can say, "Well, since you don't have anything to really compare, why don't we take a few minutes while you're here to see what the figures look like on paper? Then you'll have the numbers to compare, and you will know exactly what you need to make a decision! Fair enough? Follow me!"

That's it; we're going in to buy a car! If I can get the people to sit down and discuss figures with me, I have an excellent chance of earning their business. Think back at this point on how far we've come. We came from just looking, and not driving today, to wanting to think about it, to sitting down to look at the figures on paper.

We are basically overcoming objections. I like to think of a fish bowl full of small envelopes. Each envelope has either a yes or a no written inside. So each time we ask a question or have an objection, we pull out an envelope and see what's inside. We either get a yes or a no. Ideally, I want all the nos I can get because once the nos are used up, there won't be anything left but yeses!

As I begin showing, driving and answering objections, I'm using all the nos! Now when I move the customers inside and seat them, will I be in a good position to sell a car if I have a fish bowl full of yeses? Yes! Use up all the nos, and the yeses will be there.

Remember these words spoken by the Immortal Vince Lombardi when he was the Green Bay Packers King, *"Given enough time, I'll win any ballgame!"*

12 LET'S NEGOTIATE — THE *OFFER* PROCESS

We know now, that once a customer has taken a test drive, that our odds of entering into negotiations are vastly improved. We are hoping at this point, that the excitement is great enough so they will want to begin the buying process, and we also could have tried to find this out in the beginning or on the demo. You must be careful to not continue testing the water so much you make waves, but if you listen more than you talk, the customer will most often give you more information than they intend to.

Questions you can ask if you meet resistance at any point can be as simple as, "What did you hope to accomplish on your visit today?" Here's another thing to keep in your subconscious; when you first begin to qualify your up, most people will answer with, "This is the first place we've been." Later on when you've spent time with them, and have taken a test drive, if you ask them, "Out of all the vehicles you've looked at so far, which one do you like best?" Funny thing, but the majority of people will respond with an answer, forgetting that they told you they just started looking. So don't try to qualify the customer too soon, as their defenses are on high alert. Earn the right on the ride.

There will be an occasion where a customer wants to discuss the numbers without a test drive up front. There can be many reasons for this request, so go slow, don't push in the all too typical manner.

We are well aware that the demo drive sells, but just roll with it. It is best that we ascertain which exact vehicle they want to see figures on if you can first take them to the inventory. If they are unwilling and just wish to discuss generalities, go along with it and seat them inside. Now offer refreshments and bring out some scratch paper. I need to mention at this point that my scratch paper is always a write-up sheet or two, along with a customer statement (credit application) folded over (of course), so only the blank sides are visible. Now I am in a position to discuss *anything*. The customer may have legitimate reasons for their actions, and if you make this investment in time and offer to buy refreshments, it could just be the easiest sale you ever made!

I have found that in a high percentage of these scenarios, you are dealing with a highly courteous and conscientious buyer, who has genuine concerns over not wasting *your* time until they know they are qualified to make a purchase. They will be reluctant to waste your time on a test drive, and this why I say go along with them, but try to persuade them to accept your coffee, soda, etc., because when they do, you now have an exceptionally loyal and solid buyer. Oftentimes they have credit concerns, and many people feel their credit is worse than it really turns out to be. This is why you have a customer statement under your scratch paper.

You can now offer to have the manager run a free credit check. Many people also are unaware that you can do this without a cost to them. A lot of lenders will charge them for it! Now, before you rush off to pull the credit check, slow yourself down and think for a minute about what you are doing! Here is your qualifying opportunity and you can find out very innocently what they have in mind should your dealer find a way to help them obtain a bank loan. Since there are no actual negotiations taking place, you easily get a rough idea of how much money they are able to invest at this time (cash down) and what their monthly budget (desired payment) will be.

Now your desk manager knows how to guide you in selecting the proper vehicle for these people. Your wants and the customer's wants are the same now. You both must be on the same page, as you absolutely have to show them a vehicle that, based on their financial position, will fit this budget! If they say yes to what you show them, you make a sale. If they don't like your choice, you now work it like a regular car deal!

You earned their trust, their loyalty, and their respect. Now you are a buying team. Everything you do from here on out will be for their benefit once you find a car they like; if you ask for more payment and down payment to hit their goal, they know you're on their side. Trust me; *you will sell* this customer a car!

Now for the customer who is really just making a comparison against price, trade, and payments based on numbers he already has from another dealer, your first objective is to make sure to select the exact same vehicle he is comparing! Try hard to get them on a test drive. They will be reluctant because they feel they already know everything about the vehicle as they already drove it at the other store. Somehow you must get the ether flowing again! If you cannot get them to drive it, you must now rely on the other salesperson having given them a good test drive, but remember, they feel more of an obligation to the other guy at this point.

Think out of the box; do you know enough about your product to maybe have some fact or feature about the car that is a plus? Maybe even a slightly better equipped model that is not a whole lot more expensive? A new feature that just was added? I've made a lot of sales by pointing out a seldom discussed feature that although the customer thinks was on the other car, that I have created enough doubt that it turned out to clinch a sale. Sometimes all the buyer needs is a reason to complete the sale with you, even if an item of equipment is most certainly on both vehicles. Remember now, we're talking about Mr. fairly honest Customer who just wants to buy a vehicle without offending the last salesperson. If you can create an argument that your car is better equipped than the other car, and for the same dollars, even though your customer knows better, you will win! Reason being; these people are not really all that loyal to any salesperson! All they need is just some tiny excuse to get their conscience off the hook, and they will buy from you. Then if the last salesperson follows up, which is doubtful, they can innocently defend their buying from you. When the other salesperson explains that his car had the same options, he or she will believe it was their own fault for failing to give the customer a proper presentation. In actuality, your customers will appreciate the fact that you created this opportunity for them to save face and protect their honest image, even though you both know they have no genuine concerns over the salespeople involved. Once people feel they have done enough research and are at the point of being able to make a decision, they just want to get 'er done.

Two motivating factors that prompt buying decisions are a fear of loss or a hope for gain! Fear of losing this rare car may be just the perfect tool if you can pull it off! The customer we are discussing is again, a very cautious and also a very courteous customer. They don't expect you to spend any extra time with them if they do not intend to buy from you at the time. They will take your time only when they are ready to make a buying decision. Until that time, they are respectful of your time, and are aware that you do not receive a salary, and get paid only if you sell something.

Your key to these people is to find that chink in their armor that gives them an *excuse* to let you serve them. The "I want to drive it myself, ride along with me" line works perfect for this type of shopper. Remember, "A shopper is a shopper, 'til he meets a salesperson!" So true — and to be a salesperson, you must overcome objections! Asking a customer a question, such as, do me a favor — drive it and give me your opinion, is more of a command. Use the reason, "I haven't had a chance to drive this car yet, as they don't allow us to just 'drive' cars. I'm glad you came, so I could test it out." Other commands, can be as simple as, "Turn here, pull in there, read that mileage to me if you would," and so forth. Soon you will be saying, "Sign here."

From the test drive, we need to transition to the inside of the store. Your dealership will have suggestions as to how they want you to take this next step. Each dealership has its own style that they prefer you to use.

If you have good weather, you can keep the customer with you during the next step. If they have agreed to look at figures, you are in a position to expect information. First, you will need to write down the numbers on the car they're buying. You will need the stock number, mileage and VIN. Yes the VIN (vehicle identification number). It may not be required that you do the VIN, but get it anyway. Trust me. When your manager enters the stock number in the computer, and an error message pops up because someone entered the VIN improperly when stocking in the vehicle, you will save a lot of time by having the VIN on *your* paperwork! Sure, it happens a lot. Like every damn day! It's your income, protect it. Time is critical, and you can't be using it up chasing your tail.

If you have properly asked your buyer if the car they drove in with is the one "they're replacing," then your next step is to have your customer accompany you to the trade-in. If the weather is bad, then you will have taken the customers indoors, and selected a place for them to sit, and then you can go back outside and get the information off the trade. Ideally, take the husband back out with you. Why? Because you want him to be there, not to read you the numbers, that's *your* duty only, but so he can observe his own car! *You* will record VIN, mileage and *all* equipment on the trade. Don't miss anything. Make sure you note every option, as your income depends on it (I'll show you why later). Every paint chip, windshield star, scratch and dent should be silently touched by you, and in front of him or them. It's always *best* to have them *both* there naturally, but go with the flow. People never remember all the scratches, dents and stains they accumulate on their present car. Maybe the wife gets a dent, the husband gets a scrape, the son spills a coke, the dog chews a seat corner, a door doesn't close properly, the windshield is cracked, the headliner is torn; you get the picture. You do not have to say a word, just reach out, rub the dent or scrape, as though to note how deep or long it is, and make a note or check on your appraisal sheet. You will be required to either carry an appraisal, or will have gone to get one from the office, so use it to your advantage. Touching a dent or scratch lowers the customer's expectations of value. You are now reverse-selling. You are deducting dollars from their trade-in value.

You *never* want to look up from your appraisal slip and say, "You people are really slobs!" You will silently get your point across *without* insulting your buyers. Many people who have piggy cars have piggy homes as well, but with today's hectic lifestyles, a lot of people use a car as a tool to get a job done. They don't feel it is necessary to impress anyone, and don't have the time or desire to do anything more than drive it. They may shovel it out once a year, and the rest of the time it is abused.

So why do a silent appraisal? Because, chances are, they aren't even remotely aware of how much is wrong with it. By silently touching and making even *imaginary* notes on your slip, you are decreasing the value of the trade in their minds. Of course, *don't actually write* all of this stuff down, because you want to leave all the bad stuff to let the appraiser look for! Therefore, drive the value down in the customer's mind by finding the problems, and *raise* the value in the used car appraiser's eyes by noting every possible accessory, option and all the good stuff. Find every extra option on their trade, because it's all going to increase your paycheck!

Certainly, if my customer tells me it has a bad transmission, I *will* make note of it. We never cheat our employer, but it is just like the case of the used vehicle that each customer that sees it finds something more wrong. Your job is not to decrease your trade value, except in the eyes of your buyer. The silent walk around also *prepares* your buyers for a low appraisal. If you choose not to do this step, you are setting yourself and your closer up for a much more negative and vocal reaction when the appraisal is shown to the customer. You don't want to have the closer list all of the problems they didn't realize their car even had, because then he becomes the bad guy! Sell the appraisal! This way your buyer is prepared for a lower number and won't react as negatively!

What if the man is aware of the dents and dings he put on the car; the wife remembers the stained carpets, and the time she backed into the steel post; and they are each unaware of the other's damages. Your ability to point out the accumulated items that decrease the value, without being critical, is key to setting the buyer's mind up for acceptance of less than they thought the value would be worth.

Don't beat 'em up over condition, just make them aware that the used car manager will see it all. Another good way the customer knows you're on their side is to make a comment like "I'm not going to write all of this down. Let's hope the appraiser is busy, and misses this and this, and that, etc.!" You're on the customer's side, and you need for them to feel you're working *for* them! You can also ask if they have the trade serviced regularly, and where.

Conversely, make copious notes if the customer is selling you their car. If they tell you that all services have been performed at your service department, including oil changes, don't you think that's worth a lot to the appraiser? You bet it is. He will know that it's been well taken care of, and that any serious problems have likely been taken care of as well. He may short cut even driving the car, and may not notice the bad brakes because of it, and your appraisal may end up a lot higher, which puts more money in your pocket, as things like that are very seldom ever a cause for adjusting appraisals later on plus, that when they're selling you on its virtues, you'd better act like you're making notes of everything!

Now, if you cover up a bad transmission by fast talking your appraiser, you may expect to be charged back against your commission, and you should be fired! Don't steal from your employer.

If the weather outside is frightful, and you are going to go out and fill out the appraisal sheet on your own, just hold out your hand and ask for the keys, then offer to get your customer refreshments. There is a knack to this, and you need to learn how to do it! Something as simple as a cup of coffee or a soda can make a *big* difference! Remember those people who don't want to feel an obligation? Let's obligate 'em good!

Some dealerships have free coffee for customers. They all have snack and soda machines. So here's what I do — Since I carry a money clip, it's easier for me, but money clip or wallet, reach in your pocket (you ladies need to lock up your purses, and carry I.D. and money in a wallet of some type) and with your money showing, ask; "May I get you some refreshments? Coffee, tea, soda?" Why the show? Because I want to cement an obligation; and I know of no better way! Another reason is that no matter what happens, a customer will always finish their free drink before they leave. This buys me at the very least, 10 minutes. Also, they at least will feel obligated enough to meet your sales manager, used car manager, or assistant manager or senior salesman (for a turn).

Even if the dealership has free coffee, show the money, offer the coffee, tea or soda, and even if they take the free coffee, you have indicated to them that they are important enough to invest your money in them. Later, as you're negotiating, or after they have accepted, don't forget to offer refills. Also out of courtesy, point out the restrooms. You want your customers to be as comfortable as possible. No, *do not get yourself* a drink; you're on duty, and even though you feel it would be polite to join them, forget it! It isn't good!

Next, you will be expected to do what will be basically referred to as a *write-up*, or offer to purchase. This may be labeled work sheet or any one of many terms. That's why *we* refer to it as a write-up. You come up to a manager and say, "I have a customer who wants to buy a car," and the manager says, "Write 'em up!" That's our normal term, just don't call it that in front of the customer.

A write-up in most parts of the country consists of an information sheet, or work sheet that will have room on top for the customer's name, phone number, address, email address, the description of the vehicle they wish to buy, including items such as VIN, mileage and license plate number (if pre-owned). That's the basic information normally called for. There may be more, may be less. You may be asked to also enter the trade-in basic information on the worksheet as well.

Depending upon your state laws and dealership requirements, you may also be required to complete a customer statement, which is a credit application. Here again, rules and laws change. Throughout my career, in most stores, the salesperson asked the questions, filled in the blanks and had the customer sign it to verify that the information was correct. Many states require that the customer fills out the form personally. Many customers object at this point because of eyesight, arthritis, and so many reasons, so if you are allowed, fill it out yourself. Always!

If I am able to ask the question, fill in the answer, and keep firing questions, I can fill out the entire application quickly and efficiently. If I allow the customer to do it, the process will be slow and laborious, and anytime there is a silence, the customer gets nervous. Silence to them compels them to think of questions. You can't just say "shut up and write." So time drags, and time in negotiating a car deal is critical.

People have deadlines. Kids to pick up, medicines to take, shots to inject, dogs to feed and let out, you name it. Especially people who only came in to look, and here they are ready to make a car deal, and five minutes before handshake time their phone rings, the ether wears off, the excitement drops down and runs under the door, your sales manager hates you, you just lost $2,000.00 in commissions, and you kissed goodbye to a great effort! Shit happens! You need to be constantly aware of time constraints!

If a customer says, "We only have a half hour," as we are coming back from the test drive, I know I can't possibly get it done, so I need to know *why*. Maybe it's as simple as picking up their daughter from school. Great! Tell them, "Hey go ahead, and let's pick her up in your new car!" Have them head for the school. Picture the ride back to the dealership with the daughter saying, "Can we buy it Mom and Dad, can we please?" Been there, done that and the time element is handled, and we just bought all the time we need, and you have another ally and a few more refreshments to buy! Use time to your advantage, but be cognizant that it's ticking!

Now let's get back to that customer statement (credit app). If I am allowed to take the customer statement, by the time I am finished, I probably know more about these people than their parents! Once I have answers to all of these questions, I am closer to these folks than anyone. I have become almost like family. You need to get inside their heads, and if you are allowed to fill out the app and don't do it; you are making a major error. A lot of salespeople hand the customer the app and a pen, and say, "Here, fill this out, and I'll be back." Then they go stand in a circle jerk, smoke cigarettes so they can smell bad to the customer, and short cut their chances for a sale! Don't ever ask me how I really feel! Stay with your customer, even if they must fill it out themselves, because they will have questions. Make sure the app is complete. If the application is not complete, you will catch hell; and deservedly so.

You don't need to be anxiously awaiting a page to bring your customers to the business office, and instead being paged there yourself, and having a disgusted finance manager toss the application to you and saying, "Go finish this properly," or, "Do it over," or "Everything is in the wrong place!" A delay like this, or having to have your customers fill out a new app because you didn't see they did it wrong, could just be the last straw after intense negotiations that will cause your customers to just bolt for the door! If they do, you will likely never see them again, as they have jumped through all the hoops they're going to for you! The only way you may get them to return another day may be to make them a far better deal than they had. A far better deal to them means a far reduced commission for you!

I wouldn't even mention this if it didn't happen *all the time*! Do everything right the first time around, because customers do not have much patience for the grueling process of negotiating, let alone having to do things twice!

Once you have the customer statement completed, the trade-in appraisal sheet, and have the customer's keys in hand, you are ready to begin work.

Here's where dealerships vary their processes and procedures.

ENTER THE FOURSQUARE

Since the majority of my career has involved using this foursquare write-up process, I am very comfortable working all facets of its' many angles and the endless scenarios that can evolve from what at first look seems like a very basic and innocuous way of negotiating.

Most dealerships today will likely be using some more modern and more seemingly sophisticated write-up process. When I say more sophisticated, I do so tongue in cheek, because the newer methods have evolved, in my opinion, due not so much to a better way, but as an easier way. It takes a lot less talent and training to just sit down with a printed offer and point; "For ours; for yours," and so forth.

The real reason the foursquare has died out is because it takes a tremendous amount of training and expertise in the art of negotiating! It is far easier in today's dealerships to have even less training in selling than ever, and with more attention to product knowledge and presentation; the kinder and gentler crowd. There are still some true professionals out there, but the talent pool is rapidly evaporating. We're getting back to the German Shepherd with the note around its neck!

If your dealership is not using the foursquare, then you may just bypass the rest of this chapter, because it just gets into the real basics of the killin', skinnin', and cleanin', rather than eatin' off the menu. Or, you may wish to see how the other half lives and stay with us.

A true foursquare presentation will be carefully created by the salesperson by asking innocent-sounding questions and discussion of price, trade allowance, down payment and monthly payments. Information is supplied by the desk beforehand and will be off-handedly brought out by the salesperson, as though his or her numbers are strictly from memory and reference to previous and similar transactions that they are aware of.

Everything hereafter is designed to test the water, and slowly back into a customer offer without actually having any offer from the sales manager directly to the customer. This process is probably the least confrontational of all, because when this customer makes an offer with the help of the salesperson, everything is very low key and loose up to the final "we'll buy and drive it home now!"

The reason that the foursquare method differs from other more direct methods of negotiating an offer is that it backs into an offer rather than beginning with a proposal right out of the chute.

As the car business has transitioned through its various new ideas and modernized strategies, it has become popular to advertise the new customer friendly ways to buy a car. Dealers trump the no hassle and full up front disclosures. We advertise to show you all the numbers, including down payment, monthly payments, trade allowance, and of course; all of this from a discounted price! How much friendlier can you get? These new methods have new dialogues, planned presentations, and different ways to get the buyer involved in the negotiating process, but it all gets back to the same thing; we offer, the buyer counter-offers, we negotiate more, and the results will be the same. As I previously mentioned, I prefer using the foursquare, as it gives me an edge in setting up the negotiations, and it seems to be easier to smoothly transition into a write-up!

WORKING THE FOURSQUARE

You may be required to take the keys and the appraisal to the sales office, pick up a blank credit application (customer statement) and get a hit figure. I will go into detail at this point on the type of system where the salesperson constructs the making of an offer.

Allow me to outline *exactly* the way this system is carried out. Once you have seated the customer, taken care of the appraisal, obtained the keys, supplied information on restrooms and bought refreshments, we are ready to go to work on the sale.

You will say to your customer, "Excuse me a minute, I'll give the trade-in keys to my manager, get some 'scratch paper' and be right back." You take the keys and appraisal to the desk. The manager who will work your deal is normally referred to by the slang term, the desk. Too often I've seen salespeople often make the error of referring to the sales manager as the desk in front of the customer. Imagine the picture in a customer's mind when imagining a huge Jabba the Hut type, rectangular, talking, wooden desk! Anyway, the desk manager is the one who you will report to, and who will be working (desking) your deal.

The desk manager will book out your trade. This means he will enter all of the information from your appraisal slip into the computer. It is imperative that you carefully write the serial number (VIN) on the appraisal sheet, as the first thing the manager does is to enter this number. If you have made an error in a letter or number, the process stops, and you shag your butt back out to the trade-in to do the job right! This translates into lost time, and you need to do it *right the first time*! The accessories you have written on the appraisal will also be entered. I'll add a note here that will make you a lot of money: Let's say that you fail to note an accessory. In this case, a power moon-roof that adds $600.00 more value and the retail price is raised by $800.00. Good job for failing to write it down. I say good job, because that's what the used car manager will be thinking, because the car gained value, and he didn't have to pay you on that additional $600.00 of wholesale value. Now if you are paid 25% of the sale profit, you just cost yourself $150.00! Write down *all* accessories and extras you can find! You cannot count on the appraiser to find things you forget. The appraiser is primarily concerned with condition, paint, tires, engine, transmission and overall appearance; and not in wiping the nose of an inexperienced new kid! Often a used car manager may not even tell the desk it's worth more, because if he plans to sell the trade-in through the auction, he makes a bigger profit and his numbers are better!

Now conversely, if you know of a problem the customers mentioned about the trade, then write it down and tell the desk about it. Mistakes in not mentioning a major and costly repair means the hit figure you get will be too high, and when found later, you or the closer must now take something away from your customer. Giving them a lower estimate up front and preparing them for a reduced appraisal is better than coming back later and reducing a value they thought they had!

I know, you're thinking, in the first sentence I mentioned to get a hit figure; "What the hell is a hit figure?" I did that on purpose to see if you could practice keeping your mouth shut! Most salespeople have trouble with that! The hit figure is derived from your desk manager calculating what the estimated wholesale (actual cash value) is on your trade-in, which is obtained by taking the wholesale book value of your trade-in, plus or minus a mileage calculation, and where the vehicle value is (in relation) to this book figure. Say for example that the estimated value based on your notes and comments on the trade-in condition, the value of the vehicle is estimated to be $25,000.00. Now of course this is subject to the trade being as you described, and prior to an actual appraisal. To allow for flexibility in this estimated value, and for the fact that the customer may accept a lot less for it (increasing your gross profit) you may be given a hit figure of $20,000.00. You will need to remember it and *not* write it down. Now in case you're still wondering why this amount is called a hit figure, it is because the normal comment from the desk will be, "Hit 'em at 20 grand." So you see why we call it a hit figure, because you hit" 'em with it! I know, we have a lot of slang in this business, and you'll soon be acting just as crude as the rest of us.

So now, you pick up the customer statement (credit application) in the sales office, and it just screams at you, "Oh no, this will take hours!" If you go out there and lay it in front of your customers, they will probably think the same thing won't they? I mean, after all you just got through telling them you were going to get some scratch paper, and now you're coming out with a questionnaire from hell!

So, fold it over! That's right; just fold the questions to the inside! Now pick up the worksheet (write up) and fold it over also! Why write up? Because we're gonna' *write 'em up*! Now you're armed with your hit figure on the trade and your scratch paper.

This is where using my suggested body language comes in. Now, *learn this*, and *practice it*, because if you do it right, you will be so *cool!*

As you are sitting down, you will be making eye contact with your customers, so have your papers (2) positioned with worksheet on top, and credit app on bottom. As you are sitting, just peel the top one (worksheet) off, and casually slide the folded app off to the side as if it's just extra paper. Unfold the worksheet, and proceed to fill it out.

We begin with the worksheet. Never try to start with the credit application, because you have not earned the right. Your customer will not give you his personal information until you discuss figures; as you promised. After agreeing on what it will take to earn his business, he will be glad to!

To make this part easier to understand, since you don't have the actual forms, take a piece of paper, and let's go over the basics of a worksheet. As I mentioned at the beginning, this is *one* method, and it will be as good as anything to show you how it works and why.

The top section of the foursquare will have space for customer information, the vehicle information on what they're buying and what they're trading in.

Now, just take a plain 8½" by 11" sheet of paper, and dissect it by a vertical line and a horizontal line, forming four equal size squares. Assume that the other information on top has already been completed, and now we casually begin our write-up.

This is what we call *working the deal.* In the upper left square we write the full selling (list) price of the car they want to buy. There is a proper way to do everything, and you need to understand that *every word* you use throughout the negotiating process is not only important, but many are critical to your success! Something so simple as flubbing a sentence can drastically affect the outcome of your presentation. This is why we practice until we have it perfect!

As you write this full selling price in the upper left-hand square, you say aloud, "Tom, Jane, the price of the car you're buying is $——."

As you say it, you write the price down. If your price is $38,500.00, you *don't* say 38 thousand five hundred dollars! The proper pronouncement is, "Thirty-eight five." Make the price sound *short*! Never draw it out if you can shorten the impact. By the way, did you catch the *price of the car you're buying* statement? Yeah, it was subtle huh?

Conversely, just like a *trade-in* that's worth $19,500.00, you never say your trade in value is "nineteen five;" you say your trade value is "nineteen thousand five hundred dollars!" See how that sounds so much larger? On *Wheel of Fortune*, you'll note that Pat Sajak will always say, you won nine thousand three hundred and fifty dollars! Never does he say $9,350.00. Remember, *shorten* the impact of the selling price, and *lengthen* the trade impact! Just like *Wheel of Fortune*, when Pat draws out the number the contestant won!

When you write the price in the upper left, you always preface it by addressing your customers by name. We want to have their undivided attention, and saying their names gently fixes their attention on the square. This brings up the point that when you are at the vehicle, you need to write down the list price from the car in front of the customers, so if there is a price concern, you can address it out there! If there is a problem or misunderstanding of the price, it will now come up. Any objection such as, "We aren't paying that for it" will surface here. If there is no trade-in, we can rest on this square for a bit and discuss the price. If we have a trade-in, we can just say, "Well folks, I'll work with you on the price, but since we have a trade-in, let's see how the total picture looks, we can see what the bottom line is, and then we can work on the total difference. Fair enough?"

Now's where you pull your hit figure out of memory, and put it in the next square on the top right. Here again, the words you use are critical to making this a smooth process for maximum profit. Say we have $38,500.00 in the price square (upper left) and the hit figure you were given by the desk was $20,000.00. Now if you had been privy to seeing the actual estimated value of $25,000.00, and you were told to hit 'em at twenty grand, you couldn't pull it off could you? That's why you aren't told what the value is hoped to be; so *you* can be convincing. I should mention here that you shouldn't give your customer too much credit for their knowledge, and don't think for a minute that they'll know the real value of their trade. They don't. That's the reason we test the water! We can always give more if we have to, but that comes later on.

Now, in the upper right-hand square, we need the hit figure. An easy way to deliver it is, "Folks, when I was in the sales office, I took a peek in our trade book, and I noticed the last time we took in a car similar to yours, it was stocked in for twenty thousand dollars; is that what you had in mind?" *Write it down as you ask it.* This approach is simple, straightforward, no beating around the bush and non-confrontational. Now, had you just sat down and said, "We can give you twenty thousand dollars for your trade," that may have just ended any chance of further negotiations, wouldn't it? Since you have not made that offer, and referred only to another vehicle, and *not* theirs, your question will be answered without an argument. We *expect* the customer to object. Everything we do is asking for the maximum profit, and if the customer just rolls over and accepts one of our trial closes, we either make a huge profit, or find out they just escaped from the loony bin!

There are many ways to deliver the hit figure. Some stores have you say, "I asked a senior salesman," or, "If I remember right, the last time we took in a trade similar to yours," etc. The main thing we want to do is set our price in the customer's mind, look for objections, trial close the trade allowance, and basically that's what we are doing. That's right, we're getting all the no's out and what's going to follow? Lots and lots of yeses!

I personally like to refer to the *record book of all trades.* This has some credibility, and if the reaction is that it's ridiculous in the customer's mind, our out is that, "Its' condition must not have been as nice as yours!" Or, "If I remember right, I think that other car had a lot more miles on it!" You may be wondering, "Why it can't just be like; here's ours, here's yours and here are the numbers." Now you sound like a customer! The reason we don't lay it all out up front is because we like money! Not only that, but in this method of constructing a write-up, you never just lay out an offer that will give you a yes or no without room for negotiating. We are trial closing without risking the customer being offended.

If we make it like walking into a restaurant, and hand them a menu, then the prices would all end up being the lowest, and the trade allowances would be the highest and I'm back to selling cars through the aid of a German Shepherd with a note around his neck! You will be paid the big bucks if you learn to do this job well. Just remember, you were hired in lieu of the Shepherd!

Now, let's see what happens when we hit this customer with $20,000.00 for their trade. *Of course* they'll object, and sometimes very forcefully! Maybe mad and loud, "What! Are you nuts! That's crazy!" Don't panic! People react in different ways, and you must always stay calm and remind the customer that, "We haven't even had your car appraised yet!" Sometimes you have to raise your voice to even be heard and to bring the customer back to earth! Just be cool, and say, "Tom, don't worry, that was the last one we took in, and I'm sure it wasn't as nice as yours, but I was just curious as to whether that was what you felt yours was worth, *just for my own information.*" Justify why you hit that number and diffuse the situation!

At this juncture, we are just probing the customer for reactions and setting low as possible expectations in their minds. We use a hit figure to plant a seed and test the water, but the real appraisal will come back as an *exact* number. We are simply setting the stage for the next act.

A relaxing statement at this point will be, "Don't worry about that right now, once your car has been appraised, I'm sure you'll be happy with the numbers." Generally, the customer has tossed out what he wants for his trade-in, and it's advisable that you *not* write it down. We don't want it written down as a demand, as then, whatever happens when we counter, we must cross out his offer and we're then taking something away from them. It's never a good idea to take away. Better to give *more* than the number that you wrote down than to *cut* the number *they* wrote down! Just don't write it down!

I always told my salespeople to not worry about the trade allowance, but if it was a *key point* of contention and of *major importance* to the buyer, then to just *circle it* for me. When I came in to close the sale, if I saw a circled trade-in figure, I knew automatically that I had to concentrate on the trade allowance more than the other factors. If it was not circled, I just worked the whole deal on monthly payments and brushed over the trade allowance, as it works best in able for us to make the most profit. This is where a close working relationship can be the key to success.

Next, let's transition to the square on the lower left. This is where we find out how much down payment the customer is prepared to make. This is *important!* We have a saying in the car business that *cash is profit!* The more cash down you can get, the higher the profit we can make. Think of it this way: If a customer can hit the payment he will buy the car at with $1,000.00 down, but our profit margin is $500.00, then if he can put $3,000.00 cash down and will take the same payment, that extra cash down can go directly toward profit, and you can keep his payment at the exact same figure, and roll the additional $2,000.00 to our side of the equation, and you now have a profit of $2,500.00.

Most buyers are payment buyers. By this, I mean they have a budget allocated for their payment that they will buy at. Keep the payments where they can handle them, and they don't care much about trade, price or anything else. Never forget that statement, it's important enough that I'll say it again! Cash is profit! A lot of customers will come in and say, if you can keep my payments where I'm comfortable, I'll buy a car. You get enough of this type of customer, and you'll know there *is* a Santa Claus!

So now we go to the lower left square, and you say, "Well folks, as you know (*they don't know*, but by paying them a compliment assuming they are knowledgeable they won't contest your statement), most lenders require one-third cash down. Based on these figures, we should be looking at (mentally calculate approximately one third of the list price) about thirteen thousand dollars (⅓ of 40,000 list price), can you handle that okay?" At this point, you may run into a myriad of objections, and just expect them. They may take many forms such as:

- Customer: "What about the value of our trade-in doesn't that count?"
- Salesperson: "Oh yes but, banks just like to see that third down in cash."
- Customer: "Our bank doesn't need any money down."
- Salesperson: "That's good, but just in case they may need something, how much would be possible?"

You can see where this could get confusing, so don't over complicate it. Just get a number that they could use for cash down, and write it down in the square. The customer has likely done this a lot before, so they know the drill. They'll give you a number.

Your dealership may now want you to calculate the approximate payment. Here, I should remind you that this training is upper level, and you won't get into this for a long time in most stores, and maybe never. But if everyone stayed home and only you and your manager showed up for work, you could sell cars without missing a beat. If they want you to use this system, you will spend many hours training, so this is just to give you an idea of one way to do it.

Let's take a look at what we have next; only *the most important square in most transactions!* The payment box is in the lower right hand corner. Take a look at what we have:

- We have a price of $38,500.00.
- A trade allowance (hit figure) of $20,000.00.
- Let's say the customer said he still owes $10,000.00 on the trade.
- You were able to get them to agree to a cash down payment of 4,000.

We need to *mentally* calculate 38,500 minus 20,000 equals 18,500, adding back in the 10,000 still owing and subtracting the 4,000 leaves us a balance to finance of $24,500.00 doesn't it? Don't worry about anything other than rough numbers. We just want to again test the water by suggesting a payment. Whatever balance you have, mentally round it to a number you can simplify for calculation and multiply it by 3. In this case, think 25,000, so 25 x 3 = 75. An approximate payment will then be $750.00.

So you tell the customers, "Okay Tom, Jane, based on these figures; you should be looking at a payment around $800.00. Can you handle that okay?" Yes, I always round up a bit for wiggle room. The customer *will* object. Expect it! Say they tell you, "That's too high!" *Instead of asking what payment they want* (it'll always be lower than you need), just say, "Well you *could* handle about $750.00 couldn't you?" Upon receiving another objection; your final question should be, "Tom, Jane, let me ask you this; how close to $750.00 could you come, and still buy the car right now?" and write it down. Now, all you have to do is recap what you have. "So folks, what you're telling me then is, if we can take your car in trade, four thousand cash down, and keep your payments at $650.00 a month, you'll buy the car and drive it home now, right? Okay, go ahead and sign here and I'll present your offer." Have them sign it. If they won't, then recap, and ask again. You *need* a commitment! You have likely been already taught to not use the word *sign*. Most trainers tell you to ask them to "O.K." the figures. I like to use the word *sign*. It's stronger and works better. I want the strongest commitment I can get.

This may have seemed like a complicated scenario, but in actuality, it only takes about fifteen minutes. Once they have agreed to buy and made the offer, set the offer to the side, open up your customer statement, and start filling it out. You already have their names and address, phone number, and the basics. Now here, you can take the application in an hour or fifteen minutes. Let me give you the 15 minute version. First of all, when you're taking a credit application or any other information from a customer, any time there is a *silence*, it creates an uncomfortable lull, and they will feel compelled to break the silence by asking a question. When they do, it will be unnecessary, and take time, so here's what you do, and don't change it. *Talk the app.* That's correct, ask a question, and when they answer, *repeat* it as you write. Now ask your next question, and then talk that. If you keep asking questions, talking and writing, you'll get done in *less* than half the time, and time is precious! Once you have the app filled out, signed and dated, then offer a refreshment refill, and take your paperwork to the office.

Now, if you want a one hour version, just hand the app to them, go away, and come back later on. They'll not only have a lot of questions, but it will be messed up! If you are not in control of the questioning process, then they will make errors that can kill your deal! Take the income portion where it asks for monthly earnings; the customer who has $500.00 a month sent directly to savings, so he doesn't include it in his monthly income because he doesn't see it, and he only puts down what he actually sees on his check. That may stop him from qualifying for a loan because you weren't there to explain the question! This happens a lot. Few customers even understand the difference between gross and net income.

When you're new, someone else (closer or sales manager) will be coming out now to present the dealership's offer, and you will need to make a polite introduction and then sit there and *keep your mouth shut!* Always keep absolutely quiet, and *never, ever say a single word unless asked* by your manager.

There are many sales managers and dealers around the country who still bear the memory of being kicked by me under the table when they spoke. I remember at a big dealer group meeting one day when the general manager of a large dealership came up and shook my hand, and said, "I still remember you kicking me, and you always wore those exotic cowboy boots! I can still feel it, but I learned a valuable lesson!"

Believe me when I say, speaking when someone is closing your deal is grounds for termination in a lot of stores. It is probably the *worst possible* thing you can do! I have sat for as long as half an hour after asking a closing question without *anyone* speaking. Then the customer reached out and shook my hand. Think about it. A half hour of silence; a man and wife, my salesman and me. The couple passing a calculator and notes back and forth, and me counting holes in the ceiling. Finally a deal! Had I rephrased the question or spoken at all, the pressure would have been off and I'd have lost!

Write this down, or etch it in your brain — After asking a closing question, the first one who talks, *loses!* I've had customers even say, "This is a lot of pressure." I do not reply, I just smile and keep my mouth shut! If they break the silence with some kind of question, then I answer it, and rephrase the question, or ask another one and then I again shut up! Think about the poor salesmen I kicked. Not only did they have painful shins, but they most likely also lost a sale, because they talked first and lost!

To all those people, I do *not* apologize, because they learned a lesson that some salesmen never do. No, I never had to kick a lady. They seem to learn faster, although I do remember having to nudge their shoes slightly, or giving them a look that could kill.

I know we went through the foursquare system rather quickly, but my intention is to give you a glimpse into a system that while not largely used anymore, it was the mainstay of the car business that began in the eastern United States, then to Indianapolis, and jumped out to the west coast. It was called the Hull-Dobbs System, and it went so far as to hide trades, throw car keys on roofs, and they pulled every crooked scheme you could imagine. When you wonder why people don't trust you, it's because your predecessors earned the reputation that you have to live with. I could write volumes on the dishonest and ultra-sleazy methods, but it's best to let the past fade away.

Most of today's systems will be a lot easier than the manual, do it all from scratch foursquare method, so let's examine some others. The foursquare method is a more casual and seemingly innocent way of backing into a transaction. More modern presentations are being created to continually upgrade the selling process. You at least have an idea of what can always be done if your computers all die and you have to learn to write!

A sales manager will take the same basic information on the vehicle you're selling; the trade data, and based on the credit score of the customer, will be able to print out a proposal. The proposal is then shown to the customer and the dealing begins. As I said, the foursquare backs into a sale by never directly making the customer an offer. You make trial closes and suggestions, but you never confront your customer with an offer up front. Do it only after setting the stage.

In this other method, you may advertise a new way of doing business, and dealers do! They go to great lengths to blast the media with a no obligation, "We show you the figures up front, and let you make the decision!" The preliminaries are the same. You still go through the same process. The difference is that you don't have the same script.

Once you take the initial paperwork to the desk manager, they will print out a proposal. Now *your* job is to present the numbers to your buyer. It will have the figures all neatly printed. The selling price, trade allowance, payoff on trade, and payment and lease options will be shown. Many of these proposals will give *many* options for payments based on cash down, and *many* options on terms. Most of these proposals also have a section of lease options. If you are selling a used vehicle, there will *not* generally be a lease option.

This plan is similar to the foursquare in that we show the customer a proposal, and he reacts to it. No major difference except in this more direct form, you don't need to ease into the agreement. You make a proposal, and you get an immediate reaction. You therefore must know how to react, and be prepared to do it quickly if your customer balks, or reacts by getting to his feet. You may have to swiftly diffuse the situation, and it never hurts to quickly react to a strong negative pushback.

I normally just say, "Bill, keep in mind that this proposal is the best case for *us*, but what do you feel would be the best case for *you?*" Now, he will sit back down, and show you exactly what you need to do in order to earn his business. Keeping in mind that he just gave you his best case deal; he knows that he's being overly optimistic, and you need to remind him of this. You can say something like, "Okay Bill, this is best for you, and this other one is best for my boss, so where do you think we can get together in between?" As you ask this, follow up with a *split the difference* offer of some kind. *Not an even split*, but something close to what your initial proposal presented. So if your trade allowance was $11,000.00 and the customer says he will accept $18,000.00; you should ask him if he will trade for an allowance of $12,000.00. That's a split! If he challenges me by, "You asked me if I'd split the difference! $12,000 is not a split!" I'll say, "I didn't say an *even* split! (With a big smile!)"

You're job now is to get all the price, cash down, the least amount he will take for the trade-in; and ask the important question, "So Bill, what you're telling me is (*recap* what he had agreed to), and if we can do all that, you'll buy the car and drive it home now, right?" Now, you take the offer to the sales office, and you are back in the same position you were with the foursquare. In this method, you really only have to deliver the numbers, get all you can and turn it in. You see, there is nothing really complicated in selling cars. You just offer, get the customer's offer, and present it to management!

SETUP AND INTRO FOR THE CLOSER

Whenever a closer is to be involved, a proper setup is mandatory. You must be careful of the relationship that you have established with your customers and everything you do must have a benefit to them. You cannot afford any surprises. Surprises in a car deal are disastrous. I can always picture the shocked look on customer's faces when other closers suddenly appeared with a loud, "Hi folks, I'm John the manager," and just sat down. No setup, unannounced, and unwelcome! Don't ever pull these surprises on your customers!

When you have a written offer, handle it like this; "Mr. and Mrs. Customer, when my boss hired me, he told me that if I ever needed any help, to just ask. Well, looking at these numbers that you want, I would sure feel a lot more comfortable having my boss present your offer to our sales manager. He has a lot more clout than I do, so if it's all right with you, I'd like to ask him to join us? His name is _____ and he's a really great guy!" Of course your customers will be all for it, because they feel that you have their best interests at heart! Now you depart to turn in your paperwork. When the closer comes to your table, immediately stand up (even if you have left a chair for him) and make your introductions. Show your closer respect, because you need your customers to feel that he is an important person to you and not just another salesperson playing a role as boss.

REMEMBER, YOU'RE ON STAGE

It is important to initially select and test drive a vehicle that the customer has a desire to buy. Make certain that your buyer and the decision maker are *both* present.

I will not go into any more detail on systems because the dealer you work for will have the way they want you to work the deal. Learn the way they want you to do it, and practice with your manager and your peers. Many salespeople are reluctant to role-play, because they feel embarrassed to make mistakes in front of other employees. For those people, I say, "Who would you rather blow your lines in front of; your fellow salespeople or a customer?" An in-house goof doesn't cost you money! Besides, you may all learn something and draw others into your session!

You are going to be on stage when you are with your buyer! Consider the automobile purchase as a *play*, because basically it is. You have an entrance, you have scripts, you have places to stand, and places to move to and to sit. You also have changes of scenes from into a car, on a test drive, to inside the showroom, and to sit down at a desk and deliver your lines. Your customer also delivers their lines, and hopefully the play ends with a handshake. The only real difference between a car deal and a Broadway play is that in a play, people buy tickets up front, and the car deal pays you after it's over. If you do a lousy job of delivering your lines, the play closes due to bad reviews, and in our business, your bad reviews are no sales, and your play with the car dealer also closes, if you fail to improve your performance.

If your manager doesn't use role play in training, then ask him or her if they *will* practice with you. Get together with your peers and practice these presentations. Everyone practices in order to perfect their skills. Your dentist practiced drilling and filling molds before ever working on a patient. Your auto mechanic went to school and worked on school vehicles before he ever opened a customer's hood; your minister, priest or rabbi practiced on fellow students, and they all memorized tons of material before ever taking the podium.

You will keep hearing that *"You never get a second chance to make a good first impression!"* I've heard that ever since I knocked on my first door, and met my first customer, and to a point I agree, however; if you have a stupid moment with a customer right off, you will normally be given a few minutes to make up for it. People understand dumb comments because everybody makes them, and if it's not a serious error, they can picture themselves doing the same thing, and will allow you a short recovery time.

The secret is not really a secret at all; it is called being a professional! If your career and your job are important to you, then why not invest enough time in yourself to do the job right? Learn your lines so well that you can't fail; once you have memorized and practiced your basic presentation. So you have it aced, then no matter what happens during your sale, you can get right back on track! You may miss a line, but you won't miss a sale.

Learn your product, learn your demo route, learn your lines and practice until you're as good as possible. Learn from mistakes (we always learn more this way) and try to never make the same one more than five times! See how easy this is?

Hey, the car business is very forgiving. After all, it's not like anyone else will ever know it when you ruin a chance to sell a car. *You will*; but you always have another customer on the way in. The sales business is very forgiving of failure. If you don't get a customer to drive a car, who knows why but you? If you say goodbye after a test drive, who knows why or what happened but you? Only the numbers will eventually tell management that you are succeeding or failing. A jet engine mechanic must do the job right or a plane crashes! You have *many* opportunities to crash, and *only you* will know. You owe it to yourself to get off the ground and stay there.

OUT OF AREA DEALER CAN SELL CHEAPER

So let's say your customer is a typical *cheap mooch*; that's car talk for a price conscious and intelligent, educated shopper. He tells you that the dealer in the next suburb or city can sell the same vehicle cheaper, and to earn his business, you'll have to meet his price. The buyer is well aware that wherever he buys the vehicle, the factory warranty will still be honored in your shop.

My pitch is simple and believable; "You are absolutely correct Mr. Customer, but there are a lot of items on this car that are *not covered by the factory warranty*. Now, the factory doesn't show these exclusions, so most people aren't even aware that the dealer pays for them out of his pocket! Naturally we don't run around telling people about all of the adjustments and maintenance items that the manufacturer leaves to our good will, but we accept these costs as a part of doing business. It's always been like this, and that is why in the past, dealers would not perform any adjustments or take care of paint problems or other nuisance items unless the customer had purchased from them. I'm sure you've heard that the service departments always checked first to see where you bought it. Even though it drives the manufacturers' nuts, there are still the occasional dealers who bow their backs and refuse certain freebies. Our dealer does not allow that kind of treatment and we welcome everyone, so you have no worries no matter where you buy. I just wanted you to know why we're at this price. Can we just go ahead and buy it now?" Long explanation, but use it if you have time, because it's true and people will understand and you'll win most of these sales. Where the customer won't fade, go for a bump and compromise enough to get it done! This explanation should be used where the other dealer is just slightly less than your price. All we're doing here is giving a logical explanation as to why we are a hundred or two hundred dollars higher. We are not asking for anything more than to even the playing field. Naturally you need to make sure he lives near your dealership and will be coming to you for service, otherwise this argument won't work.

13 ENTER THE CLOSER

I n this chapter we are going to cover some closing techniques, and most oft-used objections.

Whether you are a closer or a line salesperson who must close your own sales, the close is where it ends in a sale, or the customer walks out!

I'm going to address the closer, assistant manager, sales manager or whatever title your dealership assigns you. A closer is normally the person who runs the sales crew, trains the sales team and actually closes each sale once the salesperson has a commitment to purchase signed by a buyer.

I have personally closed over 17,000 automobile sales in my career, and am proud of the fact. I even had license plates that said "Shutter." That's a slang term often used, for those of you new to this business. I closed or shut the sale once my salesperson lined it up; thus the origination of the term line-close or liner-closer system.

The reasoning behind this system makes a lot of sense when you think about it from a dealer's perspective. The ideal sales force for a car dealer would be a team of *experts* in all facets of the car business! Unfortunately, the costs of hiring the best of the best would be over and above what any dealer could afford. Reason being, is that once a salesperson reaches the point where they are considered to be excellent, great, or super or whatever adjective you would assign, they make a great deal of money. They also are likely to have a prima donna complex, such as most of us do. Some of the top salespeople are the best in their own store, and their job is made easier because of the mix of abilities in the sales team. Some weak, some better, and only a few of the best.

Put all the top salespeople in the same dealership, and you would create utter chaos! That would be like a pack of alpha male wolves or a herd of bull elk! It wouldn't work! Plus that, to try feeding all those egos and paying this huge talent pool would bankrupt the dealer. Therefore, the solution is to have a well-balanced sales force with great and well trained salespeople whose job is to sell the car or truck, but they don't have to worry about the negotiating side of the equation.

Your best salesperson seldom makes the best closer or manager. My better salespeople have always been *great people* people; meaning they could gain instant rapport with customers, and develop a genuinely friendly and close relationship. They had patience and understanding, and the ability to relate beautifully to the customer. I, on the other hand, probably would not make that good a salesman. I always say if I wanted patience, I'd have been a doctor! My forte´ is negotiating; to develop a quick rapport, keep it business like and professional, make the deal, and — next!

This liner-closer system works because a dealer does not have to worry about a good salesman also being a good closer. *All* customers are now funneled through the dealer's most talented negotiators; the closers! For the closer, which this chapter is dedicated to; you *owe it* to your dealer and to your sales people to spend time in training them!

If you have a management position, then you have a higher obligation that to just sit on your ass until a write up hits the desk, and then work for a bit, and then sit on your ass again! I'm dead serious when I say that there are a lot of assistant sales managers, sales managers and closers out there who aren't worth a damn! There are also a lot of genuinely talented people, just not as many! Yes, I'm critical of closers who do not help their people to be the best they can be!

Let's analyze what I feel a closer should be: First of all, have you *ever* been late for work since you were promoted? Why? There is no excuse, so don't even bother, unless it was a death in your immediate family! Closers should *never* be late!

If you are a closer, and you just tuned in directly to this chapter, you will learn something your salespeople already did. Never be late! Buy two alarm clocks; one electric and with a 9-volt backup battery, and the second clock should be battery only. Set them apart from each other, and set the battery alarm 10 minutes after the first alarm.

You have responsibility as a manager to lead! If it takes you 20 — 30 minutes to drive to work, then you should leave one hour early. Giving yourself this time means that barring any emergencies, you will always be there when your sales team arrives. If your car breaks down, you can still call a cab! This shows your team respect! I hold my upper management accountable also. If my general manager is holding the sales meeting, then I expect that manager to be there on time. They don't have to beat me to work, but I damn well expect them to at least be on time! If they aren't, take them aside and tell them! Obviously they owe it to all of you to respect their staff!

I also have no tolerance for salespeople coming to work late. Be strict on what you expect, and make certain to *always* lead! The reason I am so absolutely strict on punctuality is that if people are late for work, it means they are unhappy with their job, and if I can't do something to turn them around, then we need to part ways!

If you have just been promoted from the sales force, and some of your former peers are on your sales crew, they will be a little harder to control, as they will remember *all of your bad habits*. Change those habits quickly, and learn to manage by example!

Now, for the next step; do you hold a quick sales meeting before each shift? If not; start. If someone is late for your meeting, start on time without them, because it's disrespectful to the others to wait. Chew out the late arrival afterward, and privately. Have a topic prepared. It doesn't have to be anything other than a daily kickoff. Go over contacts and follow-up, any new leads you are handing out, or any methods you want to improve upon.

You may have discovered a perfect place to pause on the test drive to present the car and change drivers. Let them all in on it. Take your sales crew out to the bull pen to check out the new arrivals and fresh trade-ins.

Make it a habit to go outside often. I always made sure to take my crew to the used car inventory. Just walking down the rows will make everyone aware of what you have in stock, and possible *switch vehicles* to be used when needed. Discuss each vehicle as you walk by it, and share knowledge.

If you have been selling long, then you are aware that your bigger gross profits are generally made on used cars! You can also do your inventory walks through the new cars and trucks, but salespeople can do this on their own. There is only one of each used vehicle, and since you make more money on used, make you, and your people, get out among them.

Your meetings should last about a half hour. Occasionally, and when first forming your team, you may need a little more time on occasion, but respect your people's time. Make your meetings ½ hour before shift, and let your people get on the floor when selling time begins. Anyone who was late can stay behind to hear about your two alarm clocks, and respecting their crew members by showing up on time!

These pre-shift meetings are excellent for a little role play, and asking each team member for "how they do it." You'll be surprised how much participation you will get from your team when you ask for, and listen to their solutions to such things as; test drives, routes, methods and other parts of the process. Compliment your people on sales and clever ideas. All negatives need to be done privately, and one on one! All salespeople like to share good ideas, and your praise will enhance their prestige and cement your team.

Make your team as strong as you can. Praise them when they outdo the other teams!

I used to put on contests a lot! One year, I went on a real kick of high gear competition. Every month, I put up a contest for my team; every time they were the top crew for the month, (we ran 2 to 3 crews) I treated them to an evening at the casino.

First, we all met in the bar and I had an open bar. Then I treated to dinner, and then I handed everyone a few hundred dollars in cash for gambling. They drank first, ate, and then gambled, and everyone went home sober. Funny thing, it never got old. We all looked forward to it, and that year we went to the casino twelve months in a row! What a team! We were unbeatable, because I genuinely cared, and so did they!

You need to build a strong team, because your livelihood depends on them. If you have a weak link, then get 'em up to par, or make 'em go away! Period. Some managers carry salespeople longer than their mothers' did! A lot of them say they don't have the heart to do it because "He or she is such a nice person." If you really feel like that, then replace them anyway, and have them swing by to see you on paydays. When they come in, just hand them a few hundred dollars in cash to help them out. No joke! You can afford to because your new salesperson will likely make you that much more anyway! Don't carry dead weight! Also, when you do this, do you not send a message to the rest of your team that you're weak?

Retaining your job is dependent on how well you produce. Having the lowest sales team in production for the store, means you'd better be watching anyone who comes in to apply, because they may be interviewing for *your* job. You can't afford to carry weak people, so make them strong! It's your job to turn your people into stars. You need to work hard for them also. Give them training and direction. You also need to *study* sales techniques and keep learning!

Your salespeople need to be comfortable with you. It is not necessary to go out drinking and carousing with your team. In fact, it's *bad!* They need a leader and a mentor more than they need another buddy. You should know how each member of your team works. They need to know you, and be able to interpret a look or a gesture; that's called teamwork!

Teach them to *never, ever* speak when you are seated with their customers. You and *only you* will talk from the point you sit down! My people knew that if a customer asked them a question when I was sitting with them that they were to look over at me. If I was looking back at them, they *knew* to answer the question. If on the other hand, I remained looking at their customer, they were to *keep* looking at me — the customer would see the salesperson looking to me, and the buyer's eyes would automatically divert back to mine, I would then answer the question. This silent communication and reading of each other's body language was rehearsed on a regular basis. My people knew every gesture I made, and every look I gave them had its' meaning.

Not one of the managers I worked with had a team as well trained or as disciplined as mine. I always treated my people respectfully in front of the customers, and they were always very respectful and subservient to me; calling me sir and Mr. Swanson, not because of my request, but out of genuine respect. Some of it was definitely a bit much, but the customers ate it up. After a while when we were working the deal, the customers began treating me like *their* boss. It was amazing; the relationship we developed with our customers and among ourselves!

You must be perceived to have a genuine authority, as customers are used to being passed from one salesperson to another, and the good cop – bad cop games are old hat. If you are a manager, then *act* like it. Don't put yourself or your team in the position of appearing to take turns using the company brain. Practice your moves so well that you know what's coming.

For the salesperson: Where you have a closer or any manager that will be coming in to negotiate the deal, a proper set up is a must! Once the paperwork is ready for the salesperson to turn in, it is *necessary* to put the customer on notice that someone else will be entering the arena! There is nothing worse for creating sales resistance, and scaring hell out of your customer than suddenly having a closer appear, and you introducing this person as your manager! You might as well just say, "Folks, just forget about all the rapport we had, this manager is going to rip your hearts out!" How stupid is a system that has no set up! I don't care how you're dealership does it now, just don't you be a slob! Do it my way!

Set up your manager, and here's how. "Mitt, Ann, at this point, I am going to need some help. The offer you want me to make is a long way from where we should be, *as you know.* Now, I have a great relationship with my boss, and he/she helps me whenever he can. I want to see you get this car, so I think I'm going to ask my boss to *join* us, and I'll ask him to present your offer to our sales manager if that's all right with you?" (Of course it will be.) Your customers are now looking forward to getting help from your manager! They now have two people on their side! This set up for an introduction will make you a *ton* of money!

When a salesperson goes into the office, it is common practice in stores for the closer to ask a battery of questions, and try to get the salesperson's opinion of how he or she can close the sale. This is a weakness! As a closer, you'd better be smart enough to not use this approach. It is weak and dumb! You are the manager! Act like it! If the salesperson is knowledgeable enough to close the sale, then trade jobs, or just be intelligent enough to go in cold and form your own opinions!

I never allowed my salespeople to give me their opinions, because all you'll get are words of caution, and warnings about making the customer mad! Now you go in with apprehension, and tiptoe into your close, and the customer senses your weakness and takes control! Now the tail wags the dog, and you look like a weak suck! If you act weak, you will become weak! The only thing you need to know are their names, and maybe what they do for a living; hopefully your salesperson has taken the credit app (customer statement). Knowing a customer's hobbies is also a help; anything else is unnecessary and can be detrimental to your sale!

After you are introduced, your salesperson needs to stay with you, but needs to become invisible, although their presence is *necessary*. The "help *us* buy the car!" statement indicates the relationship you personally feel they have with the buyers, and they are feeling the same way! If they leave after introducing you, they have just put this relationship in doubt! They are an integral part of it, and they must remain like a mouse in the corner, but be there! I know the rules in your store may be different, but I have made a lifelong study of people, and I know what works! When the deal is made, your salesperson should react with, "Congratulations! We got it! *We!*" Many dealerships have a policy to turn to a closer and go get another up. I am totally opposed to this shabbiness! This is a team effort.

Closers; when you are negotiating, your salesperson needs to sit or stand, depending on the room, and to just keep their eyes on the paperwork. They should *not* make eye contact with the customer, as the customer will feel compelled to include them in the conversation. The salespeople need to become invisible! Also, remind them constantly, *When asking a closing question, the first one who talks loses!*

Once you and the customer have agreed on the next offer they'd like you to present, you stand up and your salesperson sits down, or if there's room so they are already sitting, they need to enter into conversation with the buyers, but never should they talk about the deal; anything *but* the deal! Their conversation should be about where the customer is going on vacation, hunting, camping, photography, anything!

Closers; upon your return the salesperson needs to immediately shut up (even in mid-sentence). They need to look to you, and smile with excitement as though they are a bird, and you are a mother bird with food! You will find that your customer will also adopt this sometimes comical look! In fact, it happens so often, it really will remind you of a bird's nest. Believe me, your salesperson needs to understand that they can chop off their conversations, and the customer won't even notice! The customer is only listening out of courtesy; they want to buy the car! I've had salespeople attempt to finish their story before shutting up. Only the first time!

So now you sit down, and deliver your new proposal! It needs to go this way until you shake hands on a deal! Then your salesperson need to jump up and shake your customers' hands and congratulate them.

Now for a clincher that you will not see done by other managers. Your salesperson needs to also thank you! My guys used to turn and shake my hand, and say thanks Gary! Why do you suppose they did that? I didn't instruct them to! Because they created a genuine bond with their customers, and if I did well by their customer, I did well by them! Besides, they knew they likely just made a ton of money! Our customers like a show, and believe me, I can put on a good one, and you will too!

By the way, are your fingernails clean, shoes shined, eyes clear? For the guys, are your clothes clean and your face shaved? Gals, nails and shoes clean? My big problem was being a heavy smoker for most of my career, and most of my salespeople were also smokers. High pressure jobs were what we blamed it on!

This is a fast paced and hectic career, and it seems to draw us high-strung types. I must have gone through thousands of boxes of Tic Tacs®, but I know my clothes still stank! I just made sure everything else about my appearance was perfect! Two and a half to three and a half packs of cigarettes a day and I finally figured how to quit. I'll mention it later in the book if you're interested.

Teach yourself and your salespeople how to sever your dependence on the cell phone! *You, as a manager, do not need to make and receive personal phone calls while at work!* Neither do your salespeople! The biggest fault I can find with a dealership sales staff is their lack of work ethic! It seems that the average sales force spends all day socializing!

You, as a closer, do not depend on being able to out call or outrun a salesperson to an up, but your people do! For the very reason that cell phones and driving don't mix, is the problem they are to your success as a closer. Your salespeople on a phone, will lose a second or fraction of a second at the very least from their reaction time when an up comes in! The human mind cannot drop one thought, such as concentrating on a conversation (phone or in person) and pick up a new thought, such as calling an up as fast as a salesperson who is concentrating on the next car coming in!

I always wished my people could all stand silently with a rock in their shoe. The pain would keep them awake! Your people need to be alert, and off the phones, and even though *you don't need to think fast, you need to think smart* and set a good example by staying off your own phone! Cell phones will kill you if you don't get smart, and put the hammer down! What do you have to lose? If your people would rather talk with their friends than sell cars, then send them home so they can have all the time they want. Sound too strong? Then be a weak suck and let your salespeople work when they feel like it. You keep quiet and let them be lazy. Soon their incomes will suffer, and they'll quit you anyway, and if you aren't fired yet, you can go back on the line and remember how nice a manager you were! Yeah I know; nice guys finish last!

Salespeople are notoriously lazy! I am, that's why I gravitated toward car sales, because I wanted my customers to come to me. I was fortunate in the fact that I started out in management, as I'm just lazy enough that I don't really know if I could have worked hard enough to be a good salesman for a long period of time. As a manager, I could never afford to be lazy. This was great for me, because I was forced to succeed!

You need to *force* your sales team to succeed. The greatest talent often needs to be harnessed and used, to make it perform, or it will soon fade and disappear into mediocrity. You cannot afford to waste a talented individual who has come under your wing. You owe it to them, their dependents, and yourself and your dependents; not to mention the managers above you who made you their manager in the first place. Awesome responsibility isn't it? I guess that's why it's called work!

Once you have shaken hands on a deal, your work is basically done. Your salesperson should take the sold vehicle to cleanup, prepare stock tags for the trade and introduce the customer to the finance manager. You need to be aware of what is happening, but hopefully by now you will have another deal working! As a closer, you may be very busy at times, and you need to be able to work multiple deals, one after another, and keep focused!

The toughest time I recall having was one busy weekend when I worked in a dealership with two sales teams. Saturday morning rolled around, and both sales crews came on shift early, as we had a huge ad budget hitting TV, full page in the newspaper and a barrage of radio ads. Sixteen salespeople and me; the other crew manager called in sick! We had a large showroom with 16 round 6-chair tables. Because of our volume, we didn't use the showroom to display cars, just for seating. The large fireplace was blazing and the tables started to fill up. Deals started to hit the desk, and I started working like a mad man!

Fortunately, I had a couple of very good desk men (sales managers) and they were busy appraising trades, giving me my pencils (counter offers), and I was on a dead run. I grabbed a bite of sandwich each time I went into the sales office, sneaked out the side door occasionally for a smoke, and worked several different tables each time I went out to the showroom. Our sales office was about forty feet long with a 30-foot counter, so it was made for volume sales. A 30-foot one-way glass looked out on the showroom, so we could talk about each deal, and the desk could see all of the activity, and identify with the body language going on out on the floor; and we could all see where our attention was needed next.

At any one time for hours, I was working ten deals simultaneously. Sometimes I would take out five or six offers in a folder, and go from one to the next presenting a counter, getting another counter, or a handshake, putting it back in the folder, and pulling out the next one. Every time I walked on the showroom, dozens of eyes were watching, and it was a circus atmosphere! Whenever I shook someone's hand on a deal, the other tables would clap for them. It was contagious! It got so I would holler across the room to tell a customer, "You made a deal, congratulations!" while I sat down with a different customer. Sometimes I'd give a thumbs up to someone across the showroom (we're talking 60 feet away), and a lady would scream out, "Is it really ours?" and I'd give another thumbs up, and everyone would applaud and shout encouragement! It was really a fun circus, and I had all the rings to myself!

It wasn't long 'til I had so many customers that my finance managers couldn't keep up and I was sending salesmen, with their customers, down the street to our separate finance building for paperwork and financing! I seem to remember closing 35 deals that day; however it could have been more or less, because car guys normally exaggerate.

Although I know I made some really big bucks that weekend, as Sunday was also huge! I never really kept score by numbers, just by income earned! Good job that weekend Brad and Kevin! I tell this story not because I think I was so great, but so you realize how important the team is, and the communication level that is so important! Also, communication between the closer and the desk must be as automatic and smooth. Everything we did was automatic!

These desk men knew that we didn't need to talk about each deal, they just wrote down (penciled) the numbers with a felt tip Sharpie®, and piled up the manila folders on the counter. I came in and left the folders and counter offers I had just negotiated, and told them what I had that needed explaining. Then I picked up my stack and went back to the showroom. I took the folders off the stack one at a time, sat down and kept negotiating. I remember it slowed down some time around dusk (November), and we finally got a breather.

When you have a team you can trust, from the salespeople on up to the top, you can whiz through car sales so fast that the average dealership couldn't even comprehend the coordination! So I say to you closers; lead, follow or get out of the way! A closer is in a unique and strategic position; you are in the position of being the go between that is directly in control of whether or not both sides come together on a car deal! The desk needs you, and your salesperson needs you!

TAKE IT AWAY

When a customer is being evasive and does not even want to go inside the showroom after you have found a vehicle that seems right for him, what do you do? Most salespeople will *turn* the customer at this point, but a turn should always be a last resort, because most of your buyers will have enough experience in buying that when they find that they are being turned, the savvy buyer will use this as an excuse to leave.

Make another attempt at your buyer and put yourself in his place. Perhaps he has purchased enough cars in his lifetime that he is aware, even if subconsciously, that every time he finds a car he likes and goes into the showroom that he ends up buying it! For once, he feels that even though he likes your car he would like to do things differently this time and genuinely look around. Knowing this may be his only reluctance to going inside, test the water with a pressure relieving question. Ask, "Bill, let me ask you this; you don't have to buy right now do you?" When he answers it may be your key to getting him inside. He says, "No, I don't," and you should reply, "Good. Since this isn't something that you must do on the spot, let's step inside and I'll show you what the figures look like on paper." Simple, relaxing, and highly effective! The customer is now totally relaxed and his guard is down because he feels that you are in his same position of not having to *sell* today. Little does he know that the sale is all but consummated. All you have to do now is casually enter into a write-up.

This can be little different from any regular write-up, but be careful to keep it on a more casual basis, such as; "Bill, I know we are not doing anything now, but when you do get ready to buy, assuming this to be the right car for you, would you be paying cash or carrying a balance?" Go through all standard procedures here; get his trade appraised, ask questions prefaced by, *if you were to carry a balance,* would you be leasing or financing through the bank? When you do get ready, what kind of money will you be expecting for your trade?" You should go so far as to get some sort of hit figure from the desk if you are able.

Now continue with everything being informal until you know what he feels he should have for his trade, how much cash is available for his investment (down payment), and what monthly investment he is comfortable with. At this point, I normally just lean back in my chair and say; "Bill, I truly believe that you will be back, but I have a really important question." Now I pause and as I slowly come back to a straight up position, I ask; "Since the car you want is available now, you're here, my boss is in a good mood, and even though it sounds like we're a long ways from your figures (a longer pause here); if I could do what you said it would take (short pause), is there any reason why we couldn't just go ahead and do it right now?"

At this point I am leaning forward on the desk and making direct eye contact. If he still won't enter into negotiations, follow with a quick "Why not?" Then recap the fact that the figures that *he wants* are what you're talking about and not your boss's numbers. Remind him that what your boss gave you for numbers is a long way from what your buyer wants, but now give him reasons why you feel that right now is the perfect time to get management to make his deal! It could be the ending of a factory incentive, a dealer contest your boss is close to winning, allocation time for new vehicles where the factory will replace this hottest selling model with another, or anything that makes sense. Remember, the two main motivating factors; *a hope for gain* and *a fear of loss!*

Once your customer comes inside with you your battle is half won, because just like he knew when he objected, he is sitting in the buyer's seat once again and he's about to become a repeat impulse buyer!

14 PROFIT

Remember this in your career; you are entitled to make *all the money*, as long as you don't cheat, lie or steal! Profit is not bad. It is why we are in this business.

The longer you spend in the car business, the more it will sink in to your head that if you give people a break, just because you like them, or because they have been so pleasant, they will seldom if ever thank you. I learned early on that people really don't appreciate any favors you tell them you're doing, and they generally are suspicious and feel that you were just probably trying to cheat them in the first place, and the bank wouldn't let you do it, so therefore your nice guy act is lost in translation!

This rather cynical look at people didn't come to me overnight. I learned by trying to do nice things for people, and either got no thanks as I said, or a cynical retort that made me just go back to the "I want all the money" idea. The only place I draw the line is really elderly or handicapped people, and single mothers. Outside of them, there is nothing wrong with making the maximum profit.

I remember a customer that I was working with early in my career in Wisconsin. I was finance manager, and had a tough time finding a bank to make him a loan. I finally pulled some strings and the bank really gave me a super deal for him. When he came in for delivery, I brought him into my office and then I laid the great deal on him — I presented what I had been able to do for him because he was really a nice guy. I saved him several thousand dollars, and this was in the late 1960's! Did he thank me? Did he jump up and yell excitedly? No, dammit! His *only* comment was, "Where do I sign?"

That was it! My bubble had burst! It was probably good for my career that it happened at that point, because that one incident made me a ton of money later on! No more *Mr. nice guy*. I was genuinely crushed! Here we are 45 years later, and I still remember that puke! I realized that, as I mentioned, people really don't appreciate the gestures that save them money. They don't trust us, and anything extra we do is considered to be part of the show! I know they feel that our entire process is scripted, which a lot of it is; but whenever we do something to benefit them, they feel that it was all pre-planned, and that's why they don't trust us to do anything out of kindness, or to be courteous or fair.

I am not speaking now as a cynical or jaundiced sales manager. I am trying to prepare you for the realization that most people will look upon you as a defanged rattlesnake. You may be harmless, but you're still a snake. Just roll with it and enjoy yourself; knowing all the while that you are earning more money than 80% of your customers. This message is to not only prepare you for your career, but so you realize, as I did, that our customers will always feel that we made too much money on them. You will not change the customer's belief that they are paying too much, so; since they are that sure, who are we to disappoint them? Let's not disappoint them by trying to change their opinion, instead; just *make all the money*!

Don't worry about everybody on your management team high-fiving after one of your deals. Don't feel bad when you find out that the low profit deal you thought you had turns out to be a six grand hit ($6000.00 profit)! I can assure you that your remorse will fade quickly when you find out that your commission share is $2,000.00!

I can truthfully testify to the validity of the statement; "It's not the deal the customer got that's important, it's the deal he *thinks* he got!" Some of my highest profits were made from people who really had a good time! They'd come back just to stop in and chat over coffee. They'd bring cookies and other treats! These people were very loyal, and they didn't mind paying a high profit, because they enjoyed the show! I always treat everybody with a show! It's a genuine show, but still a show.

I have fun when I'm closing a sale, and I'm comical and serious at the same time. You know you're doing well when the customers who just paid your mortgage payment, thank you for "the best buying experience they've ever had!" This means you've done a good service for the customer, the dealer, and your family. These customers will stay loyal to you, but don't ever look down on them because they paid a profit!

15 LEASING – THE HISTORY, THE CALCULATION AND PRESENTATION

Leasing is possibly the least understood element in the car business. I'm going to cover this subject with more information than you will ever use, and likely more than the majority of upper automobile management is aware of.

To understand leasing is to realize what a lease is. It is a contractual agreement for the use of a motor vehicle, for a given amount of time, at a specified dollar amount. When you lease a vehicle, you do not have an ownership interest, but rather, a rental.

Leasing is often misstated, oversold, and in the past, always carried a certain amount of mystique about it that had sort of a snob appeal to consumers. Leasing had always required a higher credit score in order to qualify, and for this reason, in its' formative years, was generally reserved for companies and their executives.

Early on, in the late 60's and a ways into the 1970's, leases were calculated as open-end leases. Remember this terminology when we discuss this further, but it basically means that at the end of the lease, the forecast future value of the leased vehicle needed to come out to what had been predicted or the person leasing it would be responsible for any shortage; thus the reason for the high credit rating requirement. We'll go over more on this concept in a while.

When a car dealer leases a vehicle, he *sells* it to a lease company and *they* now are called the *lessor*. The customer who signs the lease is called the *lessee*. This explains the relationship, and you can see that the lease company is the new owner of the vehicle. The dealer has guidelines and structures given him by the lessor which he must adhere to in order to have them purchase the lease; just the same as he must do when he sells a car by financing it through a bank. The difference is here is that the lease company becomes the registered owner instead of the customer as he does when he finances through the bank.

Back in the early 70's, the leasing industry changed the leasing structures to closed-end, which means that when the end value (residual) is estimated at the outset of the lease, the entire responsibility for the value rests with the lessor. The lessee has no responsibility other than vehicle condition and maintenance. The reason everything changed so dramatically, was in the time around 1973, there was an extreme fuel shortage in the United States and prices of gas shot up. Suddenly, values of gas guzzlers plummeted; not so much because of costs, but because you couldn't get any fuel!

I remember in the Northwest area, gas stations would open for a few hours each day. When they ran out of gas, they closed. People dropped their cars off in line at the stations in the evenings to secure a chance to be able to get gas the next day. In many areas, you were only able to buy gas by your license number, whether the last number was odd or even. When you can only purchase a limited amount of fuel, you need the most fuel efficient vehicle you can find.

Since the majority of companies who leased vehicles as a perk for their executives, leased fancier luxury cars that were as fuel efficient as Mack trucks, guess where their values went? Now, the leases that were coming to their end, that normally would be turned in and a new lease began, ran into a major problem! The open-end lease made the lessee responsible for the value of the lease turn-in.

I watched Cadillac and Lincoln values plummet to twenty cents on the dollar. Take the lease end (residual) value that was estimated to be $10,000.00, and because of the fuel crisis, it now was worth $2,000.00; *if* you could find a dealer to buy it, and most wouldn't! In order to end this lease, the lessee would have to pay $8,000.00 just to walk away.

What happened is, these companies all contracted with the lessors to extend the leases; in most cases for an additional 24 months. Of course, after the next two years, the crisis was long over and now there were a lot of very high mileage lease returns out there.

The leasing industry had to make a drastic change, or their business would have stopped. Immediately, the closed-end lease was adopted. From that time on, the vast majority of leases have been calculated more carefully, and are on the closed-end lease; which leaves the end value the responsibility of the lessor only! I say they now calculate more carefully, because you don't really need to be as cautious if you have a lessee responsible if you miscalculate the residual. In fact, back before the change, I had companies ask me to purposely change the calculated residual so they could give their executive a more loaded car. Company guidelines generally just gave a monthly lease allowance, and by raising the end value, it would allow a more expensive vehicle to be leased, and the company would have a happier executive, and the board wouldn't ever see the checks written at lease-end to buy out the excess residual.

I worked as a lease manager for an Oldsmobile dealership in Chicago at the time, and we had a majority of the largest companies as our clients. My customers were extremely loyal and happy. Leasing for two years at a time builds your repeat business tremendously! Plus that, every single one was calculated based on selling the vehicles to our lease company at full list price! It was our own company, so we really did well!

Now that I have given you more information than you need about history, let's look at how a lease is calculated, so you can see how uncomplicated it actually is.

THE CALCULATION

You should never be in a situation where you need this knowledge, other than if you know how it works, it is often a real help in selling your customer on the idea, or at least being able to explain the basics to a demanding and cynical buyer.

Today, the numbers are entered in the lease program in the computer, and the results appear. Chances are, your manager could not even explain to you how it works, and I'll guarantee you a majority of sales managers don't have this knowledge!

First, a determination needs to be made as to how much of a vehicle's value (from MSRP) will be used up during the lease term. Your dealership has residual guides from the lease company on every vehicle that you carry. These guides give you the estimated residual value for various lease terms, and with varying mileage estimations.

Knowing that if your customer leases a vehicle for three years, that it will still have an actual cash value of about half of its original MSRP, this means that its' depreciation is 50%. We refer to value in relation to MSRP because it is the only constant. Due to price discounts and the ever-present negotiating, a standard must be determined, and that is the MSRP.

This makes it easy to calculate monthly depreciation, because the total calculated depreciation is, in this example, divided by 36 (number of months). In the case of a $50,000.00 vehicle, your monthly depreciation is $50,000.00 X 50% = $25,000.00 ÷ 36 = $694.00. The depreciation is $694.00 per month, which is the *basis* for the three year monthly lease payment. Add to this, the money costs and the profit for the lessor, and you have a payment.

I'm not going to go into details on how to manually calculate a lease like I had to before we had computers, but let's look at how to sell it.

People must normally need a higher credit score in order to lease, because lease companies have fewer restrictions. A lease company will generally accept carrying higher balances, where lenders may have more cautious down payment requirements. If a dealer carries a negative equity forward on a lease, instead of the customer having to lay out a bunch of cash up front, the lessor will allow a dealer the latitude of sliding it into the payments! If you are able to sell your client on the idea of leasing, you may well find your commissions will be a lot higher, because cash down is the hardest part for most customers. If you are able to carry more money forward, you make more profit!

THE PRESENTATION

Many customers these days have preconceived notions of the pitfalls of leasing. Any attempt at converting them may be met with hostility. Many people have heard horror stories about leases, and there are a lot of them.

Do I think leasing is great? Yes! Do I think it's good for the average consumer? No, not at all! However, since I am not teaching seminary students, we need to make all the money we can, each and every time. Let me refresh our goal; as long as you do not lie or steal, there is nothing wrong with making all the money!

I recall when I was structuring a lease for my dealer's uncle when in Chicago. I wanted to be careful and fair since this was my employer's relative, so I went to his office to discuss the profit margin. I showed him the profit scale that I had from high to low. He asked, "Is this how much we can make?" I answered, "Clarence, it depends on how much money you want to make." His answer; "Gary, *always remember, I want all the money in the world!*" His uncle loved the car and we made all the money!

Many dealerships will send out your pencil with monthly payments on both purchase and leasing. The offer sheet will show Plan A and Plan B. Plan A will show the price, trade allowance, a high cash down amount, and a payment. Plan B will show the same trade allowance, maybe zero cash down, and maybe even a lower payment. Depending on how your dealership wants it presented, make the pass, and when the customer sees it, they will ask about Plan B because it sounds better doesn't it?

When you mention that Plan B is a lease, they may be very vocal in their objection. They may say, "I'll never lease!" Don't be taken aback when you get a strong objection. Take the time to ask, "Why?" Just a quiet and innocent question, as though you are trying to improve your personal knowledge. If you politely ask, they will pour out all of their fears. When the no's are out, then you can work on the yeses! I used to ask, as though I really didn't know the negatives. Be careful, because you can't pretend you've never heard any negatives or they'll call you on it! Be genuine, while explaining that you really want to know, since there are so many people that lease time after time from your dealership.

The main objection I always heard first off was, "I want to own my car, and leasing doesn't allow me to." An easy comeback to this is a quick, "You don't own the one you have now! You owe a balance to the bank." Don't make this sound like you are arguing in favor of leasing, because you need to sound impartial. This statement is something that most people don't think about, but in reality, buyers that finance cars, always are carrying a balance. *A good argument in favor of a lease is one I used to quote, "The experts always advise a person to buy something that appreciates and lease those things that depreciate!"* Go on to add, "Why would you want to *own* a car? You seem to trade every three or four years, so why don't you just lease for three or four years, and then you never have to worry about trade-allowance again!" This works perfect for the guy who tells you he never gets what he wants for his trades!

Let's look at some different selling points that can be used to promote leases. I do not instruct, nor do I condone any of these ideas, and am merely reporting to you the options that are out there, but you need your dealer's approval on what you can use: A lot of what we do borders on hype, so I leave it to your dealer. I'm just the messenger.

<u>Selling points on leasing</u>

- "Most of our business people and executives lease rather than buy."
- "Why would you want to own a car when you can lease one for less money?"
- When you finance a vehicle, you are taking full responsibility for fluctuations in market value. When you lease, the lease company takes the risk."
- "I'm sure that when you bought your present car you intended to keep it for a long time; didn't you? Now here you are, trading it already."
- "Why finance for a long period of time to get a comfortable payment when you can lease for a much shorter time and still have a low payment?"
- "You say you want to 'own' your car, just like I always used to do when I traded. *Each time* I thought, this is the one! Then I'd turn around and trade again! Then I discovered leasing and it all changed!"
- "I suggest in your best interest; lease the car! Then, at the end of the lease period, if you really like the car and want to keep it, just exercise your *option* and complete the purchase! Now you have the best of both worlds; a low monthly payment with less cash down, and the option to own it for the small purchase option at the lease-end!"
- "You never have to worry about having negative equity again! Let the lease company speculate on the future value of the car.

If at the end of the lease, if it's not worth what the residual value is projected to be, walk away from it! However, let's just say for example that before your lease is up, you come in for my used car manager to give you an appraisal. No charge of course. So, what if he says the wholesale value of this car is $20,000.00, and he's willing to pay that much for it? You can see that your residual is only $17,500.00. This means that for a few minutes of paperwork, you can exercise your option, buy the car, and turn around and sell it immediately to my used car manager, and put twenty-five hundred dollars in your pocket! Hopefully then, I'd sure want you to lease another one from us. This happens an awful lot! Now on the other hand, if it's not worth more than $17,500.00, let it go back! You see that a lease is a win-win situation for you. If it's worth more than its residual, you make money. If it's worth less, it confirms the fact that you made the right decision to lease."

- The customer objects to having a mileage limitation. Here's where salespeople and thieves have a lot in common. I said before that I don't condone trickery, but my duty is to give you your options. It's up to your dealer; the amount of latitude you are given. A *common* answer to the mileage limitation question; "Oh don't be too concerned about the mileage (discuss their current driving habits here)." Now, answer, "Of course I can understand your mileage concerns, and we can certainly build in some extra miles if you'd like. Your payment will go up some, but we want you to feel good about it, because I know you're going to really love leasing. Keep in mind however, that you are not likely ever going to be concerned about your mileage anyway, because at the end of the lease, you'll probably trade it in or buy it! That's what happens most of the time, because our cars hold their value so well, and it'll probably be worth more than the residual at the lease end. Combine that with the fact that the lease company

152

sets such a ridiculously-low residual anyway, because they don't want to take any chances on it not being worth it, that I know, without a doubt, that you'll sell it for a profit, or trade it in on another lease!"

- "Another advantage of a lease, besides less money out of pocket and a lower monthly payment is; the fact that you get what all Americans want; a shorter trading cycle! Unlike now, when you trade a car that's half worn out, you're going to always be driving a new car when you lease!"

- "Another thing that my lease customers tell me, but I myself don't mean to even suggest that I recommend this; is they don't spend nearly as much maintenance money on the leased vehicle as they used to on their own car! The oil and filter changes aren't done that often. They aren't afraid to take the lease car through the brushes at the automatic car wash, and they don't pay as much attention to selecting a "safe" parking spot, because the "door dings" are part of "normal wear and tear" in the lease agreement. Kind of like renting a car at the airport. I'm not advocating that *you should not care* about the leased car, but it's just not your personal pain every time it gets a small nick."

- "Since your lease payments will be substantially lower than a finance payment, you could actually get more options than you could on a purchase contract, because you are only paying for a small increase in your monthly expenditures to step up to the moon-roof, leather, etc. You owe it to yourself to have a nicer ride as a reward for working so hard to keep the great credit score that *entitles* you to lease!"

- "Naturally once you qualify for a lease, other *lenders take note*, and your credit score should begin to go up. It has always been true that only the best credit risks can lease. We know that it's fortunate that our managers could pull strings to make this happen, as your current credit score is not all that high! I don't know how they pulled it off, as it must have taken some work! As a result of this, I would imagine that when other creditors see this lease on the books, they will respond by looking very favorably at a huge raise in your score. This lease will not only help you on this car, but if it also raises your credit score, it will save you money on all future interest rates! Congratulations!"

- "Over the years we have found that people who are able to qualify for a lease, will definitely lease, and those who can't, will finance."

- "We go through life with car payments. It's just the American way! As long as we are going to have one anyway, why not get the *most* car possible, and for the *least* monthly payment?"

These are some arguments that can be made in favor of leasing, but make sure that your management allows this dialogue. Most managers will be cautious, as some of these pitches are overly optimistic to be sure, but by the same token, these pitches give you a nucleus to build around.

16 CLOSERS JOB ONE – TRAINING ON CLOSING SCENARIOS

losers — this is an important factor in your success. I have selected some of my favorite techniques for this book, and have placed them in no certain order.

As standard practice, I would take part of my daily sales meeting to enact some role-play with my team. We would go around the table, and each member would take a turn as salesperson, and also as a buyer. We found this role-play to be invaluable, and with the salesperson taking the buyer's role, playing hard to get, it makes the other salesperson work hard to make the sale!

The manager needs to set the stage, and then give each person the opportunity to act out their part. Nothing but constructive comments here! You cannot embarrass a participant during these meetings, and you must compliment them on their positives! This training gives everyone the chance to see each other in action, and you can all learn from each other. I did this training constantly, and when I saw someone having a problem with a particular closing scenario, we worked on it later in a one-on-one situation.

Select *one* close, and spend ten or fifteen minutes practicing in your crew meeting. Explain your reasoning, so your people will want to participate, by the philosophy that "there is no wrong way!" You can give the reason for this practice by saying that you have seen some excellent closing techniques that your people are using, and since you are all a team, you'd appreciate them sharing with one another. You'll find that they will begin having fun, and as with most of us, we like to strut our stuff. Besides, isn't it a lot easier to make a mistake in front of your peers and learn to correct it, than to err in front of a customer? Conversely, a good close that is shared, makes every team member that much better!

This brings up another point, and I believe that it's probably the most important thing you can do as a closer and team leader. *Always* keep your salesperson with you during the closing process! Many closers will meet the customer after the offer is written, and take over the negotiating from then on, and dismiss the salesperson until the deal is done. I cannot accept this method as anything but detrimental to a sale, and to both closer and salesperson! The only reason a closer would not want the sales associate to stay on board, is if the closer does not have the confidence in his or her own ability, and being afraid to look weak in front of their salesperson. To this closer I say; "Force yourself to keep them with you! Your salesperson may be experienced and good at selling, but *you* are the manager, and you were chosen as closer because you have the obvious talent for the job!" Don't second-guess your managers, and don't worry about erring in front of your salesperson. They aren't sitting in judgment of you, they are your partner! You both want the sale! Of course, they are only to act from this point on as a silent partner, but they *must* stay there with you!

Keep your salespeople involved all the way! That's how you build a team. Besides, it makes you stronger, and shows your people that you have confidence in your ability! Be strong, and they will support you. Act weak, and they'll laugh behind your back!

Why do you suppose that I previously stated that I honestly believed that if a salesperson worked for me for at least six months to a year, that they would be qualified to be a closer in most any dealership in the country! I can make this statement, because I was not only selective in whom I hired, but also in their ability to learn. I trained my salespeople to be as good as I possibly could. I taught them

156

everything I could, and I often adopted some of their techniques. Over my career, I lost a lot of great people who were offered management opportunities, and I was always proud to have helped them to achieve success. When you constantly have a winning team, every person is very important, and even though they are all individually competitive, each team member wants the team to be the best. Don't worry about losing them when they become your clone! Take pride in the fact that you helped their career. My people always gave me adequate time to replace them when they were offered a promotion. That's loyalty! This is another positive reason that your salesperson should stay with you during negotiations. They will be able to learn from you, and when they see that you are helping to further their career, they will work harder to be as good as they can, to reward your efforts!

CAR SHARKS AND CLOSERS

17 HANDLING THE MAVEN
(For Salespeople and Closers)

What is a maven? Call them second basemen, third base coaches or other terms; this person is a friend or consultant in whom the buyer trusts to advise them as to whether or not they should buy from you!

Maven is a Yiddish term, and this person is so common in their culture that I do not recall hardly ever making a car deal without one of them along. So now, you not only have a customer whom you need to present to and take through the whole process, you have another assistant buyer whom you must address.

Normally an advisor will accompany a single buyer, and although the husband and wife will occasionally bring a third party along, that person is generally the wife's father, brother or close friend. Since the wife will normally be your decision maker, she will choose the person who she feels will be an asset to her, and it won't likely be someone chosen by her husband, as she knows he will buy anything! That's a fact.

Be extremely careful in these situations. This is the worst nightmare for most salespeople, and the majority have no idea whatsoever of how to handle it! This includes a lot of trainers! I remember attending meetings where speakers advised salespeople to adopt an in your face attitude, to treat this person like they are stupid, and just do everything possible to discredit them! My answer to this is; WRONG!

I have seen salespeople and a great number of managers just turn, rudely and forcefully, to this person and demand, "Are you paying for this car? Is your name going on the title? Then why don't you just stay out of it, since you don't know what you're talking about!" I've heard these exact words, and a lot worse over my years, and trust me, this is no way to handle this advisor.

First of all, *your customer* brought this person along for a reason. For example, let's assume your customer is a single lady. She's heard all the horror stories about buying cars, and maybe the car she's driving was given to her for graduation. She may have picked a friend from work, church, her friend's husband or someone she feels comfortable with. Often times she will not bring her close boyfriend, as the ladies seem to seek out an *impartial* advisor. Keep in mind, this person has not likely been picked for their expertise, nor their negotiating skills, but just for moral support. Therefore, to make up for their lack of knowledge, they may adopt a negative posture as a bluff.

For this reason, I have always been amazed when car people develop that in your face attitude toward a poor person who is totally unarmed when it comes to negotiating skills! The big, brave salesperson slam dunks a poor companion, who just asks a few questions, maybe just to feel they're contributing something. Here they ask what to the salesperson seems like a confrontational question, and the sales rep comes unglued, and reacts like a total fool! This kind of amateurish attitude needs to go away. If you embarrass this person, you are also insulting your buyer's choice, and her intelligence. You may as well turn this customer, because you're all done! If you're too damned proud of yourself to have manners and be polite, then find another profession!

Here's how to schmooze your way into a sale in this scenario. When you are introduced, and you write down the customer's name (you'd better be doing this), also make certain to get the maven's name and spelling, and write it down. This person will generally respond with, "I'm not buying, I'm just a friend, so don't include me." Sometimes they will seem quite rude, but don't let it bother you. They are there to protect the buyer, and *you* are the enemy!

I generally will respond to this with, "You must be here for a reason, if only to protect (buyer's name) from some shady car person." You may draw a laugh (it's a good sign), but you have established and acknowledged acceptance of this person's importance to you; get their name and give them your card also! Continue in our normal manner, as though the maven was simply a parrot on your customer's shoulder. Don't sell to this maven, as they will see through your game. Whenever this assistant asks you a question, answer it completely, as they have a concern, and you *must* address this question as though it was asked by the buyer, even if the question is stupid! Without being phony, you will win this person over in a professional manner. If you can, find out what your customer does for a living, and I always ask the third baseman also, but often you will find out they are closed-mouthed about their background. Don't worry so much about it, because the closer will find out. Oftentimes, they won't tell you what they do, because it may diminish any value in their presence in your eyes.

An offer has now been written and the closer now enters the picture. This is the point where things can go to pieces fast! A closer must develop a rapport with the maven as soon as possible. Chances are pretty good that at this juncture, a salesperson may not have developed *any* relationship with this person. Whatever the case, the closer is going to be perceived as the big bad wolf!

The closer must now tread lightly; as obviously, the buyer wouldn't have brought an assistant unless he or she was leery of the process, and dreading the experience. Build rapport slowly by reading aloud the proposal. Maybe when you come in, there is no actual proposal, and the salesperson needs your help to even get a commitment. Listen to whatever the advisor says, and try to find out the reason the buyer selected this person as a helper in the first place. What level of expertise qualifies this person to be here? Maybe none at all, just a perceived need on the buyer's part for moral support.

During the process of negotiating, I almost always found a way to get the third base coach on my side. Since quite often, you will find it very hard to find anything at all to like about this person. Some goofy dork that you wonder how anyone could see any value in their opinion, having a say in your sale is sometimes hard to fathom. Look harder for something good to say! I'd wait until this inconsequential idiot lucked out and said something semi-intelligent, and I'd strike, "Wow, I never thought of that! No wonder Sally brought you along! Let me ask you this Dave; were you in the car business before? No, then you must be a banker aren't you?" Then, continue, and make sure to address this response directly to the assistant buyer before looking to the customer; "Most people would never think about that, but if I could get my sales manager to do that, could we earn your business Sally? Okay, well, let's see if I can get it done! I see why you brought Dave along! Keep your fingers crossed!" Sure, it's deceitful, but whatcha' gonna do? She brought this guy along to help out because she trusts him. If I can turn him into an ally by complimenting him on his knowledge, he now likes me, right? Now we're buds! When I return with the next counter offer from the desk, it's him and me against her. I'm going to present the offer, and I'll include him in the equation. I'll come back with another pencil, but I'll preface my remarks with, "Oh, by the way Dave, my boss said if you'd ever like to get in the car business, he'd like to discuss it with you; now Sally, Dave was right on with his idea, so here's what my boss said he'd do --------------." I present the offer, and I just made a car deal! Be careful when you fake your sincerity in complimenting the person, and don't make it too flowery, but if he has an idea that, even though obvious, makes sense; then compliment him!

You will *never* make a deal by being rude to this third party. You may win the argument, and embarrass the person, but you won't make a sale, and you lost your customer, and everyone she knows, and also anyone else he may be helping. It's not worth it! Yes, it's the ultimate in schmoozing! Where do you think the idea of the Judas goat came from? Welcome this lead sheep into your store, and let him lead his lamb in with him. Besides, you have your salesperson to make a deal for, and I'm sure they don't care about your stupid pride!

18 A FEW SHORT CLOSES

TAKE A POTTY BREAK

You've been negotiating back and forth, and you now bring out what you hope will be the last pencil. You discuss it with your buyer and one or both of them listen, but before they answer, they take a bathroom break. *You just sold a car*! They may come back and ask if you can do a little better. Tell them no, you did the best you could! *It's all over*, and don't even bother to run back to the desk, you are all done negotiating. They made up their minds to say yes, and the pressure was suddenly off; *that's why* the potty break. So, when they relieve themselves, it's a welcome relief to the closer! Always watch for this sign, and I'm sure you will from now on!

KEEP YOUR VOICE LOW

Here's a quick close that you can use, *carefully*, and it's a devastating close if handled right. Use this when it's down to the final pencil, or after you have made the offer — counter offer and need to end further negotiating. Make solid eye contact, lean forward, and in a low tone, say "Darren ---, if you were my own brother, I'd tell you to buy the car!" When he shakes your hand, just say, "Congratulations," in the same quiet, low tone. Put emotion and sincerity into it.

SPLIT THE DIFFERENCE

An easy close if you're near a deal is a split the difference offer. Let's say you're $1,000.00 apart. The customer wants $5,800.00 for this trade, and you're offering $4,800.00. Just say, "Danice, why don't we split the difference? What if I give you $5,000.00 for it?" The customer will normally say, "That's not a split! An even split would be $5,300.00!" Just say, "You're right, you have a deal at $5,300.00!" Shake her hand and you're done. Make sure of course that you know where you're at, and that you have the authority to make deals like this!

ANSWER QUESTIONS WITH QUESTIONS

This must be done professionally and smoothly, but I've made tons of money doing this. Virtually tons!

- Customer asks: "Would you give me six thousand for my trade?"
  - Answer: "If I could, would you buy it right now?"
- Customer asks: "What's the least you'd take for the car?"
  - Answer: "What's the most you'd pay for it?"

There will of course, be more dialogue than this around these replies, but you get the gist of the technique.

Now if you handle the questioning properly, your customer will tell you what you have to do to sell him. Just remember that before you throw out numbers and answers, just keep this sentence in your mind. "If I could, would you?" Or, as you will hear it in car talk, "If I could would ya'?"

I used to answer the best price question with, "The most you'll pay, and the least my boss will accept," as an icebreaker.

IF YOU HAD TO GUESS?

A lot of times a customer will be reluctant to spit out a number because they don't want to commit unless they really know exactly. So, I ask how much they owe on their trade, and they say, "I don't know." So I ask, "*If you had to guess?*" They say, "About six thousand."

This simple and subtle question works on everyone. You ask your manager, "Boss, how big was our profit on that sale?" He says, "I don't know." You say, "If you had to guess?" He replies, "About $7,500.00."

You will find you can use this question in everyday situations, with friends and family as well as customers. It works wonders!

People who are reluctant to quote something they don't want to be held accountable for if they're wrong, will guess without hesitation. The answer will be the truth.

19 TIPS FOR SALESPEOPLE

PAINT A FUN PICTURE – SMALL TALK THAT HELPS TO CLOSE

When you are at a point where you are awaiting an appraisal or other lull where small talk is appropriate, ask a thought provoking question such as, "Where are you going on your first trip in your new car?" Then tell them about your other customer's trip last Christmas; "They purposely arrived when they knew everyone would be there, and when they pulled in their parents' yard, they blew the horn. The windows filled with relatives, all straining to see who it was, and then everyone swarmed out of the house to see their new car!" Paint a picture in your customer's mind; they will mentally see themselves in the story, and you created a positive image adding to their desire to own the car! Now they can't wait to show it off, and you make them feel excited to make it theirs! Have them see themselves sitting in the vehicle. Dealerships used to have lots of walls covered with mirrors, and you could see customers on the showroom sitting behind the wheel, and looking at themselves in those mirrors. It was fun to watch as these buyers would change positions, and practice looking cool.

DON'T SELL COLOR TO WOMEN!

Never try to sell color to a woman! Learn this well, and don't ever forget it!

Let's say your customers are looking at a one of a kind car. The only one you have, and a very scarce vehicle; the car is light blue. They both like the car, and the husband likes the color. The wife says, "I don't really care for the light blue." Keep your mouth shut, and she may accept it. The problem is that some salespeople think that if their lips are moving, they're selling! In this case, most male salesmen will start pushing the advantages of light blue; "Easy to see on dark streets, and highways, easy to keep clean, most popular color for resale which means greater value retention", and the worst one of all; "You're wearing blue," or "it matches your eyes." Stick a fork in it! You're done! In this scenario, she may decide to buy it, but if you and her husband start *selling* her on it, you will both lose; every time. Know when to shut up. You never get in a peeing contest with a skunk, and you don't sell a woman on a color! Let her buy it by herself.

SUCCESSFUL DELIVERY: CATCH THAT WATER SPOT!

Here's a little tip that will bring you good factory surveys and referral business. Be aware when your customers come out of the business (finance) office. The finance manager should page you to pick up your customers, but even if they don't, have a cleaning rag with you. It's great if your customer comes out, and there you are, personally wiping their bumper or some place on the car where they can see you. If you are escorting your buyers out to the delivery area, and you suddenly stoop down to wipe off a water spot, it will have the desired effect.

GO THE EXTRA MILE

Ask your customers what radio stations they prefer before they go into finance. When they come out for delivery, have the stations preset. Also, make certain the clock is set correctly.

Keep in mind that the buying process takes a long time, and although a proper delivery should include going over the operation of the entire car, including radio stations, clock and all the rest, your customer likely will be tired, and not want to take any more time. This is especially true if the negotiating was long and tough, then the finance manager had presented and sold more items, your people may be exhausted.

Go over the *basic operation* of the vehicle so they are comfortable enough to drive it home, and set a time for them to come back tomorrow to cover a proper delivery! Spend as much time as they need. Time spent is a great investment for you.

Be careful to cover the requirements of the factory survey, and remind the customer to answer in the affirmative if they have questions on whether or not you completely explained the vehicle *on delivery*. Of course, if your customer is willing, go over it on the day they buy! Make certain no matter what, that you set the mirrors for them.

Giving your customer a small gift, such as an accessory from your parts department, or a CD of their favorite music is also nice to do. Another very good idea is to schedule a *return visit*, for a week or so later, to again go over all the things they forgot. This is something that seldom is done, but so important! Allow me to digress to emphasize just one glaring example. Once, a gentleman traded in his absolutely beautiful and immaculate Lincoln Mark VI, and his main reason was that it was uncomfortable to drive; it was less than a year old. As I closed the sale, he just mentioned to me that the new Lincoln steering wheel was so much better feeling! After he took delivery, I went out to see what was wrong with the trade-in. The steering wheel was tilted up like a bus, and when I got in, I realized immediately what his problem had been; that year of Lincoln had its' tilt wheel directly connected with the turn signal lever. You simply pushed forward on it to tilt the steering. It was obvious to me that his salesperson had not done a proper delivery. The new one he bought had a separate tilt lever, and that's all it took. Please do a proper delivery! That's why a second visit is very important.

THANK YOU CARD

Dealerships usually all have thank you cards. If they don't, buy your own! *Before* your paperwork goes to the business (finance) manager, take a moment to make a photocopy of their customer information. You may not get a chance if you wait 'til later, because the finance manager will not allow you to borrow any papers once they are done! This is all the follow up information you will need. From this, fill out a thank you card, sign and address it, and put it in your company mail immediately! Also, make sure to add the customer's address and phone number to your contact list, along with the info on family, car purchased, etc. Before you go home that day, they must be in your computerized follow-up! Never put off this important part of your job!

BUSINESS CARDS

Even if your dealership doesn't furnish business cards, buy your own. This is the best investment you can make! You can always spend the extra money by having the reverse printed with a place for someone to print their name and phone number and a dollar amount for a referral. When you get one, drop off or mail some more cards to the person who sent the referral in; with a check of course. A rubber stamp is also good for a message on the back of your card.

You should be handing out cards everywhere you go. Every cashier, clerk, gas station attendant and just everyone you meet. If you don't think people will be interested, the next time you're in a crowded place, just shout out, "Anyone here wanna buy a car?" You will hear back, "What kind do you sell?" "Where do you work?" Everybody loves cars! Get in the habit of papering the town with your cards.

I personally like for salespeople to leave off their cell phone number, and make it seem special for the person whom you hand it to, by you adding your cell by hand. That means to them that not everyone gets this treatment!

BIRD DOG REFERRALS

Does your dealership have a referral program? A lot of stores will pay a *bird dog* fee for one of the buyers sending in a customer who ends up buying a car! Find out if your dealer has one, and make certain to promote it to all of your buyers! A great plan is to add some dollars to it. If your dealer pays $50.00 for a referral sale, then you can certainly add more, such as another $25.00, or set up a plan of your own; maybe for every three, five, etc. If your minimum commission is $50.00 or $100.00, you may not make much on some, but you will in the long run!

Most people will be glad to refer their friends to you because they feel it is prestigious to have a friend in the car business. Also, if their friend buys a car similar to the one they purchased, it validates their buying decision, doesn't it? Constantly prospect for referrals, and report back to them whether or not you sell something. Also hand-*deliver* your bird dog checks! Then, give them more of your business cards at the time!

SEND AN ANNIVERSARY CARD

Here's a tip to mark in your follow-up planner. Send your customer an *anniversary card* to arrive one year after their purchase. Their reaction will be great! Think about it, they open the card and say, "It's not our anniversary!" Then they get the message! It has a lot of value to refresh you in their minds! You may also have the same positive effect by sending a birthday card to their car!

AVOID CONFRONTATION

So what to do if the situation blows up in your face? This is primarily for the person closing the sale. Have you ever had a customer turn violent and jump up? If you haven't, you've been too cautious! Having a situation turn explosive is inevitable if you're working for the maximum profit on each deal. To be the best, you must always work for all the money.

If a customer suddenly stands up, do not stand up with him. If you do, it will end up with a face to face confrontation; the position that man and animals all are in when they fight! Stand up when your customer does, and you lose!
Remain seated and gently move your hand, indicating that your customer should rejoin you and ask him to discuss it further. Also, *never point to the chair.* Use what I like to call the gentling hand. If you point, you are treating your customer like a child or a dog! Your customer will likely sit back down, as a lot of times this explosion helps them let off pressure, and is probably more show than anything. Keep smiling.

THINGS THAT KILL SALES

Watch what you say to people! One of the dumbass statements that will make people bristle, tune you out or just leave, is to walk up to an elderly man and say; "How are you, young man?" Are you nuts? If you are using this greeting, then drop it now! Do you really think an 80 year old woman is so stupid as to respond well to a, "Hello young lady" comment? You'd may as well just say, "Howdy old farts."

If you are going to earn someone's business, then treat them with respect! Conversely, it is also stupid for an older salesperson to refer to younger people as "young man" or "young lady." Just keep the cutesy comments out of your presentation. I remember what my father told me once; "Son, people always think you're intelligent, until you open your mouth." Be careful.

SERVICE PROSPECTING

I have friends who regularly show up at the dealer's service department and greet the arriving service customers. If service opens at 7:00 AM, it won't hurt you to be there just to hand out cards. When a car needs service, the love affair may be over, and you may find a lot of extra business just waiting for you. My friends who do this make big bucks.

CALL SELLERS

Call on the for sale cars and trucks in the newspaper and Craigslist. A great many of these people are just going that route because they want more than they figure a dealer will give them for trade. You may explain to these people that a lot of the time, if they have a trade-in that you can resell, your dealership may give them a much better all-around deal because you can make two smaller profits rather than just one larger one. A lot of these sellers have no intention of turning around and buying through the same source, because they figure everyone using that media is asking higher prices as well as they are.

This type of call really works best if you target vehicles that your dealership can genuinely use. It won't work if you just get people to bring in the cars nobody's buying. It always reflects badly on you if you bring in trades that your manager throws rocks at or they're such rats that he won't get behind the wheel.

You will succeed by doing things that others won't do.

20 BUY IT NOW?

Here's something that salespeople and closers are often remiss in doing properly! When asking a customer to buy at an offer they wish to make, it is very common for salespeople and managers to make this serious mistake; they ask the customer, "Alexa, if I can make these numbers work, will you buy it today?" Then they run in and present the offer, run back and forth, spend two hours negotiating, and finally come out with that big, cheesy smile, hold out their hand and say, "Congratulations!"

Then they stare in wonderment when the customer does not take the proffered hand, but stands up and says, "Okay, I'll give that some thought, and get back to you later." The manager jumps to challenge that reply with, "But you said if we could do that, you'd buy it today!" The customer says, "That's right, but the day's not over yet, so likely I'll be back and buy before the day is over." How much time was wasted? Most often, from two to three hours! Yes, this happens so often that I took this much space to talk about it! Plus that, I can guarantee you they will leave knowing what you will sell it for, and shop you against your competition! Guess what? Now, they won't buy it from you today!

The only proper way to address this issue is to lock it in so there can be no misunderstanding or games! I prefer to do it this way; I speak very plainly, and spell out exactly what we're talking about. Address the buyer by name, and be very sincere and businesslike: "Cameron, let me ask you this; if I can sell you our car for $28,300.00, give you eight thousand dollars for your trade-in, and keep your monthly payments at $550.00 per month, will you buy this car and *drive it home right now?*" If the customer answers in the affirmative, you go present the offer.

If he hesitates, or asks some other question, answer that question, and then go back and repeat this closing question *verbatim*! If still there is no commitment, then ask a different question, such as, "So Cameron, you seem reluctant to make a buying decision right now. Were you just looking to get a rough idea?" So he answers, "Well I just wanted to get an idea to think about, because it's a big decision." I answer, "Yes it certainly is, and I can appreciate your wanting to think about it, but let me ask you this; is there a number you would do it for right now?" If still no agreement, I'll try again; "Cameron, I know it sounds crazy, and I shouldn't even suggest something so wild, but what if I could get you $9,000.00 for your trade? No, is there any number that would do it?" You see, I will not give up, and I will politely keep trying, because I have nothing to lose and everything to gain!

Now if the customer is still going to leave with no commitment, I don't want him going to the next dealer with my numbers, so I'll most likely let him out on a bubble, after going back to the sales office. I'll say, "Cameron, I hope we can earn your business later, let me get your keys; I'll be right back." My salesperson will slowly walk him out to his car, and I'll come out with his keys and the bubble. I hand him his keys and say, "Thanks Cameron, I'm sure that when you're ready, I know I can earn your business! My other manager just got back, and I ran the trade by him. Now I can't promise; but before you take less than twelve thousand dollars for your trade, come back and see me!" Remember I tried to commit him to buy with $9,000.00 for his trade, but not wanting him to just lay down somewhere else for a trade allowance of $10,000.00, I now let him out on a bubble of $12,000.00. *I did not say I'd give* him that, I said to come back before he accepts *less* than that for the trade! The customer wanted to play a game, and I played it with him. Before he buys *any* car, I'll get another shot at him! So when he comes back, I'll remind him of *exactly what I said.*

It's easy to remember, when you use the same dialogue in each similar situation. I can turn it back on him then by saying; "I'll bet no one else even offered over $8,000.00, did they?" Now, you should draw out what you *really* need to do to sell him. Sometimes when this type of buyer gets upset, I'll just be totally honest, and tell them exactly what I did. I'll say, "Cameron, I knew you weren't being totally open with me when you were here before, and I was just hoping that I might get to $12,000.00. I was doubtful, but I really want your business bad enough that I have really tried! I have been able to get my appraiser to give you $10,200.00 for trade, which I know nobody else in town can do! Okay?" — I hold out my hand. I have not lost very many of these, and you just have to be ready for the customer's reaction. He was lying to me, so I used my bubble of hope to get him to return!

21 QUIT SMOKING – HOW? – I'LL SHOW YOU!

So how about a tip to quit smoking? Yeah, I know the car business is high pressure, face paced and demanding. The car business attracts high-strung people with bad habits. I was fortunate that I never went for the drugs or excessive alcohol habits; just smoking cigarettes like a stinking chimney! When you smoke, it even reeks from your pores. You'll know when you're offensive to some customers, because some will actually be abusive about it! "Oh, you're a smoker." "No ma'am, I just work part-time in a crematorium. Of course I'm a smoker, why don't you sit down and shut up! Sorry, I'm trying to quit!"

Your hair stinks, and your clothes stink, and your hands smell. I quit once for 17 years, and one night I was having a drink with a friend, and the bartender had cigarettes there so I bought a pack figuring I'd just have a couple. I went through the pack in three hours flat. No cough, no lung pain, no dizziness, just pleasure. It was as though I had never quit; after 17 years!

The next day, I went through 3 ½ packs, and then I settled in at three packs a day. I bought a few cartons and some lighters, and smoked for another ten years. Truthfully, this was a wonderful habit for me! I really enjoyed it! But unfortunately these days, it is taboo. If you're going to sell cars, I say don't smoke.

So how do you quit? Here it is; the secret! First of all, keep cigarettes in your home and your car. You may need to keep them for a long time. I did for a year! Buy the nicotine patches. The company recommends you stay on the large patch for about 10 weeks if I remember right. I doubled it. Then the smaller patch; I doubled that time as well, then on the third step down, I think I tripled or quadrupled that term.

But that's not the key. The real key is to always have your cigarettes close at hand! Also, you must have *extra* patches with you! I had a backup patch in my suit coat, in case I forgot to put one on after my shower. I had another one in my car, in case I needed a fresh patch later in the day if the first patch started to lose effect, especially on a 12+ hour work day. When I stepped down to the lower dosage, I still kept the full strength patches for backup, in case I needed to jump back up again. I did on a few occasions, but that's the real secret. Plenty of cigarettes and patches. If you don't have them readily available, your mind will hit the panic button!

I had tried the gum, but that caused gas on the stomach, and the high dosage patch has a good dose of nicotine. I don't buy the fact that the habit can be replaced by having a fake cigarette or other gimmicks. If you need something to put in your mouth, then chew plastic pens. It works. Good luck!

22 DEVELOPING A RELATIONSHIP

Your initial contact and your body language; I've already covered assisting the newly arriving customer in finding an easy to get to parking spot, and I sure hope that you've been smiling and friendly-appearing. A flourish with your hand is a lot better than pointing to the spot you wish them to park in.

A respectful tone in your greeting is best, with a, "Welcome to XYZ Motors, how may I help you today?" is an easy greeting, and it's one that gets to the point quickly. Asking cute questions such as, "What did you come to buy," or similar off the wall questions may be funny, but not professional.

Now, if the customer begins being humorous the minute he gets out of the car, it may be he is trying to break his nervousness! Maybe when he gets out, he says, "I want your best deal!" Depending upon his demeanor, you could come back at him with most anything. I have responded with, "So you're interested in buying the dealership," or "Darn, I just gave it to those other folks. How about the second best deal?" Realize that he is trying to break the ice and go along with him. If he says, "I want to talk to an honest salesperson," I'd come back with, "He just quit, he couldn't make a living! How about me instead?" If your customer is joking around, feel free to have a few moments of levity. They'll love you for it. Never take yourself too seriously.

Personally, I have always clowned around all through my entire closing scenario with the customer. It fits my personality, and I have said the most outrageous things and never had a negative reaction, because I always smile when I say something wild. A customer asks, "How do I know I can trust you?" I say, "Don't take a chance, and you won't have any surprises!" Or when a situation gets too serious, I'll put my hand on a customer's shoulder and say, "Trust me, I'm a car salesman!" Anything from taking myself too serious and I have learned that customers respond very favorably to the levity.

You have to learn how to relax your customers, and you must realize that people are leery and uptight when they come in. You need to relax them quickly and keep everything easy from then on! There is a great value in saying aloud what you know the customer is thinking; such as a car salesman's reputation! I've even used the line; "Hey folks, the last poll puts us *above* politicians!" They laugh!

23 OPEN THOSE ARMS!

Pay attention to your customer's body language. Let's say you're delivering your message and making a presentation of all the arguments as to why your customer should buy this car, and just as you begin, your customer leans back, folds his arms across his chest and listens intently to your entire pitch. He objects after your presentation is over, and won't tell you his main objection. He leaves, and you sit there trying to figure out where you lost him. Go back to where he first folded his arms. He didn't do that to be comfortable, or to give you his undivided attention; he did that to tune you out! Whenever a customer folds their arms, shut up, right then and there! Folded arms mean, "I've tuned you out! I'm not listening anymore, talk to the hand!"

As a factory representative, I once addressed a large group of automobile dealers and their managers. The group numbered several hundred people, and it was a very stressful situation, because I and the other speaker were there to announce a factory price increase, and everyone was apprehensive, as the dealer body felt it would make them less competitive with other makes. The audience looked like hundreds of Buddha's. Most every person in the room had folded arms. Believe me; I had to talk fast and furious about supplies increasing, to better and faster response to their ordering procedure, to national and regional advertising support. Gradually, arms began to unfold, and I was concentrating on only the arms that were still folded. Once I could no longer see any folded arms, I delivered the price increase to a totally receptive audience.

Had we just handed out the new price sheets as everyone came in, and tried to discuss these increases with a totally hostile audience, the place might have erupted! This was an auditorium full of car dealers and sales managers. I was just thankful that I had learned a little about body language early on!

24 HOW TO CALCULATE A PAYMENT

Calculate an exact payment with a pocket calculator. This information is for your personal use only. Do not even *think* about using it in your everyday sales.

As a closer, I always avoided even thinking about whether or not the payment given me by the desk was close to accurate, or packed by $100.00 a month. That's the reason I could deliver my message so convincingly! You must be sincere when you are working a deal! *Never once*, in my entire career, did I even try to second guess the pencils I was given. Well; maybe once!

I give you this formula for your own personal use outside of your workplace. The formula is:

P x % ÷ 365 x 17 x M + P ÷ M

This may look complicated, but it's just a quick matter of substitution. "P" is the principal or balance to finance, % is the interest rate, "M" is the number of months to finance for. Let's take an example; say we want to finance $28,000.00 for 72 months at an interest rate of 6%. Your calculation will look like this:

28000 times .06
divided by 365
times 17
times 72
plus 28000
divided by 72
The payment is $467.00 per month.

This will be within two or three dollars from the exact calculation. Now let's look at a *Factor Chart*.

APR	NUMBER OF MONTHS						
	24	30	36	48	60	72	84
4.00	0.04342	0.03508	0.02952	0.02258	0.01842	0.01564	0.01367
5.00	0.04387	0.03553	0.02997	0.02303	0.01887	0.01611	0.01000
5.50	0.04409	0.03575	0.03019	0.02325	0.01910	0.01634	0.01437
5.75	0.04421	0.03586	0.03031	0.02337	0.01922	0.01645	0.01449
6.00	0.04432	0.03598	0.03042	0.02349	0.01933	0.01657	0.01461
6.25	0.04443	0.03609	0.03054	0.02360	0.01945	0.01669	0.01473
6.50	0.04455	0.03620	0.03065	0.02371	0.01957	0.01681	0.01485
6.75	0.04466	0.03632	0.03076	0.02383	0.01968	0.01693	0.01497
7.00	0.04477	0.03643	0.03088	0.02395	0.01980	0.01705	0.01509
7.25	0.04488	0.03654	0.03099	0.02406	0.01992	0.01717	0.01522
7.50	0.04500	0.03666	0.03111	0.02418	0.02004	0.01729	0.01534
7.75	0.04511	0.03677	0.03122	0.02430	0.02020	0.01741	0.01546
8.00	0.04523	0.03689	0.03134	0.02441	0.02028	0.01753	0.01559
8.25	0.04534	0.03700	0.03145	0.02453	0.02040	0.01765	0.01571
8.50	0.04546	0.03712	0.03157	0.02465	0.02052	0.01778	0.01584
8.75	0.04560	0.03723	0.03170	0.02477	0.02064	0.01790	0.01596
9.00	0.04568	0.03735	0.03180	0.02489	0.02076	0.01803	0.01609
9.25	0.04580	0.03746	0.03192	0.02500	0.02088	0.01815	0.01622
9.50	0.04591	0.03758	0.03203	0.02512	0.02100	0.01827	0.01634
9.75	0.04603	0.03769	0.03215	0.02524	0.02112	0.01840	0.01647
10.00	0.04614	0.03781	0.03227	0.02536	0.02125	0.01853	0.01660
11.00	0.04661	0.03828	0.03274	0.02585	0.02174	0.01903	0.01712
12.00	0.04707	0.03875	0.03321	0.02633	0.02224	0.01955	0.01765
13.00	0.04754	0.03922	0.03369	0.02683	0.02275	0.02007	0.01819
14.00	0.04801	0.03970	0.03418	0.02733	0.02327	0.02061	0.01874
15.00	0.04849	0.04018	0.03467	0.02783	0.02379	0.02115	0.01930
18.00	0.04992	0.04164	0.03615	0.02937	0.02539	0.02281	0.02102
20.00	0.05090	0.04263	0.03716	0.03043	0.02649	0.02395	0.02221
22.00	0.05188	0.04363	0.03819	0.03151	0.02762	0.02513	0.02343
25.00	0.05337	0.04516	0.03976	0.03316	0.02935	0.02694	0.02531
30.00	0.05591	0.04778	0.04245	0.03601	0.03235	0.03008	0.02859

This was a vast improvement over the payment books of the early days, where you had to add up columns of numbers. I still have made a practice of having a factor chart available in the event of a power failure at work. Where your interest rate and term meet, is the number to multiply times your balance to finance.

Not but a few years ago, the entire power supply for my dealership went out, and at a very busy time we quickly sent someone to a store nearby that still had lights, bought candles, and set up about ten showroom desks and the sales office with lights. I pulled out my factor chart, and we used pocket calculators and wrote the contracts by hand! We sold a lot of vehicles that night and saved the day.

I will advise both salespeople and managers to leave this factor chart for what it is for; emergencies! Do not make the mistake of using this chart when you are negotiating a sale! Let the desk control everything. I give you this to improve your knowledge, but not to kill your sales, which *you will do* if you try to get cute and attempt your own closing style!

For closers and desk managers, I will say that I seldom ever needed to ever make a decision where I could not get back to my main computer, but there were times at remote events and sales where it was handy. Where you're working at a remote sale, like under a tent at a fairgrounds or any off-site location, it can be handy. I have had times when sitting under a huge circus tent with fifty picnic tables, and surrounded by an inventory of six hundred vehicles, and power cords going in all directions, where I had to make deals on the spot without a computer.

Things today are so much easier with laptops, tablets, and cellphones, but just so you know the basics, let's look at our chart. This is just an example, but let's say you wish to finance $20,500 at an interest rate of 8% for six years: Go down the APR (annual percentage rate) column to 8.00 and across the page to 72 months and you find your factor of .01753. Next multiply 20500 times .01753, and the result is 359.365, which gives you a car payment of $359.37 per month.

You can also use this factor in reverse if a customer says they have $1,000.00 cash down, and are approved at their bank for a six percent rate for five years, but can only afford a maximum payment of $450.00 per month. Go to the 6.00% on the factor chart and over to the 60 months, and your factor is .01933. Divide $450.00 by .01933 and you get a balance to finance of $23,279.88. This is the amount of money that the customer can finance to meet his payment requirement of $450.00. Add to this his down payment of $1,000.00, and you can sell him a car for $24,280.00 to be dead on his goal.

From this point on, it's all selling. You sell the customer on putting more money down and accepting a higher payment, you sell the bank on longer term financing, and you just build value and excitement! If you need to tailor make a couple of factors to write down for your wallet, pick your favorite term and interest rate, and either figure it yourself on the computer, or just ask your finance manager. You can see your factor is nothing more than a multiplier for a quick and accurate calculation.

Another example such as 8½ percent interest on $1,000.00 for 84 months gives a payment of $15.84 per month, and gives a pay back of $1,330.56 including interest. If you borrow $10,000.00 for the same rate and term, you pay back $13,305.60

Since most dealerships set first payments out to the legal limit (generally 45 days) the payment will be slightly higher, as the factor is set at 30 days 'til first payment.

25 EARN A BONUS

How about a bonus? I always try to pick up a bonus on every sale! You notice by now that I have a favorite way of prefacing a closing question. I begin by addressing the customers by first name, such as, "Marvin, Vicky, let me ask you this…" I say their names because people like to hear their names, and I say them in a low but audible tone, so then when I say let me ask you this; and pause; they know something important is coming. I never get tired of being repetitious when using something that's as big a money-maker as this! I now use this close one last time, at the *last* pass! I have already taken my last pass; I have the most the customer will pay and know I'm *all in*! My sales manager has agreed to take the deal, but now I'm going to ask the customer to pay a small bonus! So now that I have a deal, I want to try for a bonus for my salesperson and myself!

I approach the customers, and they are filled with anticipation. I am now going to use my "Let me ask you this" line, but I will do so *before* I fully sit down. As I sit, and as I have their undivided attention, I ask, "Would you let one hundred dollars stand in your way?" Most of the time they will grab my outstretched hand, and I picked up an extra $100.00 profit. Now if they should say, "Yes, we would," I quickly react with, "Good! That's what I told my boss! Congratulations, you bought the car! In fact, I told my manager you wouldn't pay anymore, and he bet me five dollars, and I won! Thank you." *You must be ready* to react quickly, because if you don't you may just lose the customer. It's such a risky close to try, you have to be really on your game, but I've never lost one by running this bluff. If you do this correctly, you will get almost every single one. When I first created this close, I had some people just scare hell out of me by standing up and getting mad! I learned to talk fast!

If you're a closer on a ten percent commission, you pick up an extra ten dollars on each sale, but the really important thing is, if your salesperson is on a 25 percent or a 30 percent commission, you just made them another $25.00 or $30.00 *on every sale*! If they're selling only a dozen cars a month, that's three hundred dollars, which amounts to $3,600.00 annually, and all because you made a little extra effort. Always show your sales team that you will go out of your way to make them as much money as you can. Maximize every sale. If you're closing 70 deals a month, that's a healthy bonus all around.

I've never seen anyone else use the "Let me ask you this...," but it made me twelve to fifteen thousand dollars a month for a long, long time!

26 SWITCH CARS – WHY AND HOW

L et's talk for a minute about why you must switch customers to a vehicle other than the one they picked out. Of course when I say must, this is usually what an alert sales manager will insist on!

Let's say that the car you are selling is the very one that is going to appear in tomorrow's newspaper ad as *the price leader* vehicle. Since it's going to be on ad, if you sell it, you *must* disclose the ad price; otherwise you'll be guilty of fraud. Even if they never know about it, your dealer would be a fool to take that chance. In the old days, a dealer would simply change the stock number and sell it to the customer anyway, and the ad car that appears in tomorrow's paper would have been already sold. Today's dealer will just figure a way to switch the customer to a vehicle that won't be on ad. Now, you must be creative to switch someone from the vehicle they first decided they wanted to own. Oh, you ask why not just go ahead and sell it for the ad price? Because you will not make any money! Your dealership will not make any money, and your closer will not make any money. Any more questions? Besides all that, legally speaking, that vehicle should be on your lot when the ad hits.

Depending on the sophistication of your buyer, this is not really all that hard. The desk will generally set up the switch in one of several ways. You can go out with a too high payment or a too low trade allowance. Then, when the time is right, the closer can say, "I have an idea; if I had an identical vehicle, just a different color, and I could lower your payment (give more for trade, etc.), would you be interested?" Of course they are. Then the closer departs to check the possibility, and returns with a big smile, "I have great news! I didn't know if I could do this, but I told my manager about what nice people you are, and I happened to know about this other car exactly like to one you picked out, but it came in just before the dealer cost went up, so we own it for less. My boss gave me permission to substitute this one, and I'll have (salesperson) bring it around." Boom, the figures improve to what will fit the customer's budget, and the deal is made! Depending on the negotiating skills of the customer, or their understanding of how the numbers work, the deal is started in the beginning to have enough room for the switch and still hold full price! Everything leading up to this is all planned from the very beginning! The salesperson won't be aware that the switch has been preplanned, because it must be at the proper time, and it will all appear to be natural and smooth! You may also luck out and have another one in the same color they want!

Let's just say that in a particular scenario, there is no vehicle available for a substitution. Now a dealer must try to give enough of a low trade allowance to *steal the trade*. Since the customer has no knowledge of this car being an ad special for the next day, we negotiate the deal based on the list price. Once we have shaken hands on the deal, and both the dealer and customer are happy, it's now a simple matter to walk back in and adjust figures. If we know that the price on this car tomorrow will be $3,300.00 less than it is today, we just say, "Mr. and Mrs. Customer, if it would be okay with you, the dealership can save some taxes if instead of the selling price where it is, we'd like to drop it by $3,300.00, and to keep everything the same, we'll drop the trade allowance by the same amount." No customer ever refuses to do this. Now tomorrow, if by a chance (extremely rare) the customer sees the stock number on ad, it's exactly what they paid for it, right? Being as how this is a dishonest way of doing this, I am not recommending it; just explaining how it's done! The buyer will likely be extremely upset when they realize how they were tricked, but they *got the ad price*!

If there is no trade, we can explain to the customer that we need to raise our finance profit, and we'd appreciate it if they'd allow us to raise the rate a little, and we'll drop the price to keep everything the same. Again, easy to do, however here we can't hold all of our profit, or the customer will refinance elsewhere, so we can't raise it to make up for the lower price. We just have to bite the bullet. Now a lot of dealers don't have such *loss leader* ads, but I've worked where we advertised one to two thousand dollars below true cost! Our specials were really special, and we'd lose a sale before taking this loss *before* the actual ad day!

Keep in mind, the ad specials were only used to draw traffic, and before the laws got tough, dealers hid the ad cars, or made up phony stock numbers that didn't exist! When the customer came in; the car was already sold! This still happens today, so not everything has changed.

Due to these con games, some attorneys general began insisting that instead of stock numbers, that dealers had to use the actual VIN (vehicle identification number) in the ads. Larger dealers would then store a lot of these vehicles on other lots, or just put them as far away from the showroom as possible. On many large car stores, with hundreds and hundreds of vehicles, all parked in long rows, and sometimes bumper to bumper, it made it easy to hide them.

I recall seeing a salesperson say goodbye to a school teacher one day after they had both searched all over the lot, looking for an ad car to no avail. The salesperson wanted to sell the car, so it was a genuine effort. *Four hours later*, here comes the teacher in the door, and he called out to the salesman; "I found it!" He had actually spent all that time looking at serial numbers!

27 SOS AND YOUR BODY LANGUAGE

We've discussed different clues to derive from a customer's body language in order to see if they are buying or open to what we are saying. Now, let's talk about the body language that you must project and practice!

It's always amazing to me how surly some salespeople seem to be. I'm sure that anyone who makes a living based on what they sell, or even partially on a commission structure would never intentionally project a bad attitude, and yet many do! Smiling is not a natural state for people. It must be practiced! Observe most any person in a private moment, when they are relaxing or concentrating, and you'll see that while the face may be in a relaxed state, it most likely is closer to a frown than it is to a smile. Maybe it's because of all the stress in life, or the pressures of the work environment, but think about it for a moment. If you observed someone sitting by themselves with a smile on their face, would you maybe register concerns about their sanity? Many would! That shows you that a smile generally needs to have a cause.

Salespeople must practice smiling! At first, it may be necessary to force it. Certainly it's a stressful moment to walk up to a total stranger's car with a smile, when your mind is racing through all the things that can go wrong when the car door opens. It very seldom happens that a customer will jump out of his car with excitement, and say, "I want to buy that car, right now!" No, to the contrary, the odds are that he is afraid of you, thinks you're a crook, hates the process, and you can make a long list of negatives that you are faced with! So you ask, "What the heck is there to smile about when I'm about to jump into this fire?" Well, if you don't have the proper attitude, don't even bother, let someone else wait on them!

Let's look at what we need to succeed; remember the fake it 'til you make it saying? There is more to that statement for salespeople than for anyone! If you project a poor attitude, you have no chance of selling! Successful salespeople need to send an <u>SOS</u> to their brains! The *Smile Of Success* does more than anything else to sell you, and when you meet a customer, the first thing you have to sell is yourself!

If you approach someone with your *Smile of Success*, they feel comfortable with you because you are happy to see them! You will be accepted at face value, and run a lot less risk of the just looking answer! Most people are just looking, until they find a salesperson whom they can feel comfortable with. Send that SOS to your brain, and begin practicing in front of a mirror!

Now you approach the car with a nice inviting smile. Where are your hands? Not in your pockets I hope! Never have your hands in your pockets, period! It's rude. And dumb!

Where are you looking when you meet the people; to them, or through them? Make good eye contact! You don't want to stare them down, but you do need to constantly be making eye contact. A lot of salespeople find it uncomfortable at first, but the easiest way, without your eyes flitting from one of their eyes to the other, is to direct your gaze at that spot on the nose between their eyes. People will not know you are doing this, but it will relax them, and they will feel comfortable without your eyes jumping back and forth.

Ask your question, get your answer, and break the contact briefly so it doesn't become a stare. This is also comforting to people with a crossed eye, because your gaze will not keep noticing this flaw. Practice this with close friends and relatives, and get their reactions until you feel relaxed doing it. This sniper technique makes you a better conversationalist.

When you're asking a question that you want a "yes" answer to, it helps occasionally to emphasize your question with a couple of slight nods of your head to lead them to join you in affirmation!

Develop good body posture. Open hands, facing them, don't slouch, and just practice a confident and open approach.

Be yourself! Don't fake an attitude you don't have. Be sincere, and not over-flattering! If I ask you about the Camaro convertible, don't give me the, "Excellent choice, you sure have good taste" crap, because that sounds insincere! Avoid telling a customer how wise they are, or fawn all over them for making certain selections. It's phony! Even if it would be a sincere compliment, it will most likely be perceived by a customer to be false. It's best to save the praise until later.

As an example, if you really believe the vehicle they pick is the best choice for them, and you tell them so, what happens later if they can't afford it, and you have to switch them to something else? Odds are, they will not be able to save face and buy something else you show them, and you come across as just wanting to sell them anything. In this scenario, if you had not already played the phony best choice card, you could later compliment them by saying, "I really believe this would be a much better choice than the first one you were looking at." Save the big compliments for the handshake when the deal is done!

Going back to your S.O.S. (Smile of Success); statistics indicate that 75% of buyers who answered the surveys said that the impression they formed when first approached by the salesperson had a major bearing on whether or not they made a purchase on that visit!

Those knowledgeable students of body language tell us that non-verbal communication is more telling of a person's true feelings than the spoken word. Remember when we discussed making a good first impression? We know that if we flub it, we can still have a few minutes to turn things around.

Keep your hands out of pockets, and open. When you sit, relax and avoid crossing your legs. If you notice your customer's arms and legs are crossed; remember, this means they're not receptive to the present topic you're discussing! You must get the customer on your same wave length. Get that person leaning forward and arms open and receptive. Picture in your mind, a man sitting with his legs crossed, and the image says, "relaxed and in a casual conversation" doesn't it? Now picture him with both feet on the floor. Notice how in this mental image, his body is leaning forward and closer to the table? Now mentally place a pen in his hand!

28 SEATING YOUR CUSTOMERS

S eating your customers is important. I have worked in dealerships where we had offices (closing booths) that were very cramped, offices that were open in front, and then what I consider to be the most relaxing for selling cars, and this is round tables on the showroom.

Many dealerships are now being built with the open designs. It is very expensive to have showrooms of massive size, and certainly, the idea of a nice display area for the new cars, trucks and SUVs is the best way to show off our product; it's even more necessary in exceptionally hot or cold weather. It's difficult for a dealer to find enough room to display product and still have an open sales area, especially in older stores with limited space, and any expansion would intrude into the parking lot, which is likely too small anyway.

I have worked in stores where tables were placed all over the showroom, between and among the cars and trucks. I hate desks! The first thing I did when I bought my dealership was to turn all the desks against the walls, so my customers and my salespeople sat alongside each other. You never want a barrier between you and the customer if you can help it, that's why I like round tables, because even if they are across from you, it's still not a barrier.

Also, when you seat your people, you need to place them *properly*! By properly, I mean that most all married couples will naturally sit down across from each other, like they do at home at their dinner table. This, you *don't* want! As they sit down, have them move to where they will be positioned with both of them facing you! Then, when the closer comes in they will be facing her or him. You never want your customers to be able to make eye contact where you can miss it, and they need to be able to see all papers as presented, without shuffling back and forth!

I have closed an awful lot of deals where neither customer wanted to be the first to commit, and they both sat there. So, I asked, "Can we go ahead and wrap it up?" Then, I made eye contact with one, and acting like they nodded agreement, held out my hand to the other person and shook hands. Then I went back and shook hands with the other one. Each person thought the other had agreed first, and they probably never even realized that neither one had committed first. Not that it matters, but in many relationships, people are always playing the blame game if anything ever goes wrong, so nobody wants to go first! We do, and they're happy ever after.

Had these people been in their normal facing positions, this type of close couldn't happen, and they may not reach agreement, and decide to go home and think about it. Anytime they come out of the feeling of excitement, and the impulsive buying urge, you lose! In addition to this, there is nothing more difficult than having to present to one person, and then turning to present the same figures to the other! You can see why everything in this business must be so structured, and each action has a purpose and a way it must be performed. Closers, make certain to train this process! Seating must benefit the presenter.

29 BUILDING RAPPORT

Although a sale can be made strictly on a business only relationship with no personal connection being established, this is a very difficult and uncomfortable sale. Without any rapport being developed, the customer is also unlikely to give the salesperson and the dealer a favorable factory survey. They may not complete it at all, which is still a *failure* from the manufacturer's point of view. You must always get the buyer to *return* this survey!

This type of customer is most often one who has been burned in the past, and not only hates the process, but also has a disdain for all dealership people he must, out of necessity, come in contact with. More than likely he is buying a price leader ad car, and has a chip on his shoulder. If you even try to switch this person, or attempt to sell him any extras, he will be offended, and since most of these type are aware of your factory report card, he will threaten you with retaliation if you even look at him sideways!
Personally, I would rather just turn this guy up front, but if your supervisors allow you to make a quick and smooth transaction, just make it pleasant, and get it done fast!

Now, with most people, this is an exciting adventure! They are looking forward to going home in a new vehicle (new or used, it's new and exciting to them) and you need to keep it fun!

Build your relationship on genuine interest and concern for giving the customer the best service possible. Don't just fire questions at a person like your filling out an application. "So what brought you in today?" Keep it light and airy. "What kind of work do you do?

Who for?" These are what I call light and airy; like you might do when casually meeting people at your kids school or a party. This type of questioning, such as where the person works, must be asked after you have ascertained their needs and are en route to show them a vehicle.

When your customer answers, you must show a genuine interest by asking them to elaborate on their actual duties. This is especially important! The majority of people are bored with their existence. They go to work, spend the day in a likely mundane activity and go home. Now here in between does anyone, including their spouse, show any interest in their work day? Doubtful. People love to have someone express an interest in what they do for a living! You will quite often be listening to someone pouring out a passionate story of their daily work experience, when their spouse interrupts with, "Oh Charley, he doesn't care to hear about all that!" Be careful here to respond with, "Oh, to the contrary, I am really enjoying this, but I guess we can finish up after we get the sale done, but I do want to hear more!" Just because the spouse doesn't care, make sure to be genuine, and when the sale is done, remember to get the rest of the story. People seldom get a chance to discuss what they do for employment, and if you want to make a real friend; ask and listen, and then respond. I always not only find out exactly what a person does for work, but by the time I'm through, I'll know both spouses employment and their hobbies!

Make certain that during this interview and fact finding process, you are constantly calling them by name. Don't make the mistake like I remember having happened years ago: I'm closing a long negotiation on an extremely expensive motor home, and as I always do, I first say their names, so I say, "John, Peg, if I can do this and this, can we go ahead and wrap it up?" Silence while they are thinking, then Peg says, "Well should we go ahead Jack?" We shake hands, and I said, "Peg just called you Jack, is that what you prefer?" He said, "Yes, I haven't been called John since college." Tough way to learn a lesson! My salesman had introduced them as John and Peg, and although they never corrected him, I knew all too late that neither of us had really developed a close relationship! Certainly it was very friendly, it had to be, because the new coach was a super-expensive purchase, but I think back as to how much better it would have been if the salesman and manager had been calling him by the name his close friends and family used! We left money on the table on that one!

That's almost as bad as Mr. and Mrs., and sir and Ma'am. I think respect is great when I first meet someone, but I get on a first name basis immediately. If your introduction is hurried, or you don't catch the names properly, start over and slow down! You may be in a rain storm, snow or sand, whatever; get under shelter, or in a car or out of a noise situation. Then begin again and always ask what name a person prefers to be called by. Repeat their name or nickname, and write down what they tell you! Use their names as often as you can. People *love* to hear their name!

Make certain to preface important closing questions with the customers' names, and pronounce them clearly. Older people cannot usually hear as well as others, but will rarely admit it. Watch for signs; such as leaning toward you, watching your lips when you speak, and if they ask you to repeat something. Then raise your voice a bit, and *keep* the volume up! Once you have been made aware, there is absolutely no excuse for not speaking loudly!

Try to learn something about every person's employment. What their company does, what they do for the company, and something important about their particular position. I promise you that this knowledge will be of great value to you in the future! I have closed countless sales much easier because I knew a lot about people's jobs and employers in general, due to previous customers elaborating on their jobs at the same companies.

30 THE COLUMBO CLOSE

I have always picked interesting and effective methods of body language from every source available. Early in my closing career, Peter Falk starred in the TV detective series *Columbo*. After the first few episodes, I had developed what I called the *Columbo Close*, and it has made me *huge* amounts of money! Columbo always had a semi-stumbling method of investigating crimes, where he would be leaving a room, and suddenly turn, as if deep in thought, and say, "Just one more question." I liked it so much, I immediately adopted the technique and tailored it for the car business.

When closing a sale, the pressure must be eased from time to time. Whenever I make the next pass, I try to get all of the movement I can. I'll present the numbers given me by the sales manager (or myself, if I'm doing it all), and I know that I must get all the movement from the buyer that I can. It is important that both sides continue to give, and end up compromising with a mutually acceptable agreement. If the customer just moves a little toward my offer, then I must move a lot. Working a deal means structuring the plan whereby we can make a deal by meeting in the middle. Now if the customer is fighting the process, and wants to rush it, I'll do it in stages, and here's where the Columbo Close comes into play. I'll write down what they just offered and start to walk away, then suddenly I pause, turn and either lean on the table (if there's room without invading the customer's space) or I'll oftentimes just stand there, or even just squat down alongside, *without* sitting, and say something like, "Now, just in case the boss says he wants blah, blah, what should I hit him with?" Customers see this is a sincere concern that I feel their offer will be turned down, and "I want to do right by them." They will give some answer which is usually an indication that they may be willing to go higher but, "See what he says." Now when they answer; I sit back down, but just on the *front edge* of the chair, like I'm planning to depart quickly. In actuality, I *now* will push for a higher offer from them! My purpose is to make as few passes as I can, as if we run back and forth too many times the customer will perceive this as us grinding on them, and eventually we'll wear out our welcome and lose.

Columbo enables a person to cut the negotiations in half if done properly. I can make a pass, get a bump, use Columbo, sit back down and get another bump! My salespeople immediately noticed my new technique, because it was a natural for selling situations. Whenever there has been a confrontational situation with a customer, I immediately diffuse the situation by taking what they offer, depart, and show them it's going their way, and then using Columbo, I'm back in the driver's seat! Remember, your customers will always pay more for a great performance! They want a show; give 'em one!

I realize that I have dwelled on the Columbo Close for a long time, but the art of negotiating is so important that it needs to be perfected, and one cannot prepare too much! Practice this technique with a close friend or your spouse, and they can help critique your performance.

Especially important in keeping a long negotiation from getting tense, is to not drag out the grinding. You know you need a big bump, and yet your customer has reacted negatively, and given you just a token increase and has gotten tense; you now diffuse the tension, and use Columbo to reopen your request, and not totally sitting back down, keeps them from getting tense again. This casual body language takes the pressure off, and will still get you some movement! Just the mere fact that you are squatting down alongside the table or desk, instead of sitting back down, keeps the situation from getting tense.

31 KEEP SCORE

L et's look now at how to keep score. Car sales has been an easy way to track your performance. Make money you stay, and if you don't; "See ya!"

So let's look at some statistics. An automobile salesperson needs to concentrate only on one step at a time. Your first step is to up the customer. This means that whatever dealership system you are under, nothing can happen until you get a customer. *You should strive to get ninety percent of all your ups on a test drive.* Most salespeople will end up around seventy-five to eighty percent, if they are good at their jobs.

Breaking it down to simple terms, you should end up by at least selling one out of every five people you greet. Here's how it normally breaks down:

Out of every five customers
80% test drives = 4
50% write ups (offers) = (50% of 4 = 2)
50% closing ratio = (50% of 2 = 1)

These are national statistics. Just remember that saying; "The feel of the wheel is half the deal." *Test drives sell cars!*

Make sure you select the *right* vehicle, have all parties involved in the decision drive it, and you can easily increase your test drives to 90%! Make them drive it! If they don't drive it, they won't buy it; so what do you have to lose? *Time? Invest time!* Don't be in such a hurry to get back to sitting on your butt to wait for your next up. Love the one you're with! The better a job you do, the higher the number of people that will make an offer to purchase.

Now, if the presentation and demo drive were excellent, the closing percentage will increase, because your buyers know there is no better product for them! As you learn; your closing percentage will increase, and soon you'll be at:

- 90% demos
- 60% write ups
- 60% closes

which equates to about two sales out of every five customers!

My closing percentage was a low of 65%, but a lot of times when my gang had their demos perfected, we felt like everything was a sale! Talk about having a highly motivated sales team! That's when it gets exciting to come to work! It oftentimes seemed like everyone was a buyer, and they were all ours!

Obviously in what we are looking at, the demo drive is really the *key*, isn't it? So now you are seeing a *key* that many salespeople choose to ignore throughout their careers! The only thing that controls the entire process; the ease of attaining a write up, the ease of a smooth close, a great factory survey, and great profit is *The Test Drive!* Liken this to climbing a hill: Wouldn't it be whole lot easier if you could start at the top and walk down? If you do the proper demo, it's an easy walk!

Allow me to show you an important part of selling that very few people understand, and if they do, most will soon become too experienced to stick to the basics.

Selling is a profession that has ways to keep score, but the hard part is forecasting! If you average $500.00 commission on a sale, how many ups do you need to make $5,000.00? Sure, your dealership may be able to give you a guesstimate, based on what they think they do for numbers, but that's only as good as the numbers their salespeople told them. Truth be known (and it seldom is), the average salesperson blows out more customers than the management knows! Take the salesperson who ups the *one legger* (person without their spouse), and answers a question and says goodbye. This salesperson, if questioned about the customer, says, "He just wanted to know how the car looked because his brother bought one, and he was curious. He wasn't a buyer!" Not counting this up covered the salesperson's butt and skewed the numbers.

You need your own *exact* numbers, and only *you* can compute your individual numbers. The reason being, is that only you will ever really know the truth.

I want you to keep a *60 day record*. Why 60? Because a 30 day average will not be accurate enough, as there are too many variables. You may need a card to carry with you, and transfer to another sheet each evening. You need only four columns on the card. U (for ups), D (for demos), W (for write-ups) and S (for sold). Each time you get an up, you make a mark. Each time you go on a test drive with someone, you make a mark behind D. Each time you get a write-up, you make your mark, and a mark behind S for every sale.

Now, at the end of 60 days, you total all four columns. Let's say that in the 60 days you had 172 ups, managed to get 135 demos, and had offers (write-ups) of 60 and sold 30 vehicles. Since you had 135 demos out of 172 ups, you divide 135 by 172 and your percentage of demos drives = 78%. Now you managed to write-up 60 of those you drove, so divide 60 by 135, and we see that of your people you test drive, you are able to get 44% of them to make offers. Next, you sold 30 people, so out of 60 offers, you managed to close 50% of them. You have now established your individual sales index.

- Your demo rate is 78%

- Your write-up rate is 44%
- Your sales rate is 50%.

This tells you that out of 100 customers, you should sell 17.

Let's take a look at it. 100 customers X 78% = 78 demos, times 44% of them that you will get to the table, which is 34 people. Out of those 34 write-ups, you will close 50% which equals 17. Let's analyze these numbers. Your goal is to demo 90% of your ups, to write-up 60% of them and to sell 55 to 60% of your write-ups. That's the *goal*; but let's only be concerned to start with your demo percentage and your write-up percentage. These are your *immediate* goals; especially if you have a closer coming out to close your sales. You can do your job better, and hopefully with better preparation and closing skills, you may improve.

You may need to better qualify customers to make sure you are showing the right car. You need to analyze your demo route, and make sure your demo drives are safe, enjoyable and interesting. Since this is the most important element in your sale, you must *perfect* it. Ask your managers and your peers for tips. Take your manager on a test drive, and have a genuine interest in picking as many brains as you can for tips and advice.

As your demos get better, your confidence level will improve, and your percentage will go up. Also, as a result of better demos, you will find it a lot easier to get people inside to increase your write-ups, because your customers will be more convinced that they want your vehicle! The more sold your customer is on the car, the easier they will be to close, and your percentages and personal sales index will improve. The more they like the car and you, the easier job a closer will have, or if you close your own sales, your expertise will increase.

Your 60 day test will give you numbers you can count on to continue as long as you maintain the skill level you have now. If you do not improve, then you can count on needing 100 customers to sell 17 cars. After a month or so, as you gain more experience, conduct your 60 day test again. Some of my people kept an ongoing record by dropping 30 days each month off the back, and constantly charting their last 60 days performance. This, plus bigger paychecks, is the only way you can tell if you're getting better, or repeating the past like *Groundhog Day*!

When you get up to 90% demos, even if your write-up percentage stays at 50%, which is still low, you will write 45 people out of 100, and even if your closing ratio stays low at 50%, you now close about 23 sales out of 100. That's six more than your previous percentages and the increase can be easily brought about by improving only **one** skill; DEMO DRIVES!

So going back to goal setting; if you now wish to make $5,000 in a month, and you average only $500 per car, how many customers does that take? We know that you sell 23% of your ups, so to hit $5,000 at an average of $500, we need ten sales, which means we divide 10 by .23, and that equals 43 or 44 customers, and 23% of them will give us 10 sales!

Once you know your overall sales index, your numbers will stay the same unless you improve. So let's say, using our same index that you want to set a goal to amass a down payment for a house, boat, car or anything. It now all boils down to a numbers game, doesn't it? You can easily chart your average commission, and set goals *not by how many sales you make*, but by strictly the number of ups you need. Period! Your numbers may not always work out *if you are inconsistent*! You need to keep constantly improving of course, but the whole key to selling is to remember that it's all *just a numbers game*! This numbers game requires a consistent and regular pattern of performance. The secret to making it work is consistency. If you lose ten in a row, you must *not* sit down to lick your wounds. You must keep going, and you may sell the next six in a row! You can't stop to feel sorry for yourself, or get your head together, forget it! You're the same person, with the same skills, and just because the buyers got themselves out of the proper order, your 23 buyers are still coming out of the next 100 ups you get! If a few failures however, make you jump out of line, the buyers that were meant for you just might land on someone else, and they'll think the car gods just smiled on them. Actually, those were your buyers. You took all that abuse going through all those non-buyers, and just when your real buyers were lining up, you were on a woe is me kick! If you have a failure, it's always hard, so take a quick break, and get back out there. *It's all numbers.*

I hope I've worn out this point, but I want you to learn what most car people never do! The car gods will always make the numbers work, so just don't mess around with the odds. Just stay on track and remember what comes after we get all the no's out!

32 IMPORTANT PREFACE FOR CLOSING

The most important thing in asking a question is to make certain to have the customers' undivided attention. If you don't, you will not get any worthwhile response.

I begin by addressing each buyer by name; "George, Barbara, let me ask you this; if I could do this, this and this (my proposal) would you buy the car, and drive it home right now?" You absolutely *must* make sure to have their full attention and present a clearly understandable proposal. Repeat their response aloud, but *do not* automatically write it down and rush in to your sales manager. You see, your customer gives you more credit than you should have at this point, because they really believe that this is all a car game. They believe that you are really in the know. Therefore, if you just rush in to present their counter, they now feel that in your mind you feel it should work! If you ever want to kill a deal, just take whatever they give you, and split for the office. You must always *defend* every pencil you are given, as though it were gospel. Don't try to second guess the desk! Believe the pencil, and don't even think of alternatives! If you don't convince yourself that the pencil is correct, how can you convince your customers?

Don't be too prideful! Many closers are embarrassed to play dumb, but I promise you it works wonders. I've watched and listened to closers around me for years, and I have seen them blow out customers because the closer acted like the *deciding and decision making manager!* Even in those many times that I was the sole manager, and I penciled myself, and wrote the offers in big bold figures and knew exactly where I was at, I *always* made believe my boss gave me the offer! No matter what, you must never act like you think the customer's offer will work. Even when the customer came up to where I knew was a full profit deal, I still had to leave doubt, and defend the dealership's last offer! If you *ever* just accept their latest counter, if it is *not exactly* agreeing to your last pencil, *the customer will instantly realize* that all your denials of knowing what would work have been an act, and you've been lying all the time. You must *always make one last trip* to the sales office; even if you know that you can't possibly hold all the profit they just agreed to! You can always use reasons later on to give them a better deal, such as higher appraisals and other reasons that enhance your dealership's genuine concern for their well-being; just don't blow your sale at the end. Make the final trip to the sales office, and complete your final pass by coming out with a great smile and a loud, excited "congratulations!" I cannot stress highly enough to stay dumb. Maybe it just came natural to me?

The key to this whole segment, to me, is the setup pause; "John, Mary, let me ask you this; if I could this, this and this, would buy it and drive it home right now?" "Let me ask you this," followed by a pause and a clear presentation will do more than anything for a smooth sale. I used to hear myself repeating "let me ask you this," and think in my mind, "I'm wearing out this question," but it worked so wonderfully, I just quit worrying about it. Customer response is your key. If it works, polish it and use it!

33 DEFENDING YOUR POSITION

I touched on this in chapter 32, and need to elaborate on the idea for professional closers. You know that your salespeople will genuinely believe that what they are told is the truth. You however, are well aware that the closing game is generally a series of back and forth offers and counter offers until a compromise is reached and a sale results. In order to be a professional closer, you need to stay with the basics! Stay dumb, and don't let your management title kill your bank account. What's more important to you; your *image* or your *income*?

I have both empathy and sympathy for the newly promoted closer. Here you are with your brand new position, and if you didn't take over the sales crew you were on, you took over another team. Now that you have a management hat, your fellow salespeople and managers don't see you as a different person! Just the same salesperson they have been working with, wearing a new title. You may have been a clown, or maybe one who never followed orders, did proper follow up, or came to work on time! Yes, this happens, because the best salespeople are not necessarily the best closers! Conversely, some of the laziest salespeople sometimes shine as closers.

Here's where my empathy – sympathy statement comes in. Now, when you first go in to meet your salesperson's customer, you have two concerns; how to properly close the sale, but also, how to look managerial in front of the salesperson. You will be afraid to humble yourself and act dumb in front of the customer (your best move), and risk appearing weak in front of your salesperson. Well, get the fears out of your head! You were promoted for a reason. Your salesperson is probably more concerned about your coming in and acting like an arrogant ass than anything! They will appreciate your skill in showing humility, and you'll find that they will applaud your skills afterward!

Over my career, I trained hundreds of salespeople, who because of my always running a very successful team, were usually selected for promotions. Since my people had sat there with me and witnessed my methods, they never had the worries about having to act important to their new salespeople once they were promoted; they were already important because they were the best of the best. I don't say this to brag, but when a closer has a limited number of salespeople he or she can have on their crew, it is necessary to train them to be the best, or replace them. Since for most of my career I ran with six to nine people, I could not afford to carry people who could not be trained to meet my standards. When each salesperson represents one-sixth of your income, every person is extremely important!

Closers; all your people care about are your abilities to close their sales, and training them to be better! They don't give a damn about your bigger ego; all they want you to do is to make them money! When you receive your promotion, take your 15 minutes to strut around and then get your butt to work!

34 THE $950.00 SANDWICH!

T hroughout your career as a salesperson or manager, you will always be at the mercy of your own negativity. We seem to concentrate more on our failures than on our successes. This is a fact we must deal with if we sell on commission, because it greatly affects our income! Think of a long-haul trucker; if he has a problem in his life, he will live with it like you do, but he can still perform his duty for the most part, and the personal issues may not have an effect on his income.

If a salesperson has a problem, it will *directly* affect their income, because to do their job, they must keep their minds clear in order to perform! We need to remember that in our business we will fail *more often* than we succeed! This is a fact that cannot change, so accept it! If you sell two out of every five people you meet, you still lose three of them! Get used to it, but let's look at our own worst enemy — us!

In the "keeping score" tip, we discuss keeping a 60 day record of ups, demos, write ups and sales. This evaluation should be periodically conducted on your own, because it gives you actual statistical data that pertains only to you! These are the key numbers for you as an individual. As you gain more experience, your numbers should improve.

You need to use these numbers in order to realize that sales are strictly a numbers game. Out of so many customers (ups) you will have X number of test drives, and X number of those will end up on paper and you will close X % of them.

Salespeople and managers all live with this fact, and we know that if we sell two out of every five, the order is not just meet five, sell two, meet five, sell two, but that you could easily work with ten in a row that don't buy, and then you may sell the next five, skip one, sell one, and so on. National averages will show you numbers based on what dealerships report to factories from numbers given the dealer by the sales staff. Are they accurate? Who knows? *You need to chart your own.*

The most important thing you can learn is that the number will *always* work out. You *will* sell X number of people out of X number of ups based on your individual counts. If you sell two out of five, then I don't care if you miss the first thirty sales, your numbers will always come back around! The secret you need to learn is to maintain the *same* positive attitude throughout! It's difficult!

Now, I'll give you a good example of *not* listening to the facts. This time, I'm working a rotating up system; my salespeople would take their turn, and when through, rotate to the back of the line, and work their way up again. My next man up came to me and asked if he could go to lunch. I reminded him that he was next up, but he told me he had already had three lousy ups that day, and just needed to go across the street to the restaurant and enjoy a good lunch to get his head adjusted. I advised him against it and told him he was messing with the odds, but he was so down, he didn't care, so I let him leave. At the moment he entered the restaurant, a car drove in, and when the couple exited, they looked at the salesperson greeting them, and said, "We came to buy a new 4X4 pickup!" Just that easy! They paid full price, and we got their trade for less than its' real value!

When my other salesman returned from lunch, he came over with a sheepish look and said, "I saw them come in just as I entered the restaurant; how much did my sandwich cost me?" I replied, "950 dollars!" Case in point; it's a numbers game, and don't mess up your odds by having a $950.00 sandwich! Grab a candy bar and stay up.

35 MANAGERS: HOW TO FIND GOOD SALESPEOPLE

Managers, when you need good people, what do you do? Run an ad and hope to steal someone else's well-trained and experienced people? Or, do you want bodies? Think about it. Do you really think that a professional salesperson with a good track record is going to be going through help-wanted ads? No. What you are going to get are the disgruntled people in the lower half of the rankings who feel that a job change will give them a new chance. Sometimes you can snag a good one that just never had been properly trained, but a high percentage of the applicants blame everyone but themselves for their lack of sales. I just feel that the best people don't look for ads, they look at where they might like to work, and go there to apply.

I have always gone on a hunt for people I want. Many, many times over my career, I've gone into a new position where I either had to replace a weak sales crew, or maybe had to form a new one. Because of my wanderlust, I would oftentimes get bored and just leave, or I'd get a call from a dealer who needed help, so I'd accept the challenge. I've had to many times, start from scratch. I wasn't always able to ask people to follow me, as with my desire for change, what security could I offer?

In my beginning years, before I had a talent pool that I could draw from (steal good people that would follow me), I had to go out shopping. So where did I shop? Shopping malls. Yes, I'd go out shopping where salespeople are. Have you ever hired a shoe salesman from Nordstrom? They know how to schmooze people, and they are good qualifiers. How about the television salesman from Best Buy, or the Sax 5th Avenue clothing salespeople?

I will just go in and observe, and when I am approached, I will quickly analyze the person and if I like what I see, I present my card and explain what I'm really there for. If I don't like the person, I politely keep looking around and observing the people on the floor. If a person has a professional appearance, and they can converse easily, they can be trained! I approach the target when they are free, and tell them I'm headhunting.

I have also been successful at raiding good people over the phone. I will pause here to say that for newer managers that aren't well known, that the best way is to dress down to casual clothes, and just drive in to a dealership and play customer. This is an excellent way for you to see a prospective salesperson in action. Act like a customer, but don't take a lot of their time. When you find someone you like (experience isn't necessary, but you have to like them), then explain why you're there, and invite them to come and see you. This is a great way to see exactly what you'll get!

Naturally, this is a viable option, but if you are a new manager, you have potential problems. An experienced salesperson with a good track record will likely be hard to sell on working for an untried closer, and someone who too readily comes on board may be ill-trained, or hard to train. Either way, if you can get them to come to see you for an interview, this is a great way to go.

I really never had the luxury of anonymity for long, because I started in a large store, and with our turnover, and my reputation, I could not often go to any dealership where I wouldn't bump into someone I knew. If I just stopped in to say "Hi" to a friend in a dealership, rumors would spread and I'd start getting calls from all over town asking if I was hiring on there as a manager. I've had sales managers I didn't even know come up to me and ask, "You're not here to take my job are you?" That's when you know you've changed jobs too often, when you can't go anywhere without suspicion.

One of my better recruiting tools was the telephone. My script varied, but I'd generally call a dealership pretending to be a customer. I'd tell the receptionist, "I was in a few days ago, and can't remember the salesman's name, but he was rather new there, and from what he said, it looked like he was doing a great job! He had a very pleasant personality and was really sharp!" This is basically what I was looking for; someone who was new enough to not have bad habits, a good personality, already doing well, and noticed by others for his success. Invariably, the receptionist would come up with a name or two, (because these people stand out), which I would write down, and ask to speak with the individual. Now, I should explain at this point why I was gender specific. The reason was, the dealerships I was pirating from hired very few females, and not because women couldn't sell cars there, but these were high pressure dealerships that most women would not want to even consider working at; salespeople all over the lot, running all over, and an atmosphere not conducive to anyone who wasn't ready for a lot of abuse! I selected these stores to pirate from because I knew their line-close system, and I knew before a new salesman was allowed to even approach a customer, he must have his script and product tests completed, and be good at presentation.

I was interested in, as I said, an unspoiled, but fairly well-trained salesman who may respond well at this stage to a better working environment. When I'd get this person on the phone, I'd just lay out why I called. Naturally, I had an uphill battle, because here was a new salesman, doing well and probably a hero among his peers and managers. I had advantages that I would briefly outline, but if he did not show any interest in even sitting down for an interview, I'd then ask the following, "Would you be able to recommend another salesman that I might talk with? Someone who you feel is good like you are, but maybe isn't really all that happy there?" Amazing results! This worked very well! After spending a few minutes in conversation, here he is recommending someone else for me, and he'd even go give the person my name and number, and they'd call me!

I never tried too hard to analyze why, but I hired some excellent second best salesmen by this method. Maybe because salespeople always want to be the shining star, and want their best competitors to go away; maybe because good salesmen are gregarious; maybe because, even though he wasn't interested at the time, he was curious, so he was willing to send another salesman to hire on, and if it looked good, it was an option to consider in the future. Car people that are successful are always open to opportunity!

Timing is very important in most facets of our business, and as so often happens, a new salesperson comes in, has some lucky sales, and rises to star status! In the meantime, another good salesperson has a run of bad luck, and suddenly, the old timer is sewered. It's like being in a boat race, and a new, inexperienced racer starts to pass you, and you're losing some distance when suddenly someone on your boat drops the anchor! Now, you not only hate the new guy; you hate your team, your sponsor and your boat. Suddenly you have an opportunity to race for a new team who really wants you! You're willing to at least listen aren't you? That is how I built many successful teams!

Once you have this salesperson come in for the interview, it's up to you. You'd best have a game plan, good selling points on your dealership and reasons why this person needs to work for you! Remember, you called them, now you'd better be able to find out if you really want them now that they are here. The fact that this person showed up means they are interested, so conduct your normal interview. Also, try to find out the underlying reason why they are willing to consider a change at this point. What is it they are looking for? Recognition, training; or is there a hidden problem, like they just lost their driver's license from a DUI and you're closer to their home? Remember, before you finish, you need names and numbers of *more* salespeople at their same store who your applicant feels may also be receptive.

Once, when I was talking to choice #2, he mentioned that a couple of his associates were also unhappy. I had four people show up for the interview! I hired three of them!

I always believed in training people from scratch, but where I made exceptions was when they had the qualities I required and I could re-train them to my way. These qualities are appearance, eye contact, conversational skills, body language and the basic feeling you get when you first meet someone. I can teach cleanliness, selling, dress, obedience, and scripts, as long as one has the ability and the willingness to learn.

36 SALESMANAGERS: HOW TO DESK A DEAL

S o sales managers and closers, are you desking properly? I ask this because desking a deal properly takes a lot of talent. You must remember first of all, that *you* may be paid on the overall profit of the sales department, but that your closer and his or her salesperson are paid *only* on this deal that you now are working on! Nothing is harder for a closer to put up with than a manager who is inattentive. The closer does not care if you promised to call the bank back on a deal. They don't care if you have a long lost friend who wants to chat with you on the phone. They don't care if your kid failed finals, if your car broke down, or any other thing in the world but the deal in front of you! So, your polite chit chat on the phone while they need your attention is disgustingly rude and disrespectful!

Your closer and your salesperson are required, by you, to stay focused *only* on the deal, and you owe them to do the best you can. Certainly you have necessary interruptions, but learn to say, "I'll call you back, I'm working a deal." It will be appreciated, and your level of respect will go up.

When you send the closer out with a pencil, you should have a general idea of what response you will get back, so you need a backup plan. When the closer comes back in, be ready to feed the figures into the computer, and pencil them again. A lot of desks just give a pencil more to get the closer out of the office than to have their offer make sense. This does not buy time for the desk, it wastes time for everyone, but unfortunately, this often happens.

You need to carefully look at both ends of the deal. Look at your *worst case* scenario. *Know* your absolute bottom line, and what the *least* you can live with is. This way, if the customer takes offense and just gets up and leaves, you can react quickly if necessary. You may even have to get out of your comfort zone, go introduce yourself to the customer, sit down with them, and close the sale yourself! A good manager must know the alternatives. Knowing your bottom line lets you react immediately to any offer that meets or exceeds it. You will not have the time to recalculate when the customer is heading for their car! Make a note on your deal folder of your least acceptable deal, and code it so only you can read it. This way, if you're working many deals at the same time, you can react instantly.

Remember that your salesperson and closer only will have just so much time in which to close this sale. Once they have gone through the efforts to present, demo and complete an offer, you now have the shortest allocation of time. Time is of the essence, so you need to hurry. Then, no matter what happens, even if the closer runs in with, "They want their keys," you can go out with him or her, and you can make a deal on the spot!

Trades can always be appraised before the write-up even hits the desk. You should have received the appraisal slip and the trade-in keys when the salesperson came in for the initial paperwork (credit app, write up, etc.). If your used car manager is sitting, chatting with his wholesaler buddies, get him off his ass and get this trade appraised ASAP! A good desk always has the answers before questions are asked. Used car managers generally wait 'til the last minute which is understandable, but you can hurry them up.

Most sales offices have a write up board. When the salesperson comes in with an offer, they enter the info onto the board. Unless you are involved in something else, you should be watching and entering the stock number of the vehicle being sold into the computer while they are still writing. This way you are ready to work the deal the minute the papers are given to you. The salesperson should now go sit with the customer and talk about the 3F's (Fishin', Fightin' and Foolishness) until the closer arrives.

I should mention here, that these frustrations with ineffective desk people are real. I was never that fast at desking, but I've worked for the best! I've worked for desk men that could easily work 10 to 20 deals *at a time*, and for a 12 to 14 hour shift! You have to learn efficiency and concentration! These types of managers are impressive and worth gold when you're busy — Kudos to Brian and Shawn; the best in the business!

One mega dealership I worked for never even bothered to physically appraise trade-ins. Occasionally, if they sensed a problem, they would drive a trade-in, but for the most part they maybe had the closer test the transmission, or maybe check for body damage, but mostly they just took their numbers directly off the appraisal slips filled out by the salespeople, and worked the entire deal from them. The sales office was even on the second floor, so they didn't even get to take a quick peek at a trade, other than a look from the windows down to the parking area. Occasionally, they would look out and ask some question, but no one would go out. We had a corporate used car manager who oftentimes wasn't even there on weekends. He was in charge of used cars sold by six of our area dealerships.

Any mistakes on trades wouldn't be caught until the next week when the used car manager would critique the performances for the multiple dealerships. Sure, we bought some bad transmissions and some other mechanical and body problems, but salespeople also forgot to add all of the equipment and accessories on their appraisal sheets, so the values actually went up on a lot of them. Then about Tuesday, those of us who were on the desk had to do the bullpen walk. That meant we met with the used car manager to defend our appraisals. When he found problems with our appraisal being too high, we could try to justify the dollar amount we put on a vehicle, and if we couldn't, our deal would get cut back (reduced in profit). This reduced gross profit would of course affect our income, and more directly, the commissions to the closer and salesperson. The key was to be aggressive, but not too aggressive! My store was smaller, so I actually drove most of my trades, but I really had great respect for the jobs the guys did who could work so many deals at a time. My excuse for not being as fast, was that I had to run outside every ten minutes or so for a cigarette!

A desk person must be cognizant of the time a deal takes, and the bearing each sale or non-sale has on morale, more so even than profit. A deal that you take excessive time on, to only increase your total profit by a small amount, is detrimental to morale and your factory satisfaction survey. Make your deals fast and efficiently. Too many trips back and forth by your closer, even if smoothly executed, translate to grinding. Don't give the impression that you want every last dollar from your customer. People grow resentful when you grind for small amounts!

I'll give you an example: Once I was grinding a law professor from a major university, and we went back and forth many times. I had a western theme in my dealership, and we were down to 99 cents a month in payments, and I also asked him to throw in two horseshoes for decoration on my showroom wall (he owned a horse ranch also). We made the deal, but I learned a valuable lesson. Three weeks later, he finally came in with my horseshoes. He had taken the time to cut one in half, and welded it to the other shoe to form a beautiful hat rack, which I immediately hung on my office wall. My lesson? As we shook hands, my customer said, "You notice though, you only got *one and a half* horseshoes!" He had to win! A lot of desk managers think it's cute to keep on grinding for every nickel they can get, but I was embarrassed into changing! I was fortunate to learn such a valuable lesson from a nice man! Both sides must be winners.

If you are desking multiple deals and you have two or more closers awaiting their next pencils, this will create impatience among your managers. Have things you can ask for, to get them doing something, and take the pressure off. If you don't, you will appear inadequate, and *you* will get flustered. You can't afford to lose your cool, so send them out with pencils for more info on the app, to ask various questions, anything to give the appearance of moving smoothly. You may be waiting for call backs on the two appraisals and approval from a bank, but just keep going with what you have! Sometimes you just have to go ahead and take a deal where the closer is spending too much time getting a counter. I always told my closers *not* to grind too long, "Get what you can, and come back in!" When you're busy, and the only thing holding you up is the trade appraisal, and you feel you're on board; "ROLL 'EM!"

Here's another thing you can do that helps all the way around. Occasionally, walk out and shake a hand to close a deal. A desk manager is the dealer's representative, and when you've desked the deal that took two hours, *you* at the very least should be out there thanking the buyers for their business! Get in the habit on all sales, even the used cars where the only survey you get is if they ever buy from you again!

I can look back to the times I had to desk myself as a closer, where people have asked if there really was anyone in the sales office. Thinking fast, I'd have to say, "Oh, the boss had to run off real quick, but he asked me to thank you for your business!"

Customers always are suspicious of what we put them through, so once we've earned their business, there is nothing wrong with taking them into the sales office to meet the manager inside where it all happened! Get permission first, but I've always done that! People don't stay long, but they feel very privileged to be allowed in to that special place that few people ever get to visit. Then, as a desk manager, get off your butt, smile and thank them. It really is important that you do this, and a dealer should be going around the store doing the same thing. A lot of desk guys remain seated when a customer chances to sneak a quick peek in the office. *Get up* and act professional!

Many dealers even have their sales offices on the showroom. Maybe glassed in, but visible and accessible. I've worked in many stores with these sales towers, and there is nothing at all unpleasant about it. After all, we have enough cues and clues in this business that we know what to do so the customer won't be able to read what we're doing anyway! So there is nothing we have to hide!

37 CLOSERS: CAN YOU WRITE UPSIDE DOWN?

Thison is something I just decided to do to dare to be different from every other closer! Sound crazy? It works wonders, and is just a way to have some extra fun at this closing job! I've done this for over forty years. I was first taught this by Mutual of Omaha. Part of our presentation was to write numbers on a chart that faced the customer. We wrote-in the numbers, as we made the pitch, and to make it a smooth presentation, it was necessary to write our numbers so they would be readable to our prospect without the interruption of turning the sheet around. I adapted this to the car business, and it is absolutely mesmerizing to a lot of people. This one is over and above, but I just enjoy doing things that others don't do.

Before you dismiss this idea as not being worth the effort, consider this; do you want to be like every other closer? Are you planning to succeed and be the best you can be? Are you interested in being great, or is mediocrity okay with you?

My answer is that your bag of tricks *must* contain every possible method that you can find! Learn from everyone you meet. There likely aren't any new ideas, but a lot of the old ideas that work well have been dropped due to a genuine lack of professionalism in today's marketplace.

When I began in the selling game, I wanted to learn every possible way to be successful. I did not want to be good; I wanted to be great!

To my way of thinking, if you are going to do the job, then why not learn everything possible. After all, when you work on commission, everything you learn will make you more money!

I found that car buyers are absolutely fascinated and entertained when you give them a break from the same old monotonous and worn-out presentation. When I'm presenting numbers, the offer sheet is always flat on the desk or table, and facing the customer.

This is another reason that the salesperson *must* have your buyers sitting side-by-side to properly view the papers at the same time without showing one, and then turning to the other person to repeat the process. If, when a closer first meets the customers, if the seating is not conducive to a proper presentation, then change them around, right then and there! Ask them to move and explain why. Then after the deal is done, reeducate your salesperson to do it right the next time.

As I present the figures, the buyers can examine each facet; price, trade allowance, payoff on trade, suggested cash down, monthly payments and number of months. As we discuss the offer, I naturally move quickly to cash down and monthly payment. I do not of course, spend time dwelling on the rest. I will often just point to the numbers such as:

- "For ours" (point to selling price).
- "For yours" (point to trade allowance).
- "With X$ cash down, your payment is X$$. Will that work okay for you?"

Quick, nonchalant and I ask as though I expect a yes. Now, when they object, I can address and elaborate on the points of concern to them.

Here's where your reverse writing will come in. Any changes the customer wants, I will write alongside the offer. I cross out what is there, and write what they really will accept in its place, only I do it so the numbers appear facing them. Sure, I've had a lot of customers interrupt at this point with comments like; "You wrote that upside down!" or "Where did you learn to do that?" I've had some try to turn the page around, not realizing what I had done, and then catch themselves and express shock that I had written it upside down! The interruption is inevitable; they will comment! Like everything else I do, it keeps the negotiations fun, fresh and friendly.

You may wonder why, when my whole method of closing is to stay the course, why I would open myself to interruption like this? It is the only deviation I allow myself, because I found it works to relax the buyers! They will ask how I am able to do that, and my answer has generally been, "Laziness, I don't have to turn the paper back and forth," and then I laugh. It breaks up the pressure they may have been feeling when I brought the big pencil, and hit them between the eyes with a proposal that we in the car business refer to as a ballistic pencil!

When the desk person knows they can have the confidence in their closer to not lose the customer with what many would consider to be an outrageous proposal, then they will begin asking for the moon! There is a greater skill level required to present these ballistic pencils, and I found it helpful as I began going over what they could do, rather than what we wanted them to do, it had a calming effect when I did my upside-down numbers.

If you are going to use this method, then practice! The best way is to take a sheet of paper, and neatly print the numbers 1 2 3 4 5 6 7 8 9 0 on the *bottom* of the page. Now turn it upside down, and practice writing these numbers as they appear, in their upside down form.
Fill the page, begin another, fill it, and do this until you can write neat, legible numbers.

Next, you can begin writing commas, dollar signs, and amounts such as $42,988.72, $739.46 MO., and any other combos you may need. I often wrote words upside down, and you can also try that if you're skillful. I was never all that good at words, but it didn't matter.

Since we are exploring ways to better do our jobs, if you should try this, don't worry about occasional flubs; they're bound to happen, but the customer won't mind one bit! If on occasion, you write $856 when you intended to write $658, you just say, "I thought I'd try!" They'll laugh, and you go on. I've even told an occasional customer, "It's because you're upside-down in your car!"

This is just another way that I found to keep the negotiating from getting stale!

38 WHAT IS THE REAL REASON?

Whether you are presenting an offer (pencil) as a salesperson or a closer, be careful not to overreact! A common error made by closers when they are handling objections, is they may hear, but they *don't listen!*

Normally, in a line-close system, the closer will be the person who takes the dealership's first offer to the customer. The desk will naturally make the offer that will be the highest profit maker to the house. In the stores where I worked, if the customer said yes to the first pencil, we couldn't possibly keep all of the enormous profit that was built in! Don't expect the buyer to roll over. They will object. The problem closers have, especially when they're new, is they fail *to listen!*

If your customer objects to the trade allowance, *do not* begin to even try to justify what you're offering him for his vehicle, until you understand fully what he's after! If a customer's car has a wholesale value of $8,000.00, and we offer him $4,000.00 for it, does he really care all that much? Maybe not. If I told the buyer I would give him $8,000.00 for his car, and the payment would be $600.00 and he objected, was he objecting to the trade allowance or the payment? You say both? Why?

Let's say this same customer wants $8,000.00 for his trade and a payment of $450.00 per month. What do you think he'd say if I came back and told him I'd get the payment down to $450.00 per month, but I could only allow $3,000.00 for his trade? Maybe if I had some reason that might sound logical, that's all it may take.

The point I'm making here is that all too often, a closer reacts too quickly to the trade allowance objection, when maybe it all comes down to the payment, or down payment! This is a major reason why sales are lost. I'll explain that statement: When we hit the customer with figures, as I said, we are asking for the highest and best for the dealership. When the customer objects, we don't slow down enough, and we often start writing the *customer's counter offer* without finding out the true objection!

Once a customer starts countering our offer with figures of his own, we will be faced with a new problem to overcome; we must now begin taking away what the buyer wants. If we take it slower before we just begin writing, we can save many more deals that would be lost by reacting too quickly.

Slow down! You must ascertain the real objections. Discuss each point. I always would just ask the customer in an offhand manner such as; "Folks, let me ask you this, since trade-ins are always a tough way to go because of the 'up and down' market, is the trade allowance really the main concern, or is it the monthly payment?" I will continue, *maybe before* they even answer with, "The reason I ask you this is because sometimes I can get the management to make other concessions that will get the payment down, even if they can't do better on the trade." This type of question is not only a deal saver, it is a profit maker. Now you allow the customer to answer, and the dialogue that follows may really open your eyes.

Don't ever react and start writing yourself into a corner before you've heard the real objection. Sometimes it's not any more than the cash down! We always ask for more than we need anyway. I've seen customers object angrily to the trade allowance and payment, and when I really dig deeper, it was all a bluff to fight having to put any cash down. Quite often a customer feels he will lose face if he just admits he can't put the money down.

I know a lot of closers that take their salesperson aside and ask them all about the customer, and what the buyer wants to do before they meet them. This is a poor idea! As a closer, I *do not* want someone else's opinion about how they feel I should close the sale! If you do this, your closing days are numbered! Form your own opinions, and under no circumstances do you need anyone's advice except the desk!

To avoid these unnecessary bluffs by the customer, a closer needs to go "back and forth" over all the terms of the deal to ascertain what the truly important objections are. A closer's job is to *close*. In order to close a sale, you must know what's important to a customer, and what is just a smokescreen objection.

Seldom will you find a customer who is not willing to compromise on an issue if he can see a genuine benefit. People will take stupid amounts for their trade-in if it amounts to a low enough payment. Since the payment buyer is the car gods' gift to us, we make the most profit off of this customer! Be extremely careful in you analysis of your customer's objections. Don't spend your time shadowboxing the wrong objections, and always address the entire proposal when you recap.

39 MORE FOR TRADE! NO!

When your customer objects to what you're offering on a trade, don't be too quick to defend, or rush to justify the pencil. If you hurry to the defense, you may create a snake that wasn't there.

When the customer states, "That's not enough for my trade," try something simple, light, and not defensive, like; "It never is, is it?" Or; "I know, I never get what I want either, so can we go ahead?" You can use most any comeback, but you must not dismiss his concern, and you also must be ready to address it further. In the majority of negotiations, the customer feels they must make the run.

For this reason, you must be relaxed in your comeback to this trial. If your customer hits you with a counter, such as; "Go tell them I need another $1,000.00 (or whatever) and I'll do it." You need to *end* negotiations! You don't want to even imply that there may be any more room. If you start to try to negotiate one last try, by saying, "What if I could get another $500.00?" or anything, you are giving away money you shouldn't be! Just sit there calmly, and explain to the customer that *you know there's no more room*! "I was very surprised we got this deal. You really did well, congratulations!" Hold out your hand, and the majority of time you'll be amazed when you make a deal. Get used to drawing the line.

A buyer will continue to negotiate until he feels there is no more room. If you continue to discuss the what ifs, then your customer will continue to believe there is further room. You have to learn to close it down quickly. Oftentimes, you can set the stage up front by explaining that your dealership "doesn't do all that back and forth stuff, because my dealer just tries to give the best deal right up front. He knows that our customers don't like it, so we really have our best deal in front of us." Run the bluff, and if your customer hasn't bought in (which most won't), then make it seem unusual; but "I'll sure make an offer on your behalf."

Whether you're a salesperson working straight-sell or a closer, you need to rehearse a proper dialogue, so if you tell the customer he has the best deal, then you need to express sincere doubt that there is more room to go. I will normally sit down, and review the figures, and then express doubt that there is any more room for a better deal. Then, in my most sincere mode, I will ask; "If I could, and please understand I think we're 'all-in,' but if I could get you another $100.00, would it work?" Yes, it takes a lot of guts, but that's your job! The customer is thinking hundreds or thousands, and I offer him a hundred dollars, and express doubt I could even do that? Here's where you have to act as innocent as you can, because you will get a definite response, and the type will vary from mild disbelief to loud ultimatums. Just agree to try your best to help, while continuing to express doubt that you can get it done. Realize that your customer is acting upset, just as they feel you are acting sincere. You both know that you are all acting, so keep it light and easy. Negotiations can be fun if neither of you allow it to get too serious! It's your job to maintain a light-hearted and fun experience. If a customer gets upset and accuses you of trying to con them, you can always just say, "I thought I'd try," and laugh!

Do not think that your buyer is so knowledgeable that he will recognize the best deal. The only way he will stop negotiating and buy, is when you have *convinced* him that you're all through trying *one last time*. Convincing the customer sooner in the process while there is profit remaining, that he has reached the bottom line, is the secret to earning a good living. Running back and forth with offers and counter-offers for hours is not the key to success! The idea is *not* to hurry between customers and the sales office like an abused track star, it is to sell the offer you're making! The sooner you can relay the feeling that, "This is as good as it gets," the sooner you can count higher commissions! You are not running messages from headquarters to the front! I know I'm overworking this point, but the customer only knows the negotiations are over and it's time to make a decision when *you* stop running back and forth!

40 TELEPHONE PROCEDURES

I could actually write many chapters on proper telephone techniques, but this section is a guide to the basics. Entire books have been written by dozens of phone sales trainers, and I will not do more here than cover the common sense of phone work.

I have been to BDC (Business Development Center) training in Texas, where my general manager and I spent six intensive days in study and role play, and came back and set up our own phone center in a newly built, large room in our dealership. Millions of dollars have been spent, and more millions are being invested each year in setting up "state of the art" telephone centers in dealerships. I've been in some that had over sixty phone stations in huge offices with a computer and phone at each station. These phone rooms are like a business within a business, where all sales calls come in and go out of this business development center, and there are managers and monitors on duty at all hours the dealership is open! Sales people rotate through these phone rooms on every shift.

After all these years of running loose, the modern car dealer has finally realized how much money his ineffectual telephone skills have cost him, and how much more money he can earn by getting up to date.

The training program alone, costs thousands of dollars, plus major re-models, at least fifty thousand, and on up to several hundred thousand dollars in many cases! Add to this, the cost of ten to sixty phones, a central telephone system, and computers for each station. Now, add the staffing expense by more managers, tons of support materials, throw in some visits from the BDC Company for training and follow-up visits for your success, plus from $125,000 to $225,000 for a franchise fee, and you are talking beaucoup bucks! Some of these setups can see price tags eclipsing a half million dollars. The positive side is that it doesn't take long to earn it all back. Just by the sales increase that is achieved by proper handling and follow-up of something so simple as a phone inquiry! See why I'm not going to go into detail on the procedures necessary to accomplish telephone expertise? Sure, I could do it, but I'd want ten thousand dollars per book to cause me that much brain drain!

I hope you can see how important the phone will be to your success! Your dealer will supply you with scripts and training as to how he wants you to learn. Most auto manufacturers have training on phone procedures, and all dealers have outside sources where they purchase phone training programs.

I suggest that you invest your time in learning, and practicing every bit of phone skills training you can lay your hands on! This free training is going to be worth thousands and thousands of dollars to you. I can guarantee it! It always amazes me as to how much money the average dealer invests in training materials that his sales staff seldom takes full advantage of. I guess *free* doesn't equate to value in most peoples' minds, but these training materials can make you a small fortune, and you end up with a master's degree at the U of You! Invest in yourself! As I said in the beginning, I'll just cover the basics. Let's do that now!

Dealers do not advertise to sell products! What? That's correct! They advertise to get the phone to ring. Period! Now when it rings, they expect their sales staff to find a way to bring the caller in to the store, so they can sell them a car! The dealer runs the ads, and it's your job to properly handle the phone, to bring the fish into the boat! It's an analogy that comes to mind. The ringing phone is like a bobber going down. Your conversation is like setting the hook, and bringing them in is like reeling in the line. Then once they're at your boat (dealership), it's up to your selling skills as to whether or not they end up landed, or they break the line and swim away! The ad is the bait, and your skills need to do everything else.

Your job in taking an incoming phone call is *not* to sell something over the phone. Your duty is to arouse enough interest in what you have to offer to convince the caller to come in to take a look! So, you will be taught how to answer questions without giving specific information, and to create desire without anything but painting a mental picture to build excitement in the caller in order for him to come on down! So for example, your ad describes the year, make, model, and price but no other information. The caller asks how many miles it has because the price seems fantastic! The secret you will learn is how to entice this customer into coming in, but without telling him the vehicle has 150,000 miles on it; and all *without* lying!

There are so many ways to avoid giving information, and still bringing your buyer in and ending up with a sale, a good commission, and a happy customer that I won't even begin, because on this one scenario, I could write fifteen pages of text on the options you could choose from!

The phone is going to play a major role in your success as a salesperson, and if you learn it well, you will definitely be in that top 20%! The sooner you learn phone skills, the sooner your income starts to soar! I guarantee it! This stuff is dynamite!

41 INCOMING CALLS — IS IT OKAY TO LIE?

L ying is always bad, but I guarantee you that all car people do it! All of the professional telephone trainers, and every expert I ever saw has taught salespeople to lie! So why do we teach our people to lie their asses off, and then to profess the utmost honesty when they actually come in? Because it's necessary! If you are completely honest with the caller, you likely will never get a chance to show them later on how honest you really are, because they will *never* show up!

Now, let's analyze what you're dealing with! First of all, the majority of callers that phone regarding a specific advertised vehicle, are feeling that your advertised price is too good to be true. They don't want to waste their time coming in, and *definitely* don't want to just come in to look through your inventory. They may just be cautious, or in reality, scared to death of the car buying process! We have discussed this type of buyer, and this person is the most likely to deal with the internet department if they are interested in a brand new vehicle, where they may be able to deal anonymously via emails, and not have to verbally discuss anything. This way everything is in writing, and they can slowly and carefully list questions, and read answers.

Now however, Timid Tommy calls in on the ad vehicle and you get the call. He asks you miles, condition, and all sorts of other questions about this vehicle. You go out on the lot, write down the answers, and call him back. "Hi Timid Tommy, this is Naïve Nick;

that car has 182,000 miles, a large scratch down the passenger side, two torn seats, and a torn headliner," Click. See now why you can't be totally honest? The customer's suspicions were right! It was too good to be true. Remember when we discussed the reason we advertise vehicles? To get the phone to ring, right? Do you also remember my saying; it's your job to get them in! If you tell the truth, Timid Tommy and his wife Negative Nellie will never come in to give you a chance to find a really nice car for them.

Now let's say that Dazzlin' Danny gets that call instead of you. You're listening to his conversation, but why hasn't he gone outside immediately? He's chatting, let's go closer ———— "Yes Tommy, from what I remember, that's a very nice car, but I don't see it right now, I think it's on a test drive. What's your schedule? Can you come down right now? Oh sure, I'd be happy to get that information for you. Oh wait, here comes my used car manager; let me ask him, so hold on." What's Dan doing now; he just has his hand over the phone, but he didn't put it on hold? Now he's just sitting there, and there is no used car manager in sight. Dan is just holding the phone in his hands? Okay, he's back on, let's listen; "Tommy, good news! The car is still available; I guess the lady can't buy it without her husband, so they'll come back after work. How soon can you get here? Miles; oh I forgot to even ask I was so excited, but he did say it was a real nice car. My manager also mentioned that he just took in a couple more very similar, so it looks like you'll have a great selection if you can get here quick! Can you come right down?"

So what do you think? Does that conversation create more excitement than calling Timid Tommy back with all the negative points about the car? Since the used car manager advertises the vehicles he owns for the least amount of money, what do you think the odds are that you'll ever be able to find a cream puff advertised at a low enough price to get the phone to ring? Notice that Danny gave himself an out; when Tommy shows up, and instead of a nice car, the ad vehicle is a terrible turd, Danny can honestly say, "I never saw the car, darn, the used car manager sure wasn't right about this one. He must have been thinking of a different car! Let's go see what we have that's similar, but a *whole lot nicer*!" He got 'em in, and how he's working with an absolute buyer! Most customers who are drawn in because of one of these ad specials, do not end up buying them. Once their salesperson establishes a relationship, he helps them find a car they like, and a sale is made. It is unfortunate that these scenarios must be played out like this, but once they come in you can charm their socks off! First you must get them in!

To handle the phone call any other way is jeopardizing your career. If per chance, the customer does not ask you the specifics, and you just do a great job of making them like you enough to come in because you say "it's a really nice car," what happens now? They come in, meet you, and you now take them out to see this car you described as really nice, and they now will deduce that you either lied purposely or that you don't know a damned thing about cars! Either way, you lose! Now you've wasted a lot of your time and effort, and burned a customer that someone else may have sold; Dazzlin' Danny for instance! You are always better off to tell someone that you *asked*.

Now let's look at what you need to do. When the phone call comes in, your goals are to end up with their names, phone numbers, and an appointment.

When you answer, answer with your name and a smile. If you aren't smiling, don't pick up the phone! I think that all phones should have mirrors sitting behind them to let salespeople see themselves as their customer is picturing them; yes, people can *hear a smile*, and they will form their opinion of you based on your smile, the tone of your voice, your enthusiasm, and of course, what you say.

There are many choices up front, as to how best to get the caller's phone number. I just like to start with, "My name is Gary Swanson, and yours?" She tells me "Vicky," and I say, "Glad to meet you Vicky, how may I help you?" She tells me, and I write it down. My next goal is to get her number before I give out the information. Today's caller ID systems can recover it for me, but I do it myself. I say, "Vicky, I'll be happy to get that information for you; it will take me a minute, so just in case I lose your call, give me your number so I can call you back." Now I write it down, and I'm ready to stretch out my conversation, and try to find out her needs and wants, and how she happened to call my store.

If she called on a specific vehicle, I can do the *ask my manager* move, referred to by many trainers as a pattern interrupt, or I can just keep discussing general information to secure an appointment. I also want to find out why she called on a particular vehicle, but if I am not careful, she will get tired of answering too many questions and turn off. I am mainly interested in why she called on this particular vehicle, but if I just come out and ask, "Why this car?" I risk painting the wrong picture. This customer may be calling on a very nice car, but she may also be calling ten more places on different makes and models.

By asking an open question, I can find out if she is possibly open to other choices. I say, "Vicky, I'm going to go out and get the information on the Camaro, and while I'm out on the lot, is there any other vehicle you'd like me to keep an eye out for?" She may come back with, "Oh yes, I would also be interested in a Mustang, a Charger or a Z car." At this point, I will just say, "Vicky, I have an idea. Why don't we just set a time when it's convenient for you, when we can get together and look at everything? I have so many to choose from, and that way you'll be able to actually compare them side-by-side! What's your schedule like?" I will not go into a whole lot of additional dialogue, because your dealer will give you intense training in this skill, and how they want you to learn their phone techniques.

I personally believe that a person needs to let their natural ability to carry on a conversation be their guide. You can learn an idea, as I am giving you, but it must be delivered in a way that is comfortable for you. Using a word track that doesn't fit your personality will come off as phony! Therefore, if you are given a track, memorize it and practice a lot!

Once, I was in a phone training program in Houston, and practicing answering phones in a business development center. The calls were monitored, and I was one of the few people attending that figured these were not actual customers calling in, as the dealer letting us experiment and train in his BDC wouldn't take a chance on trainees handling his actual calls. These were people hired by the training company to make the calls as though they were buyers. Therefore, I just took the general idea and played the game. I remember one call, where the caller wanted a one year-old Cadillac, and this person had the normal Texas drawl which I wish I could bottle and sell to salespeople. The man could tell I was a Yankee of course, and the conversation came around to where I was from, and I said, "You know Jim, I'm not all that familiar here yet, but is this Cadillac you want going to have to have a set of those longhorn steer horns on the hood?" We had a laugh, and I realized that I would have asked the same exact question had we been both doing our parts for real! It's my personality! You must use your own personality, and be professional, but never be afraid to have fun! Be yourself; feel the force.

42 THE INTERNET – LEARN IT, USE IT, AND PROSPER

Finally, the American car buyer got what they've wanted forever! A completely innocuous way of buying cars; or so they think!

In a few short years, the internet has gone from a source of information and inquiries to a negotiation tool for the consumer. At one time, television and newspapers attracted buyers to the products, and to who had them to sell. Then buyers were able to gather information online, and it then became necessary to call a dealer, speak to a salesman, and set a time to go in person to the dealership.

Now, a short while later, the consumer can sit down at his computer and send multiple emails to all dealers within his chosen search area. We've had separate internet departments for years now, but they have always met with mixed reaction by the sales forces.

There has always been a rather dramatic difference between the regular sales force and the internet salespeople. Early on, the type of salesperson who was attracted to internet sales was a seemingly more timid and less aggressive type of person. Your average sales force has always been a more outgoing, animated, showy and somewhat brash group of people, while those in the internet department have been more conservative in both mannerisms and dress, and their demeanor was more like a personal assistant in your local bank.

The image one has of the two styles can be pictured as the plaid jacket, white shoes, sunglasses wearing salesman, and the white-shirted, black slacks banker type.   One; outgoing, flashy and gregarious, with the loud and energetic mannerisms, and the other more quiet, reserved, soft-spoken, and clerkish in behavior. This comparison, although extreme, is likely why the type of person who prefers online shopping may be attracted to the latter.

The car buyer has always wished they could just get our bottom line without having to go through the process. People have always asked, "Why is it necessary to go through all of this negotiating? Why can't you just give me your best price up front, and let me decide on my own?" My answer to them has always been, "If I gave you my bottom line up front, I'd still not earn your business! You'd still feel compelled to shop around, to keep me honest; and when you finally realized that my price was fair, you'd be at another dealership, and instead of coming back to me to reward my honesty, you'd likely buy from wherever you were at. Besides, at that point, the other fellow only has to beat my deal by a small amount, and I'd lose anyway!" People always say, "Oh, I'd never do that," and my only answer to that is, "Why not?" I know they would, because giving out my best price up front, without any rapport, I cannot win!

You can see for yourself that the car buyer has the right idea, but there are so many variables that come into play that this is not possible. The type of person who absolutely hates the process, and gets physically upset when required to negotiate, is who this internet process appeals most to. There are a lot of car buyers to whom our negotiations are so distasteful that they are perfect candidates for the salesperson with patience and a non-emotional presentation.

A majority of the true internet buyers want to work out everything they can by email. They do not want you to even suggest a meeting until you have earned the right. They will send out many inquiries, and oftentimes they will give you all the specifics on the vehicle they want, and ask you for your bottom line price. Then, they wonder why no one wants to go first.

Establishing a relationship online is much more difficult than a face to face meeting on the lot. It's hard to build a relationship based on just the written word, but the secret to handling this type of inquiry is to build trust in the fact that you are willing to do everything the way the customer wants. You must create a trust in the fact that you have their best interests at heart, and the reason you are in the internet department in the first place is that you, also, do not like the car games that the regular retail salespeople must play. Your internet boss would fire anyone who was not completely truthful throughout the buying process! Your duty is to stress the simplicity of your department's selling procedures. Your internet buyer will understand why he or she can't have the real numbers until they come in to meet you. Establish a relationship, and let them know what to expect. They come in to see the vehicles, pick the one they like, and drive it. You explain how everything will proceed, and after they select the one they like, you will give them the best price without a problem.

Emphasize this difference in your department. Once this buyer has made a selection, you will immediately show them everything! The best price, trade allowance, payments, down payment, lease options, and all of their choices without the necessity for them to negotiate! Then they can just tell you "yes or no." You need to imply that you really like this process because no one has to run back and forth with offers and counter-offers. Just an honest bottom line deal that you're sure they will appreciate. The picture you need to paint is that, "My customers all tell me how they really enjoy this way of buying!" What you are painting a picture of is a very relaxed and uneventful process, whereby the buyer is not asked to buy anything. They select a vehicle, and we just tell them all the numbers, and if they want it, then they have to ask us. We won't even be concerned with trying to sell something, heaven forbid! "We are just here to be of service!" Sound good? You'd better practice it until it does!

Isn't this what we all want; both your customer and you? Of course it is! Now, once I have presented the numbers to the internet buyer, he turns out to be like everyone else! So he says, "I don't want to pay that much for yours, and the trade allowance isn't enough!" He now wants to negotiate! I can now say, "Terry, Deandra, remember when I said we don't really do all that negotiating in this department? Well, it's true. We try to make every sale like a fleet transaction. A fair price and a fair trade allowance. What is it that you think is wrong with these numbers?" I am now making the customer defend his statement, aren't I? I can't just come out and say, "What do I have to do to make it work?" If I do that, I've just turned everything I've said into a lie. I can respond firmly and with conviction, like; "Terry, I know that you're used to having to negotiate every time you buy a car, but that's why I told you at the beginning that we'd give you the bottom line up front. Deandra also said she didn't like the car games, but you don't seem happy now that we did it your way? I sometimes wish my boss would leave some negotiating room, because people seem to prefer being able to have some flexibility. Are we a long way from being able to earn your business?"

Your dialogue can and will take many turns, but you must reemphasize your method of selling, and how you did everything you promised to do. You helped them select a vehicle without pressure, you presented a complete proposal on a discounted price, trade allowance, and payment options, just like you promised. You also are expressing that you wish in cases such as his, that you could have the luxury of your dealership leaving some negotiating room, to make your customers feel better. Since so many people really aren't satisfied with a true bottom line, because they are so used to having to work hard to get there. "We try to give our customers what everyone always says they want, but then sometimes it backfires on us, as you're telling me now, because it's not what you want. Let me ask you this Terry, Deandra, if I had come out $1,000.00 higher, and made you beat me down the thousand, could I maybe have had a better chance of earning your business?"

Anything we do from here on is acting. How you do it will be up to you. All we're doing here is going back over our commitment to give the customer our best numbers. We are establishing the fact that he is the one who wants to negotiate, and "Even though it is against our policy, and I don't think there's anything I can do, I really want to earn your business, so what could I change in order for you to take the car home with you?"

Where are we going now? Right to the same place we'd be with any buyer that just drove in off the street! Difference being, is this is the same customer that hates the process, but somehow it has all changed now, because we are doing this *for the customer*, not because we like to. Naturally our bottom line figures are about the same as they would be with any first pencil. The main difference is that in a regular retail first pencil, we would not discount the list price. With the internet buyer, we must give a discounted selling price, or they'll come unglued. We may even have had to discount the list price before they'd even agree to come in. This is especially true when they are shopping for a specific model, and comparing prices before they will even come to the dealership. Always go out with a discounted list price for the internet buyer. The trade allowance will likely be lowered by a similar amount, so the so-called internet deal will still be at full profit, unless there is no trade-in. Then, the discounted price may not be quite as low. You see the advantage is still ours, because in all regular deals, since we always try to steal the trade, the normal number is always so low anyway!

The biggest difference is the perception the buyer feels between the internet experience and the way he has always experienced the car dealing to be. You are not really doing it much differently than when you meet a *drive in* at the door of his car. With the internet customer, your relationship begins with non-verbal communication. Trust is built through the written word, but your relationship is cemented upon actually having phone and in-person dialogue.

Once you begin negotiating after your professed initial reluctance, you continually need to express amazement that the dealership is even finding a way to improve upon their bottom line. There *must* be a genuine reason. This can be further speculation on the trade-in value, or a new bid that the used car manager was able to get from a different buyer, or some other logical and believable explanation. The reason must make sense, because if you arbitrarily just make them a better deal, then the customer will think that you were trying to cheat them with your first offer. You can never improve on your bottom line price without proper justification. The trust level *must* be maintained!

Develop your internet skills. Surveys of internet shoppers show that a high percentage of their email inquiries receive no dealer response. Find out how these inquiries are distributed. You need to establish a relationship with whoever in your dealership is in charge of this department. Let them know that you can be depended on to follow up on all leads that you are given. In our business, just like a momma bird, we always feed the open beaks!

An internet manager is rated and paid on success. If you produce sales, and are an important part of your department, you can count on being fed choice leads. Make your manager look good, and you will never have to worry about having enough customers.

Internet buyers can be the easiest kind once you establish trust. Be very serious, and keep your email relationship on the most professional level; then once they show up, you can turn on the personality.

43 PROPER APPOINTMENT PROCEDURE!

D on't let anyone steal your customer! Here's a scenario for you; you've made an appointment with a customer who called in on an advertised vehicle. The time of your appointment comes and goes, and still no customer. Meanwhile, you haven't taken any ups in order to politely await your customer. Now you're walking by the delivery area, and there you see the car you were hoping to sell! Even though you are not allowed to, you can't resist, and you approach the new owners with; "Hi folks, you wouldn't be the Andersen's would you?" They answer, "Yes, you're Jerry, right? They said you were on a test drive when we came in." It happens all the time! If you want to work with saints, join a seminary. The car business can be cruel to the naïve and uninitiated! Hopefully this book will keep you from ever having one of these moments! Some sharp associate of yours just stole your customer and your money, but without penalty!

Whenever you are expecting a customer, you need to set the proper safeguards to work. First, you need to know exactly when your customer is coming in. If you are talking with a customer calling on a vehicle, do you think they care who they work with? Do you think people care to work with you because you gave them the information they asked for? If you've spent a half hour on the phone with a person, do you believe you have developed enough rapport to have them ask for you? Well forgedaboudit! Buyers are liars, and their only loyalty is to themselves! The only person who is watching out for you is you!

Here's how to *properly* set an appointment; learn it well! As I said before, first you must know exactly when your customer plans to arrive. In these days of cell phones, it is easy. If you are developing a good relationship over the phone and you say, ask for me, and the customer promises, do you think he will? Wrong! You are in the process of learning some very important lessons without them costing you any money! This is part of your training that most new salespeople find out the hard way! You will also, because you are going to get burned at some point. This material is so I can jump into your subconscious mind later on and yell; "I TOLD YOU!"

Do it my way: Let's say my customer is making plans to come in to look at a vehicle he inquired about. He say's I'll be in to see you at 5:00. His name is Dave. I will now set the proper appointment. Option 1) "Dave, I want you to write something down. Get a pen and something to write on," or option 2) "Dave, do you have a pen handy? I'll wait." Either option 1 or option 2 work for me. You will hear him rustling around and soon; "Okay, go ahead." I'll say, "Write my name down; Gary Swanson (and spell it for him). My cell phone is xxx xxx xxxx." He says, "Okay, got it." Next I say, "Okay Dave, read that back to me." He will. Next I smile, so he can hear it over the phone, and say, "Now who you gonna' ask for when you come in?" The customer will repeat my name again! Now, even if he forgets the paper, he will likely remember me won't he? This may seem strange, unfriendly, and demanding to the new person, but trust me, I know! When you take command of your customer like this over the phone, how easy will it be to also do so in person. The cautious person calls ahead. You take control before you even meet, and they'll give you control and their trust when you meet. Now, if anything should change in their plans, they'll call you because they have your cell right? Don't count on it!

Get Dave's cell number, and always ask if there is anyone else will be part of the buying decision. If he says yes, you ask who. He says my wife, Phyl; I ask if she has a separate cell, and I get that number also, just in case. Now if he's late, and if he's driving, I call her number and say, "Hi Phyl," and I now make her my friend. Since we haven't spoken, she may have changed his plans, or maybe he forgot to even tell her he made the appointment! I not only ask for these numbers up front, I also ask; "Now Dave, if I can't reach you at either of these, is there any other number?"

If the appointment we set is not within the next hour or so, I make plans with the customer to touch base again just before they leave to come to see me. No, you're not through yet. Now just prior to the customer making the trip down, I want you to do a mental drive with him. You know where he's coming from, so discuss his route from where he's starting, past known landmarks, and ending with him arriving at your dealership. Instruct him as to what entrance to use, where to park; and then to enter the dealership and now tell your customer where your receptionist is. Instruct him or her to go *directly* to the receptionist and *have her page you*! Why such an elaborate plan? Poachers! Your fellow salespeople. Yes, your customer will come in and when he tells the person who upped him who he wants to see, a poacher will say; "Oh, he just drove out about a minute ago. How may I help you?" Prevent this crap from happening at all by telling your customer a little story that maintains the integrity and honesty of the store, "The reason I want you to go in to have me paged is that everyone thought I would be off today, so no one probably knows I'm even here, but I'll be listening for the page." Now find out what they're driving, and you've covered all of your bases.

You can always go a step further in case you're customer is naïve enough that someone may have convinced them that "you had an emergency phone call and left." The other thing you can do if your customer is coming in on a specific vehicle, is to tell your customer, "I'll have the keys with me," *and do it*. This practice will be frowned upon, but like I always say, if my income is at stake; "I'd rather beg forgiveness than ask for permission." This tip is not meant to scare you away, but you need to know what can happen in some stores. You need to be extremely careful with your income. If you can be skated out of a sale easily, then you will be skated often!

Remember that these are the dealer's customers, not yours. If you want them, then do things right. It will not matter all that much to the dealer which salesperson sells the car. He still gets the sale.

Naturally, I always ask the customer to call my cellphone just as they are about to arrive at the dealership (if they are not behind the wheel), so I can be out there to greet them. This will also prevent some clown from greeting them with some off the wall comment like, "Hi folks, are you here for the big sale?" If at all possible, be outside when they arrive; when you see their vehicle, you can guide them to a parking spot. Just tell your associates they're your appointment!

44 GRATUITIES TO PAY

Certainly you see the advantage of paying for referrals (birddogs), but are there times when it is appropriate to acknowledge others? To answer this, I have a friend who for years was a top producer every month. After I came on board at the same dealership, and a new company had purchased the dealership, and changed the rules, he confided the following to me: Every stick of furniture in the switchboard operator's home had been paid for by this man when he was selling *on the line*.

No one had ever figured out why he always got so many phone calls. They just thought he had a tremendous following. Eventually, he did have, but he was being fed heavily from the receptionist. It may have all started innocently enough, with a thank you gift that he gave her for a call he picked up that made him a nice profit.

Standard procedure for incoming sales calls is for the operator to page for an available salesperson. In cases where the dealer utilizes a business development center (phone room), the calls may be taken by a central operator, and spread around evenly, or first come, first served. In the case of my friend, he eventually worked it around where he was paying the receptionist by gifts that she was preselecting in her favorite furniture store. She purposely funneled the best sounding calls to him. This practice is, of course, dishonest and I use this only as a bad example.

However a dealership is structured, keep in mind that a small gift such as lunch, a gift certificate, or other thank yous are certainly welcome surprises from someone in the store who goes out of their way to help you. Even a coffee or soda is a nice thanks. Certainly, if one develops a good working relationship *where it doesn't get out of hand* (like bribing a receptionist to send calls direct to your cell phone rather than paging for an available salesperson) is acceptable.

Just as you tip your mail carrier, newspaper carrier, waiters, or doorman, if it fits, do it. If a technician in your service department sends you a customer, even if they don't end up buying, a tip of some sort is called for. If they do buy, pay promptly, and pay in cash! These in-house sources are your very best bird dogs. Your own mechanics likely have already made a friend in the store that they refer their friends to, but things change, and maybe you need to meet your technicians and openly discuss your referral (bird dog) program. Ask for business!

The service writers in your dealership are the people that directly deal with the customers that come in for maintenance and repairs. How valuable is the service writer you have a working relationship with? Let's say they just diagnosed the slipping transmission as terminal, and the customer is facing a $4,000.00 repair. Rather than throw that much cash at it, the person says, "I'll just trade it in, because I can use the money for a down payment, and you guys can repair it afterward!" Now, the service writer calls you to come back and meet the customer. Think about it! Your customer has trust in his service advisor, who refers him to you, so you have instant trust yourself! This service writer may have just made your day! You'd better make his, after the sale!

Bird dog payments to in-house sources had sure better be a lot higher than to your other referral sources! Word will soon spread that you know how to be grateful!

The repeat customers we get are invaluable to us, and we get them back largely because of our own follow-up skills. The plus business we get from others around us are what most salespeople fail to develop. A box of doughnuts dropped off in the business office at your dealership is nice to do. You can always check in with your service manager, and see when they have shop meetings, or employee night (where they allow the technicians to work on their personal vehicles); and drop off a couple of pizzas and leave a few business cards. Don't stay, just drop off the goodies, and just tell everyone present that you're new, and appreciate any business they send your way, and that you pay great cash referrals!

45 DO I HAVE TO TELL THE TRUTH?

When there is distrust and tension, how do you relieve it? Sometimes you can bring out your childhood bible, and talk for hours about your honesty. You can, as they say, "Talk 'til you're blue in the face," but you will not convince the customer that you are honest. They don't trust you when they come in, and they will likely not trust you later on after they buy from you.

So how much does it really matter? I don't think it really makes all that big a difference, that we should be so concerned that we make a big deal out of it! We know that actions speak louder than words, so rather than be defensive and apologetic for how we know we are perceived, let's roll with it! Have fun! Whenever I sensed that people didn't trust me, or were leery of what I was going to be like (which with a closer it's immediate when you are introduced) I'd break the tension right away! As soon as I could, I'd seize the opportunity to answer one of their questions with; "Do I have to tell the truth?" and they always answer "Yes!" To which I say, "Oh darn." All I am doing is saying aloud what the customer is thinking!

If you don't think your customer feels this way, get a life! Go to the nearest computer and Google yourself silly looking at the most hated and distrusted occupations! When things get tense, like when I'm getting up to take their latest offer to the sales office, I like to place my hand gently on the customer's shoulder, and say, "Trust me, I'm a car salesman!" Sometimes they absolutely roar with laughter! A lot of times I'll just maybe lean my chin on my hand with my elbows on the table, and look slightly up and say, "Would I lie?" They'll quickly respond with, "Yes! You would!" I then just respond with, "Just thought I'd check, in case I was getting too honest! I don't want to ruin my reputation!"

Sometimes it's the simplest thing that makes a major impact on our future. Once, while watching Johnny Carson back in the early 80's his guest that night was George Burns. Johnny asked George the following: He said; George, you've been in show business all your life; you began your career in vaudeville at age three, you've starred on radio and TV, you've had an amazing career, and now you've made the *Oh God* movies. If you could name *just one thing* that was the secret to your phenomenal success, what would that be?

I watched this famous comedian lean back in his chair, his eyes rolling upward, he took a couple of puffs on his cigar, and leaned forward and looked directly into the camera and said; "Honesty!" Then, he took a long pause, and with excitement, proclaimed; "If you can fake that, you've got it made!" I roared with the audience while I experienced a major epiphany! I had discovered the key!

This was a game changer for me. I began to hone my skills in a different manner. Contrary, I'm sure to what you're thinking; I did not begin faking honesty. In fact I created a totally opposite approach. My career makeover began the very next day. I realized that it would be absolutely impossible for one person or thousands of car people to change the public's perception of us, so I made the decision to just roll with the image we already have!

My very next customer became the guinea pig for the new me! At a tense moment in the negotiations, I put my hand on the customer's shoulder and quietly said, "Trust me, I'm a car salesman!" The customer cracked up, laughed like crazy, and shook my hand! From that moment on I used this approach continually. I found that by openly acknowledging that I knew what the customer's perception of us was seemed to turn over all the cards on the table and everyone relaxed. People seemed to make the assumption that since we all knew that I was the bad guy they didn't have to worry about being cheated. Therefore, just good, honest negotiating could take place.

Think about it; would a man who makes fun of the public's impression of his business turn around and try to con you? Don't you think the entire transaction would be to the customer's benefit? "Trust me, I'll treat you fair!"

It is surprising to see how some little, off the wall comment like this will relax people. It seems that when people realize that you're not trying to be phony, and act to be something you're not, then they have nothing to fear! It's kind of like a trust that is created by mutual need. They need a car, and you need a sale, so you work together as a team. Often it ends up as you and your closer, and the customer on one side, and the friendly adversary in the sales office. It's almost like the cougar and the squirrel floating through a flood on the same log; a temporary truce for mutual good.

Like I said, don't apologize for what you do for a living! You are providing a more important service to people than most anyone else in the world ever could! You are feeding their egos! You are making them happy, and making them proud of themselves! You are important in their lives because you are instrumental in their very success in life.

Every time they leave their neighborhood, they are noticed in their new car! Why do you think that when someone buys a new car, he suddenly doesn't have enough room in his garage? The new car is forced to sit outside for a long time, isn't it? When his admiring neighbors stop by, he quickly explains how he thought he'd better use this opportunity to make more room in his garage! He will do this rearranging until he's sure that every neighbor knows he has a new car! You did that for him!

Also, this is the same man who always just barely makes it to work on time. Suddenly now; he's there from a half hour to an hour early, and most likely has the parking space closest to the door, and in full view of every person arriving for work. But, does he go right in? No, not at all! He finds things to do in his trunk! For the next half hour to 45 minutes, everyone who comes in will notice, and come over saying; "Hey Alan, got a new car huh?" He replies, "Yeah, just trying to get my trunk organized," and he waits for the myriad of questions, and elaborates on the features. Don't you wish you could just be his constant companion for a week? Think of all the selling he is doing!

How proud would this customer be if three of his neighbors and fellow workers ended up buying the same model (different colors of course)? Do you think he needs a supply of your business cards? Also, don't you think a call asking "Who can you tell me wants to buy a new car," will work? Help him feed his ego by helping his friends get a new car also!

Does this all mean that he trusts you now? Don't count on it. You don't need the trust, as long as he likes and respects you! I don't mind people saying, "In God we trust, in Gary we have confidence."

46 A FURTHER NOTE ON SELLING USED CARS

Don't be overly concerned over the condition of some of your used cars. I know that once you begin work, you will sometimes be critical of the selection of used cars you have to choose from. Do not pre-judge what you think people will think and feel when they look at your pre-owned inventory.

The fact that you are around new cars all day, will certainly prejudice your feeling when you begin showing someone a vehicle on your used car lot. It is human nature for a salesperson to have concerns about the condition of the inventory. Naturally, it's easy to sell a flawless, brand new vehicle. There really are no negatives to apologize for, and you have learned about every feature and know the answers to every question.

Now, here you are looking at a brand that's unfamiliar to you, you don't know the exact operation of all of the features. Your presentation won't be as smooth, and both you and your customer will explore the vehicle together. You worry that without being able to run through a smooth presentation, showing all of the benefits of owning this car, that the customer will have more time to discover the dings, dents, tears, scratches, stains and other flaws! Don't be too concerned. Your customer won't be. You'll soon see that the glaring deficiencies that you see will not matter to the used car buyer. They will not normally ask for repairs to be made, but rather, they will use these items as negotiating tools. Good!

They expect wear and tear. Used vehicle buyers are not concerned about flaws; they would be suspicious if there weren't any. This person may never have had a new car, so the things they look for are miles, condition of tires, and how it feels on the road. Engine, transmission, handling and comfort are the keys. Many of your customers will tell you they buy used cars because the major part of the depreciation has already been paid by the original owner, or successive owners, depending on its' history. The guy that's delivering newspapers and putting on many miles every month would likely not even consider buying a new car. In a year it would look five years old anyway. It is strictly a tool, and there won't be an emotional trauma when it gets nicks, dings and scratches. To your customer, this is a new car, so don't be even concerned.

Also, when negotiating with the average used car buyer, don't apologize for the flaws. You don't want to give them the impression that what they point out is a major problem. They are pointing out an item, and acting like it is a real concern, but trust me, it isn't. The buyer is merely negotiating to get the price down! Someone says to me, "Look at that huge dent!" My reaction would likely be, "C'mon John, it isn't that bad! (With a smile of course.) Now you've got your first dent. You'll probably never get another one!" That, as I say, would likely be my immediate response, and then I'd follow up with, "But seriously, the used car manager most likely didn't fix it on purpose. A lot of times he will leave small cosmetic items like that in order to keep costs down. The majority of our buyers are more concerned with the mechanics of the car, and they don't want to pay the extra cost of making it like new. That's probably why it's priced so low!" This kind of a response, in your own words of course, is the best way to handle the average used car buyer. All too often, a customer points out a flaw in order to prepare for price negotiating and the salesperson overreacts; like it really is major! This kind of a reaction can, as they say, make a mountain out of a molehill!

As I previously mentioned, they expect signs of use. The big difference between the new car and the used car buyers is that your new car buyer will not want damage on the vehicle, and is likely to insist on a different car, even though you offer to repair the damage. They'll actually tell you, "If I wanted to accept a car with dents, I'd be buying a used car!" They will also most often refuse your offer to repair damage because even though the body shop would guarantee the work to be flawless, they will still know it was damaged. They will oftentimes just switch to a second color choice rather than even let you trade another dealer for a different one! They still think you might repair it, and slip it on them!

The used car buyer will, in most cases, use the damage as a price negotiation tool. He realizes that he's likely to someday get a dent, hence my first reaction. The used car buyer may be as argumentative as the new car buyer when it comes to damage, but just remember the difference is that in almost every case, a cash discount will satisfy the used car buyer. We are not talking now about classic cars, or expensive sports cars, but rather the average family sedan, sport-ute, or pickup.

Regardless of the customer's initial reaction to damage, you must react calmly, and never act like it's a big deal! If your customer makes a big deal of something right off, do not join him in his fervor, remain calm, and ask, "What would you like me to do?" You can't minimize the impact of damage on a new vehicle, as you sometimes can on a used one. Your reaction, in either case, must show that it is not a major crisis in your mind.

So much of our business ends up in mind games. I've seen salespeople misunderstand a used car buyer's vocal and animated act when they find a flaw, and the salesperson joins right in and reacts just like the customer intends. He voices his shock at finding such damage on the vehicle to the sales manager in front of the buyer, not realizing they he played right into the customer's hands. At this point, the manager is on the spot, and must make some monetary concession right then and there. It's too late for calling his bluff, or letting the closer brush over it lightly. Now the manager must agree up front on the dollar amount of concession.

Later, when other negotiations take place with this buyer, this repair amount cannot be used as part of the normal offer — counter-offer and the dealership just had to needlessly sacrifice some profit! Salespeople need to avoid playing the customer's game and stay on track!

47 TO THE DEALER PRINCIPAL AND GENERAL MANAGER

Are you at the point in life where you spend your time entertaining your peers at the Country Club? How involved are you in the actual day to day operation of your dealership? Are you above reproach and beyond constructive criticism? Are you successful because of a winning franchise, or because of a great management team and a great job on your part?

Those of you who have no concerns may leave, and thank you for your time. The rest of you, please gather around, as I want to share a few things with you.

My suggestions will be from the standpoint of sales, as it is my forte´. My only major service and parts experience came after I bought my own dealership, and came to find out that my mechanics and parts manager had been rebuilding and selling engines for years. The bad part was that the parts came at no charge from my parts department; the mechanics were paid flat rate for doing the rebuilds. The engines were then sold at retail to their friends, and the profits were divided! The real rub was that everyone split the profits except the dealership! So there were several mechanics, a parts manager, and a general manager all splitting the proceeds, and my new store had been footing the bill!

Now to the front end; do you drop in the store unannounced at times? If you don't, why not? Are you afraid your people will think you don't trust them? Whose store is it? I guess what I'm saying is that if your name is on the franchise agreement, then you need to inspect what you expect. If you never stop in on weekends, why not drop in the back way sometime? Let yourself in the back door, and go up through service, and just observe. Listen to how they page. Friends have told me they have gone with a buddy down to their store in his car, and stopping out back, they have observed outrageous behavior all over the store. Football games, hose fights, and just loose behavior. They've heard pages over the P.A. system that were sloppy, and crude, and very lax discipline.

Walk into a sales office at a slow time of day when you're not expected and you find the desk man drinking a beer with his feet up, and the whole place a mess! Shit happens in all stores unless there is a danger of getting caught!

Are your procedures being followed to the letter? Why not? Dealers must have checks and balances, and consequences if they are not followed. Have your profits declined since you became less involved? Is it the times, or the lack of your time?

Just because you are successful, don't be an absentee owner. Let me ask you this: I will ask again, are you successful because of superior management skills, or because of a winning franchise? Is the dealer with the Chrysler-Dodge franchise making as much money as you are with your Toyota-Lexus franchise? If so, you'd better get a checkup from the neck up, because your operation may have some need of improvement!

In this day and age, we find some very brilliant dealers who have always been wonderfully successful, and their faces are well known by everyone in their city. They are like celebrities, and yet, when you buy a car from them, are they so important that they're too good to come by your table and shake your hand and say thank you! I'll bet they weren't so self-important when they started out! The dealer or acting general manager should spend time saying "Hi" to all of their customers whenever possible. I really believe that this is the most ignored aspect of the car business! A dealer that's successful forgets all too easy that people are more likely to stay loyal to you if they can tell their friends, "I know the owner!"

Do you walk through your parts and service departments to acknowledge all of your employees? When did you last drop in on your detail shop, or compliment your lot attendants on a nice looking inventory? Many dealers only seem to care, or show they care, when they're struggling. Then, when they finally make it big, they become royalty!

Do you ever monitor your used car operation? Are you buying a lot of used cars from a particular wholesaler? Is all the money being paid for them legitimate? Is the manager who is making your purchases, perhaps paying a little too much, with some of it possibly coming back to his bank account? Are you buying the right kind of inventory for your lot? What is your turn time on your used inventory? Sixty, 90, 120 days? When it gets aged, is your used car manager swapping some other dealer for his aged crap, and thus also bailing out a buddy and covering both of their asses on your nickel?

I was once spending millions of dollars buying cars and trucks at auctions, and I made a point to buy hundreds and hundreds of newer cars and 4x4 trucks. If they were still under warranty, I threw caution to the wind and kept my lot full! My logic was simple; if there was anything mechanically wrong with a vehicle, my service department could get paid by the factory warranty to fix it, so I had virtually no risk. I could sell a one and two year old truck, sport utility, or car for thousands of dollars less than the same identical vehicle in our new car department and make huge profits. I really thought I was a king until one day my dealer explained to me that I was killing our new car business! I had not been concerned, because I was doing great! I started buying older vehicles, and other makes, to diversify. I now had to be more cautious and had to work a lot harder! Is this happening to your store? Used car managers and new car managers of course, need to be paid on both departments, but watch this carefully, because a sharp used car manager can easily manipulate inventory mix.

I always hated having so many wholesalers hanging around when there was work to be done, but they are a necessary part of our business. Just try to limit their visits to once a week if you can. Your used car manager won't want to be rude to them, but he may appreciate you limiting their visits. He can get more done, and you can be the bad guy!

Do you know what desking procedures are in place in your store? Do you approve?

Who attends your 20 group meetings? If not you, is it your G.M. or your partner? Do you discuss the results together afterward? You should. Are you even in a dealer group? Or, do you depend on the factory to supply your comparisons and operating procedures?

Who reviews your over-aged new and used inventory? Are you overstocked in poor selling models, and is it limiting your ability to order what you need? Who is monitoring the ordering? Is your new car manager accepting oddball vehicles to maintain a personal relationship with your factory sales rep? Doing favors for factory sales managers is okay, if what goes around — comes around. Just make sure you're benefitting by some hand-picked and hard to get models in return! Aging new car inventory can kill you quicker than the used cars can. Some new models can become almost sale-proof! Make them go away!

If your used car manager is upside down, and you can't take the hit by wholesaling, maybe another dealer is in the same dilemma; consider swapping book for book, and getting some fresh faces that way. Just don't take the same kind of junk. Like the old saying; you can't pay too much for a good car, or too little for a turd!

Do you have a factory certification program for your franchise used cars? Are your mechanics actually performing the required services, or are your managers just changing oil, giving them a bath, and checking all the boxes? How do you know for sure? Your service manager likely can't swear to it! I have personally seen a used car manager sit down at a desk and certify (check all the boxes) a vehicle in ten minutes! No technician ever saw the vehicles!

Do you have an active internet department? Is your website fresh and impressive? If not, then I suggest you get up to date. It would not cost a lot of money to modernize. You likely have some energetic young computer geek on your sales force who would be proud to enhance your web presence, and bring you into the modern age. They'll work for pennies to find favor in your eyes, and be very loyal! You don't have to pay some high-binder to spend weeks developing some program nobody will use. Your own people can do it, and then you can create an entire internet sales group. A good domain name is dirt-cheap, and web design is only costly in the time to create it!

Have you ever considered a business development center (phone room)? They work, and they will make you a ton of money! If you don't think you need one, make a few calls, and have friends make calls to your store and play as customers. See what kind of effectiveness your sales staff has! Most of you will probably be shocked by how the majority of sales people handle incoming and outgoing phone calls. You'll wonder how you've managed to stay in business! Yes, I do recommend that you pay secret shoppers to check on your operation. It pays!

How much money do you suppose you've left on the table each month by not being on top of your game? If your golf handicap and your profits are both going down, then you need to go back to work for awhile!

One more comment on your telephone procedures. Why do you think some dealers are spending huge dollars on phone centers, computers, training, and seminars? Because the phone is tremendously important, as you know! You don't need a $500,000 phone center, but I recommend highly that you hire professional trainers, and that you and all of your managers (yes, service, parts, and office staff) *all* attend! Phone skills are important to everyone who has contact with your customers!

I will again suggest that you invest some time calling your dealership from an offsite location. Have some friends and maybe your management staff present. Callers should act like typical phone pops, and go through the entire process. If you aren't absolutely shocked by what you hear, then my compliments, because you will be a rare dealer. I've sat in on these sessions with dealers who just could not believe the terrible job coming from their people!

48 SHYNESS – OR COASTING?

Are you too shy to succeed in this business? Don't confuse shyness with stage fright. Many of the best salespeople I've ever had would throw you if you met them out of their element. They possess an almost introverted personality, and you'd never guess that they are highly successful and highly paid performers. I think that last word really sums it up for a lot of us — we are performers!

Seeing my teams outside of the car business, one wouldn't know offhand how they make their living. All one comes away with is an impression of interesting people, who seem very comfortable in their skin.

Here is the rub — good salespeople often appear very shy, and that's typical of stage performers. A lot of professional actors I have met over the years have told me they get butterflies in their stomachs before every performance, no matter how many times they've performed. The more professional you become, the harder you are on yourself to perform to your absolute highest!

Shyness can be misinterpreted of someone who is engaged in constantly meeting new customers, engaging in new scenarios, and experiencing different challenges. Sometimes it's hard to pull yourself up after being hammered down in an attempt to merely sell a car! You may have a half, or a whole day invested, and suddenly everything falls apart! Different people react in many different ways to a deal going south, but it can have a devastating effect on one's morale!

Likewise, in a lot of cases, a very successful month's sales record will oftentimes be followed by a long, flat slump by the same person! I'd say a lot of this has to do with the constant pressure that a salesperson is under. Every situation is different, even though it seems like just so many scenes being continually repeated. The shyness symptoms that a salesperson exhibits are like a genuine fear of starting over with another stranger.

I remember once when I was selling door to door in southern Minnesota. It was a bitter cold day, and the hard-packed snow on the sidewalks made a loud crunching sound as I proceeded down this long block of homes. It was about 10 degrees below zero, and I was dressed in a suit, topcoat, and rubbers that kept my feet from slipping, but collected snow inside and around my shoes and socks. It was around eleven o'clock in the morning, and no one was answering their doors. I saw curtains move slightly, but no one wanted to welcome a half-frozen salesman. Then, at about the tenth house, the door miraculously swung open and the lady of the house said, "Oh, a Fuller Brush man out in this weather!" I had visions of hot chocolate, a large order, and then, the bubble burst! Her next words came through my conscious as a shock — she said, very loudly, "I don't want anything!" and she slammed the door!

Well, I went home and never left the house for two weeks! I just about didn't earn enough to pay the rent that month! I was crushed so bad I couldn't handle it! I almost had to start looking for a salaried job. This is how tough it gets! Yet, one cannot find a more rewarding career than sales!

I liken this condition to shyness, because this is how one feels. It's like if you reach into an oven without a glove, and pull out a hot pan, you get burned. Now someone comes along and says, "Reach in there and do it again, it's your job and I will pay you to do it!" You know you need the money, it's the only job you have, and had you known when you were hired that you had to do it bare-handed, you'd never have hired on, but it's too close to rent time to quit and look for work, so what do you do? You may stand there for a shy while, until you finally go for it. Then you do it again, and just when you're on a roll, the month ends and you have to start all over again; after a break just long enough to heal and forget the pain.

I always wished we could have 60 day months in the car business, because once a good salesperson gets on a roll, the month end will take a psychological toll, and bring the performance to an end! Now, it all starts over and we're back at the oven again!

We car dealers limit our successes in so many cases by gearing our efforts at 30 days at a time! Twelve times a year, our sales force must normally start over. It also works conversely of course, because a salesperson that is having a bad month is just waiting for it to end. Suddenly the month ends, and so does the drought! Why? In this scenario it helps to end the torture. The tough part is when I've had a person on a terrific streak of success, then suddenly the month ends, and the faucet absolutely shuts off! Then it takes ten days to prime the pump, and now the salesperson has only 20 days left to have a good month.

This psychological block is something that every salesperson needs to constantly fight! Try to set 60 day and 90 day personal goals, and hopefully lengthen your successful runs!

49 CLOSERS – KEEP AWAY UNTIL IT'S TIME!

losers — Are you nervous while anticipating what you will run into when the next write-up comes in? You'd better be! Of course I say that, because it goes with the territory. After a while, we just learn to roll with the punches, don't we?

Never worry too much about what you'll run into, because it's always about the same scenario, isn't it? Your price is always too high, your trade allowance is always insulting low, the down payment you're requesting is ridiculous, and the proposed monthly payment is about double what the customer can handle! Oh yeah, and, "It's taking too long!" Did I miss anything? So why worry about what's going on with your salesperson and the customer? When the deal is written, you'll get to take your shot!

The only concern you should allow yourself is whether or not it gets to the offer stage. You need to be standing by when your salesperson returns from the test drive, and observing the body language between them and their customers. If they are not proceeding with the recording of information from the car they drove, and the trade-in appraisal sheet, *your* job begins!

You *need* to be in earshot, or close enough that your salesperson is aware of your presence. If they are not able to reach agreement to at least step inside to get an idea of what the numbers look like on paper, it will be obvious! Your team needs to know that they can depend on you to do more than just close sales! Unless you are closing a deal, you need to be aware of what's going on. You should *know* when one of your people is on a test drive. I would be disgusted as a salesperson returning from a demo with no commitment, to see my closer clowning around in conversation with another manager while I was in need of help! You have a duty to be there!

I digress here not to brag on myself, but to make a point on work ethic!

- I spent thirty years on my feet!
- I *never sat down* except when closing a sale!
- I paced, I watched, and I walked.
- When my team was on duty, I was on my feet; all day, every day!
- I watched everything that went on. I also saw ups come in, and shagged my people out to get the up. I know it was tough on them sometimes, but all great salespeople can get complacent!
- I always knew when my people were on a test drive, and I was *outside* when they returned.
- If they'd proceed indoors to sit down, I followed, unobserved, and then continued to be available inside.
- If they were not going in, my people knew I would be nearby. They would look around, and say, "Folks, I want you to meet my boss before you leave," and they'd turn and call out, "Mr. Swanson, do you have a moment?" This politeness was not per my insistence, they did it not only out of respect, but because they were experts! They showed respect for the position and in turn the customer realized that they weren't just trying to turn to a fellow salesperson! I would then come over and introduce myself as, "Gary Swanson." Then I would try to make them feel at ease enough to take a few minutes to discuss what the numbers might be so they would have

something more to think about. We turned hundreds and hundreds of these innocent conversations into sales. This all goes back to having a well-oiled team where everything is professional, and courteous, and beneficial to the customer.

Above all else, the closer needs to have meetings and sessions on a regular basis, to reinforce how the role-play must be done. You can't rehearse when it's live. By then, it's too late, and you blew a sale.

I've covered this already, but you and your sales team must be able to read each other. Every action and reaction should be natural and immediate. Learn each other, and let your team know how you want them to set you up to eventually be introduced, and how to sit silently, nod, smile, grin, laugh, or whatever response is appropriate to each situation! You will soon be automatically reacting to each other as though you were repeating a Broadway play! Everything else just falls into place!

I *never* wanted to have any idea of what I was about to encounter, and I give you this advice if you are a closer; I have known countless closers who would try to listen in on the conversation between the customers and their salesperson, and I consider this a *foolish and costly* error! Many closers have their team position their buyers in certain places where the closer can listen to the entire write up process. Don't make this mistake! Remember, the customer is also acting. The script the customer follows is all negative! "I won't pay this much!" "I want this much!" "I'll walk out if you 'turn me' to anyone else!" "I have a better deal elsewhere." These are stories they are *telling* your salesperson!

When you come in as a manager, how can you act surprised, and be genuine, when you have already heard all of their arguments? You've already taken a huge crap in the middle of your own mind, you're sewered before you even meet the people, and you are likely scared

(Yes, I said scared!) to even begin negotiating! Don't subject yourself to this kind of SNIOP effect. *Stay away* until the deal is written, and go in with an open mind.

Also, do not ever *ask*, or allow your salesperson to *tell* you any secrets you should know, or how they feel you should approach things! I say this with reservation, because my teams were so professional, that if they knew any secret things that would help, they always asked the customer's permission to share these things with me, and then did so in front of the customer, and we further cemented the team aspect of our relationship! I know that a lot of closers and salespeople do not ever cement this type of relationship. The game the salesperson plays is; *customer and salesperson against the house.* The closer is kept in the dark, and the salesperson and customer work together to scheme for a better deal, with the closer left out of the loop and out of the partnership. This is stupid!

When I first started as a closer, I saw my salesman secretly make a negative sign to the customer by shaking his head. The customer made me a counter offer, and I wrote it down, and then made an excuse to ask my salesman to accompany me to fill out another separate appraisal form. When we were outside, I said, "What in hell was that signal you passed to these people?" He proceeded to explain to me that he had always worked a deal this way. He had been taught to help the customer negotiate, and to have secret signals as to when to say no, and telling them that, "I'll nod when I think we've got the best deal."

Immediately after this sale, I called my new team together, and had a meeting of the minds. I found out that everyone had been trained this way, as the trainers felt it really impressed the customers as to the salesperson's honesty. As I said, this was my first closers job, but I knew this was no way to sell cars! My new rules were; *we are a team!* From the salesperson, to the closer, to the sales manager, and the used car manager, to the general manager, and to the dealer! We are a team that has one goal — to work together on behalf of the customer to earn their business. Certainly, the customer had to know that the salesperson and I would be working closely with them to get the best deal, but there was no good cop, bad cop attitude! No bad guys — all good guys.

From that time on, any secrets were shared among customers, salesperson, and me. Then it was us against the house, but the house was on our side also, in the fact that we all wanted to sell the vehicle! Once we began this new attitude, the gross profits went up tremendously! We could still do the same negotiating, and running back and forth with offers and counter-offers, but it was always for a win-win situation. Our negotiations went from confrontational to selling upper management on our new proposals from the customer.

If you are a salesperson or a closer who currently use this salesperson and customer against the world, change it now! You and your salesperson must be totally together with the buyers. Your salesperson has to let that buyer know that you are the guru. You are the one who can put this deal together! You are the one who can work miracles with your upper management. I was always introduced in this manner; "Mr. and Mrs. Buyer, this is the man I was telling you about. This is Gary Swanson, and he's going to help us buy this car!" This is a must! Trust me! I sell cars!

50 WATCH OUT FOR THE MIND GAMES

If you're going to play the game, make sure you can stay the course. Let me give you a story that really happened, and how I lost an exceptional salesman!

Let's just call these guys Bob and Steve to cover their true names. Steve is and was a tried and true professional, but he suffered from the same ups and downs that all of us experience. Fortunately, his ups lasted long and his downs were short!

I had found it necessary to terminate a poor performer and decided to take a chance on Bob. I liked his attitude, and started him from the ground up. Bob was energetic, but he took a while before he caught fire.

Steve and Bob became pals, and Bob always wanted to beat him, but Steve was hard to get close to. Whenever Bob got close, Steve just turned it up a little and ended up with more sales.

Then, one month Steve hit his usual 25 sales and Bob ended with 22, which was his best so far! Bob had realized his potential, and justified my faith in him! I knew that he had the potential to be a super star. Both salesmen had huge profits and had made a ton of money.

The next month, Steve had a slow start and still had not sold a car the first eleven days; as often happens when someone does so well the previous month, and Bob continued his roll. Here we were on the 11th of the month, and Bob had already sold 11 cars! He was absolutely doing great! Bob and Steve were bantering back and forth, and Bob kept teasing Steve about how he was going to beat him bad this month!

On the morning of the 12th, after my sales meeting, the two guys broke away from the crew for coffee, and the kidding continued until Bob finally triggered Steve's pride! Bob said, "Steve, you don't stand a chance! I'm going to clean your clock!" Well, I remember Steve really got mad! He stuck his finger in Bob's face and said, "That's it! I'm taking you down!" Steve sold three cars that day! Bob had a few ups, but didn't get a write up. No big deal.

The next day, Steve sold two more! Bob had a couple of customers, but now he was visibly shaken by this sudden two day five to zero score. Bob had not seen Steve sell like that, because Steve never really worked too hard to sell his 25 to 30 a month, he was just steady. Things were different this month, because Steve had something to prove!

Neither of these guys even spoke to each other anymore that month, and the month ended with Steve at 22 cars, and Bob *still* with the same 11 sales he had been at on the 11th of the month!

Try as I did during the last half of the month, Bob could not make anything come together. He tried, but his customers just seemed to all be just looking. He was totally demoralized and visibly shaken. Now Steve began goading him and rubbing it in!

The next month, Bob resigned, and I lost a very good man (and he took the receptionist with him, and they got married). Had he stayed, he would have been offered a management position. Steve was; however, Steve elected to keep selling rather than have the constant pressure of management. Good choice!

I use this example because these men are good friends, and they are among the tops in this business. I use them to show how the mental part of this business has so much to do with one's success that it outweighs every other aspect!

As you progress through successes and failures in the car business, you will have people try you on. It's kind of like bluffing at poker. As you get better, your fellow salespeople may become jealous, and attempts will be made to disrupt your sales success. This is only natural, so don't be surprised when it happens. When a sales force has down time, the mind games begin.

If one can mess with the minds of the competition, it makes them easier to beat! Nothing to do with anything other than winning. No one really wants a fellow salesperson to lose money or to fail. The truth of it is that when you are winning and others can't beat you, if they can mess up your mind and cost you your lead, or at least have you join them in their misery, they will feel better! Every sales game is the same. You might say misery loves company, but winners aren't welcome. Since 20% of salespeople make 80% of the money, and since it's easier to be in the lower group, because all they have to do to become members is *nothing*; they would love to have you join them, so just try not to hang around and let them have a shot at your mind!

The interesting thing that you will experience when you get in the chosen 20% group is that you will likely find an occasion when you also will be tempted to assist an offensive associate to join the 80% club! Mind games will always be the preferred sport of salespeople. The lower 80% of the team clawing to reach the top, and if they can't, they hope to drag one of the upper 20% down beneath them so they can step over the descending body to reach success without any positive effort on their part.

Those *glass half empty* individuals need to be avoided. It's not that one cannot be friendly with negative feeling and speaking people, and maybe they will succeed with your help. Just don't hang around when things turn negative.

I have seen a lot of stories play out in my years, and the Steve and Bob story is just one example. Had Bob come back the next month and been able to overcome his embarrassment, he would have been a strong contender! I wish he had, but he's doing well, and Steve is still winning also!

TRUST CAUTIOUSLY

When I advise you to take your fellow salespeople at face value, but have trust in your manager only, there is another example I'd like to use a further reason. Back when the lottery was only a million dollars a week (seems far back now), a group of salesmen at a Lincoln-Mercury dealership in Portland played each week, as so many did.

This particular group would gather in the customer lounge just off the showroom for the weekly announcement. Service being closed, one salesman sat at the up desk on the showroom and the TV was on. Just before the drawing, a customer drove in and our up man went out to greet them; he called out to his buddies, "Somebody write down the numbers for me," and out he went. Let's call him Bud. As soon as Bud went out, one of his pals got the idea of checking the desk, and sure enough, Bud had left his lottery ticket inside his appointment book in the top drawer. The salesman quickly wrote down Bud's numbers in a random order from what was printed and returned to the TV area. Bud soon finished with his customer, and when he came back in, he sat down and pulled his ticket from the drawer and said; "Anybody write down the numbers?" His buddy began reading them aloud in the scrambled order. When he finished, Bud shakily blurted out, "Read 'em again slow!" The salesman slowly repeated them and when he had finished, Bud stood up, picked up his briefcase, and loudly stated, "You can tell Walt (the owner) he can stick this place up his ass!" With that, he headed out for his car.

I had heard this story, as it was carried throughout the city, and several years later I met Bud. I asked him if it were true, and he said it almost ruined his career! Bud said he got halfway to his car, and having just mentally retired he was so excited, but he said he suddenly had a premonition and he turned and looked back at the showroom. There across the windows were his friends all roaring with laughter and clapping their hands. Bud said he just slumped! He said, "I drove straight home and didn't even answer the phone or leave the house for a week!"

I relate this story, because you need to be very cautious in just how much you believe from anyone! Yes, even managers are prone to con games and practical jokes. This is a high pressure business, and it's a lot like pure, raw nature, where the strong survive. You may say to this; "Then it's not for me." If you can make that call at this point, perhaps it's *not* for you! If your inner being tells you that you'll never be able to run with the big dogs, then maybe it's best that you apply for a job as a clerk in a retail store.

If however, you want to make a large amount of money, and are willing to put up with the basic training, then you may be what we need! One cannot expect to develop a cocky, self-assured attitude that is associated with car salespeople without walking the walk! We all began the same way! By walking in the door and saying; "I'm here to become great;" even if only in our own minds!

Just like anything in life, you must be willing to pay your dues. Learn and keep learning. Every time you succeed analyze why, and when you fail, learn from it and try not to repeat the same scenario next time!

51 GO AHEAD, REINVENT THE WHEEL!

In the world of selling, your new employer will tell you not to try and reinvent the wheel. They will caution you to follow instructions, and be like everyone else on their cookie cutter sales crew. Fit in and be a sheep is your safest bet to start. However, once you learn the basics and have a feel for what you're doing, you may wish to experiment a little!

When Joe Girard received the Guinness book title of *World's Greatest Car Salesman*, he didn't earn that distinction by being the same as his peers! Joe earned that title by having enough self-confidence to really stand out in this sameo world.

Joe said he would attend a sports event carrying a paper bag full of his business cards, and when a major play happened and he stood up to cheer like all the rest of the fans, he acted! Taking the paper bag by the bottom, he raised it high above his head, and spun around forcefully hurling business cards in all directions!

Can you imagine several hundred business cards flying through the stands? Now, what if every one of your cards had a message on the back that said you would pay cash for referrals, and that you could deliver any make and model for less money than anyone else? Analyze it a bit! What if only thirty people glanced at your card? Curiosity would certainly get more attention than that, but let's just say only six fans actually take the time to read it, and only two people ever call? Remember, if they call, the chances are great that you will have a good prospect! So maybe, worst case scenario, you only sell one! You may only make one sale, but if your commission is $300.00, it's likely to be a better memory than the game. Joe did tell me that he really had much greater results than that, and always carried lots of business cards, just in case he had such an opportunity!

I realize that most of you will never do this, because most salespeople would feel embarrassed to do something so extreme! That is why *most* salespeople take rank with the 80% of salespeople that earn 20% of all the commissions! It all depends on where you wish to position yourself.

If however, you see yourself in the other group of 20% of salespeople who earn 80% of all the commissions; you may very well be ordering extra boxes of business cards!

You know, it's kind of funny how some of the most admired people in the world are the professional salespeople, and yet in many cases they can be the most fearful when it comes to stepping out of their comfort zone! I have mentioned that if one ever just hollers out in a crowded room, "Who wants to buy a car?" that there will be immediate questions in response, such as "What do you sell?" "Where do you work?" "Can you get me a good deal?" And all sorts of responses. Yet, actually doing something like this is too intimidating to the average salesperson. About the only product in the world that you could get away with such outlandish behavior, without negative reaction, is the *car business*!

People *love* their cars. From the first week after someone buys a new car, their thoughts range from the excitement and enjoyment of the attention, to the model they maybe should have bought, to what they want in their next car! It is an ongoing process. You are in this exciting business because you obviously recognize that the easiest and most profitable product to sell is one that people *really want*!

It's so different from selling things people need, like insurance, siding, and the more mundane necessities of life that people may need, but have to be sold on the importance.

People already know that they both *need and want* a new car! That's a fact! How much work is it to sell fun and excitement? All you have to do is enable them to find a way to own it, and they'll take it and run! Therefore, since cars sell themselves, you need to spend time learning to think outside the box! Dare to be different! Dare to be great! Get over being shy about doing new things; continually challenge yourself to try new approaches to strangers.

In order to really stand out, and be truly successful, you will need to do things that the majority of your fellow salespeople will not do! It won't do you a lot of good to emulate your team mates, because even the top 20% won't be likely to be all that different. They may not have any particular talent, other than hard work and perseverance. You need to form and develop your own persona. Why be content to just be among the crowd!

This is one of the very few opportunities in life where there are no real tight restrictions. No one will care if you spend the whole time walking on your hands, as long as you sell cars! You can say and do the most wild things, and as long as you are courteous and honest, and produce sales, you can do it your way!

I know that a lot of times my fellow closers just watched my crazy antics when I was conducting my showroom circus. But no one could argue about the results. My animated tactics and my announcing someone's successful negotiations clear across the showroom served to not only create excitement, but it also drew everyone else into the positive experience. The effect on other buyers was tremendous. Human nature is to trust what you can see, and when sales are happening all around you, and on an open showroom filled with tables, it's contagious! When other people are shaking hands on car deals, this spreads the feeling of trust and confidence that this must be a good place to buy! I always make a point to negotiate in tones that keep everything confidential, but when a deal is made, there the quiet reserve turns to vocal enthusiasm! As I have always maintained; people pay more for a show, and I make sure they get their money's worth!

Newcomers to our business may find this method of selling to be uncomfortable, and maybe not as professional as the calm demeanor necessary to sell life insurance, but get it through your head; you are not selling funeral plots! You are selling fun and excitement!

Don't worry too much about changing your personality, it will come about automatically. Within two weeks, your friends will be mentioning the change, and the better you become, the more outgoing you will become. Let it happen, and expound on it. Dare to be different!

52 TAKE A TURN (Mandatory reading for managers!)

Most every successful dealership has a turn policy of some sort. A safety catch for a salesperson who is unable to proceed further with a customer. Some stores have the salesperson just touch base with a manager, while others *require* a turn.

The caveat here is that as a manager, you must inspect what you expect. I cannot believe how many managers that can lean back in their swivel chairs and watch turns being made; or stand in the showroom and observe a salesperson introducing his or her customers to another sales rep, and when the customers leave a few minutes later, everyone is satisfied that the job was done properly!

How naïve can dealers and sales managers on all levels be? Ladies and gentlemen at the top, hear me! If you really think that your wishes are being carried out, you had better think back to your early days in the business. If you have never been on the line, or run a sales crew, then maybe you'd better do some analysis, because I promise you that business is walking away from you!

I can say this with conviction because ever since I got my first sales crew, I've observed hundreds upon hundreds of salespeople come up to a group of their associates and say, "I need a courtesy turn." Now what do you think that means? A courtesy turn in car talk means, *"Cover my ass and blow these people out for me,* so I can go eat lunch." This courtesy turn, if boiled down to its actual meaning means help me cheat and lie to my dealer! What is happening here is the salesperson has made the determination that these customers are not buyers. This turn is not sincere and a genuine request for help, but a means to satisfy CMA requirements.

My preferred method is for the salespeople to make turns to their closer or immediate supervisor. A management turn is a lot more impressive in the customer's eyes. Be careful to not try to fake the "I'd like you to meet my manager" intro though. People can quickly see through it. I know a lot of dealers train their people to introduce the other salesperson as their manager, knowing the value of it, but as I've had many buyers tell me over the years, "Yeah, we left the other dealership when our salesman turned us over to another snot-nosed kid and said he was his manager! We don't like dishonesty!"

I know that turns to management are difficult, because I was only able to take an occasional turn myself, but when I did, I could not go out on the lot to sell a car, due to the fact that I needed to be available for everyone, so I recommend doing it this way. When a manager takes a turn, his or her job should be to turn things around; to determine if there is a real possibility of making a sale now or at a later date. You have to think fast when you take a turn. If you have a feeling that these people haven't been properly qualified, or maybe not even taken out to the lot, you have just a few minutes to investigate. Maybe there is just a personality clash with your salesperson. If you feel there is still an interest in proceeding further on the customer's part, just thank your salesperson and say, "Thank you, I'll take it from here," and dismiss them. Now, call over one of your other salespeople, make a strong introduction to the customer and explain, "D.J. is my top salesperson." Then to D.J., "I want you to treat these folks special and find them a car! I'll see you when you return." This type of turn has 100 times more effect than salesperson to salesperson! Now, if a sale results, you split the commission between the two, and counsel both salespeople together, after the customer takes delivery, and have the person who made the sale explain what they did to make it happen. The one who sold it is complimented, and the one who made the turn learns and earns!

As I mentioned, I never went on test drives, all my concern was to see if I could determine whether or not the customer was a buyer. I now had complete control over this customer, because my salespeople were trained to know that anytime they received a turn from me, they were *never* allowed to release that customer until they checked back in with me. This is common sense and courtesy to the customer.

If the salesperson later comes to me, I now have a final chance to make a last attempt to close. I can then ask if all of their questions have been answered, did they find something they like, and if they would like to have some numbers to take home with them.

Look at it this way — if a customer leaves without even test driving anything, you most likely will never see them again, so what do you have to lose by trying your hardest to find an interest? So you may now ask what you've been thinking all along, "I feel that my sales force is professional and well trained, and they should be able to take care of these turns as well as anyone. Besides, I am just too busy!" Now, if this is your thinking, you have just answered your own question. The problem is you! If a sales force is really that good, then what do you think their attitude is toward each other? "If Oly is asking me for a courtesy turn, then I respect his ability enough that I *know there's nothing there.*" They now take the courtesy turn, but with the first salesperson just standing there, and number two asks a couple of quick questions and thanks them for coming in, and your customer leaves! Whose customer is it? Yours? At this point, where a manager or closer is earning a living on commission it *is yours*! However, don't forget, this customer belongs to your dealer! Don't let your salespeople make the final determination as to how and when they will *allow you* to earn a living, or to *allow* your dealer to make money!

Here's another way to look at this critical mistake playing out every day in dealerships. How hard will the second person work, if they respect the first salesperson's ability? They know that salesperson #1 is good. They know that if #1 doesn't see any reason to devote any more time to them, then even if they could get this customer interested in again looking at the inventory, and maybe going on a demo drive, that no matter what, they still can't make a sale!

Why? Simple; the better salespeople are at qualifying, the more attempts they start making to trial close *up front*. When salesperson #2 takes this courtesy turn, they know for a fact that there will be no meat left on the bone! So many of the better salespeople are riding on such immense egos that they would be highly embarrassed if another salesperson could go behind them and make a deal. It is for this very reason that before the pro makes a turn, he or she may even have offered to sell the vehicle for $100.00 over cost! Who even wants to follow that?

This next method will not work in stores where the courtesy — blowout turns are allowed, because these pros turn to other pros, so there will be no chance to effect a good turn. In this next scenario, we look at the best kind of a turn. Take the case where the salesperson just cannot relate well to the customer. This happens frequently, and a lot of the times this situation just ends with the customer leaving and *never* coming back. If for any reason, a shopper runs into an uncomfortable situation, or because of some remark made by the salesperson that they find offensive, they will leave, but seldom ever return to the dealership. This is why proper turns are a must.

Now we take the professional, who is more concerned with his or her paycheck than the big ego trip. A pro knows that by turning to another pro, they run a huge risk of the other person's mindset being,

"If he can't do it, what can I do? Is he just giving me this dud so he can get a good up?" This is the actual thought process.

Now, this pro takes a newer salesperson aside, and compliments them on the fact that they will probably be a better match with this customer than themselves. This happens an awful lot, with older, less patient salespeople and a much younger customer, where they relate like parents and children. The turn to this less experienced salesperson will be the best possible way to make a sale! The person taking the turn will be so proud of the fact that the experienced salesperson had enough confidence in them to give them the turn, that they will work exceptionally hard to make a sale happen. Harder even than they would on their own customer! Pride alone will make their chances of success better than anyone else's. The pro making this turn realizes this, and if this turn is successful, then they may just form an excellent partnership that will work from then on. I've had many teams like this over the years, and the newcomer will seek out this pro when they run into the same situation where they can't relate to a demanding customer that needs a more experienced person to take control.

The turn now works as it is intended; to make a sale! The commission of course will be split evenly between the salespeople, and many stores have a rule that if a salesperson is working on a turn from salesperson 1, and salesperson 1 gets another customer and makes a sale while the first customers are still with salesperson 2, then number 2 will receive half of the other deal. This happens regardless of whether or not salesperson 2 sells their customer or not. The theory is that had salesperson 2 not taken the turn, then they might very well have had the next up, and made the sale all by themselves. In some stores this is not a rule, but it is generally understood that if you are working for me, then we are partners, and I am working for you as well. Without a sharing arrangement like this, then you may as well just go with the courtesy — blowout turns, because that's where you'll end up!

When you try to analyze all of the possible situations that can occur, it is best to have a firm rule or understanding up front. If a salesperson doesn't want to play this way, then they need to state up front how they will or will not reciprocate, so the person taking or making the turn is in agreement. You may not feel that this can be that big a deal, but I've seen this happen so many times that I feel it necessary to discuss it further.

Actual scenario: Salesman 1 has a customer who states he is currently having marital problems and can't trade cars without his wife's approval, and she's not there. Because of store rules, salesman 1 turns to salesman 2. While salesperson 2 is listening to the customer's same story, he overhears salesman 1 meet a customer that says, "I want to buy that convertible! I've been looking all over for one!" Now, instead of just saying goodbye to the customer he just met, because there is no way he can buy anything, salesperson 2, knowing #1 is about to make a sale, decides to use the system. He offers to buy the one-legger non-buyer a cup of coffee. They sit down to enjoy a lengthy conversation that of course, accomplishes nothing, and salesperson 1 completes a sale. At this point, salesperson 2 boots out his customer and claims half of #1's commission! This deal turned out to be a $6,000.00 gross profit, which paid a commission of $1,500.00. Had salesperson 2 not overhead the conversation between salesperson 1 and the new customer, he admittedly would have immediately said goodbye to the non-buyer, but he technically, by the rules of the store, was entitled to half of salesperson 1's deal. The coffee was free, so #2 had nothing invested, but looking at the other side of it, he may have been the one to greet the convertible buyer, right? Then, had he not been with the turn, he would have had it all!

This is quite likely, because normally after spending time with someone and turning them, it's human nature to take a short break, so #1 may have not even been there to take the convertible up. Conversely, when you work on this sharing of turns, then when turning to another person, your responsibility is to go get another up, because you're partners!

Now in this situation, to further complicate matters, salesperson 1 was a long term employee and top producer. Salesperson 2 was an up and coming and talented person. So what would you do? If your rules are to split the deal, you run the risk of having salesperson 1 quit and walk out. If you don't split, then salesperson 2 may very well blowout and can still sue you for half, since those were store rules. No, I'm not going to tell you what actually happened in this case, but it gives you a lot to think about, doesn't it?

Here's another one for you. True story. One busy Saturday, I walked out of the showroom, and here's one of my better salesmen standing and waiting for an up. I said, "Dick, what's happening? I thought you had customers." He said, "Gary, the system is working for me — I had five ups already, and quickly turned every one of them. All five are still with the other salespeople, so now I'm waiting to cherry pick a good one for myself. Hopefully I'll make one for me and get five half-deals!" This store had splits, but with no reciprocal sharing, so you turned, you got half if the other salesperson sold it, but they didn't share your sale. Dick had it figured out, and although I felt it wasn't right, the people he turned to were not on my team, but since they were working on my shift (with permission) I was their designated closer! Of course, I ran with it! I recall that I closed every one of those, and Dick waited for the real nice family, with the perfect four year old trade, and made a great sale! With one and five half's, Dick then requested Sunday off! What could I say?

Turns are always difficult from both sides. There is always suspicion from the one taking the turn, and if it's legitimate, the person giving

311

the turn is concerned that the other person may not really try their best to make a sale! In reality, there are many salespeople who over qualify right up front when they first meet resistance from the customer. They don't want to take a chance that the customer who is being standoffish to them may warm up later on for someone else, but they made an immediate determination that they don't want to waste time with an uncooperative customer. For this reason, they will fire a bunch of qualifying questions at the person, to test the water. Over the years, I've heard it all.

In mandatory turn stores, I've even heard salespeople tell the customer, "Do me a favor. I know you're not buying, but we have a rule here that I must introduce you to another salesperson, or I'll get in trouble. Can you just take a minute to save my job?" Then he calls another buddy over, and says, "John, this is Mr. and Mrs. Parker, they're not buying anything today, but I just wanted you to meet them." The customers said hello and goodbye, and the first salesman walks them to their car. Stupid, and against all logic, but it goes on in every dealership. Dealers would go nuts if they knew what really goes on right under their noses. You see why I believe so strongly in T.O.'s to a manager?

The salesperson may have qualified the customer and found out that they came in to buy a loss leader ad car, and rather than spend several hours to make a minimum commission, they want to turn them. Maybe another salesperson needs one more sale for a bonus, and they would love to have the number. This type of turn is actually beneficial to the dealership, because even though this may not be a moneymaker, but having this buyer working with someone who wants their business instead of the salesperson who just pushes them through the process to get them out, will guarantee the dealership a good factory survey! If you can't make money, at least you don't want to sell a loss leader, and get a failing grade on the survey as well! That's double jeopardy!

Here's a little tip that your dealer likely will never even discuss with you. There are many high pressure stores, where their weekend ad specials are often advertised as low as $2,000.00 below the dealer's actual cost! When you are in an operation like this, you must keep in mind that selling too many ad cars can cost you your job! That's right; vehicles are advertised at low prices like this to draw traffic, *not* to sell these advertised vehicles! They won't come right out and tell you this, as in the old days, but if you want to be in good standing, don't go out of your way to purposely find buyers for these cars. You are there to make money, and even if you steal a trade, and sell a lot of extras on a loss leader, you seldom can expect more than to break even. I never was too happy going in to close an ad customer, because other than get another number for my salesperson, I knew I was spending a lot of time for little or no reward. Now, I would have a team member tied up with a no-profit customer for hours on a busy day! This, I was not at all in favor of! Plus that, if there was a way to trick the system, the finance manager would skip over these customers as long as they could. I've seen ad buyers sit waiting while other customers were slid in front of them. Finance managers want money too!

The main idea here is to show the advertised vehicle, and then try to sell against your customer owning that particular vehicle. Many experienced salespeople have ways to qualify people quickly, for example; "What brings you folks in today?" The customer says, "We saw your ad in the paper." Salesman, "Great price, I'll be happy to get you some help with that. I'm not really available right now because I'm waiting for an appointment, but I saw you come in and wanted to be of service. Let me get an available salesperson for you, I'll be right back." With that, the salesperson goes and grabs another salesperson, either a new hire, or someone he or she knows just wants to get another number. They'll explain, "I'm waiting for an appointment, but these people asked me if I could find someone to help them. I didn't get a chance to find out what they're looking for, and don't put me on half, it's not a turn." Then they then continue looking for a live one, and no one is generally the wiser. This is the way I personally hoped my salespeople would use to avoid selling a loss leader ad car!

The world of turns is vast and unending in its variations and challenges. You will learn it the way you should, but knowing all the ramifications also allows you to avoid getting a turn from a person that just needs to dump a bad turn on you!

53 WE ALWAYS COMMIT FIRST!

This is such an important part of this business, that I must single it out for its' own coverage! As we have discussed, all negotiations must come from us. Salespeople should never even enter into any discussions about selling price, other than full list, and should never, ever, ask a customer what he wants for his car! This is absolutely forbidden! Never put yourself in a position where you are *taking something away* from a person!

Our entire selling procedure needs to be for the customer to select and drive prior to entering into negotiations, and then we will make the first offer. The easiest way to handle it, when a customer starts talking about price, trade allowance, or payments, is to just answer with; "I'll be happy to get those figures when we get back inside. Then, just as a suggestion, don't even tell me what you have in mind. Then when we see what the dealership offers, we can discuss it. Who knows, maybe they'll give you a better deal than you even want! Yeah, I know, fat chance, right?" Then we laugh, and now we wait until they are in love with the vehicle! New salespeople are often confused by this method of refusing to discuss figures until later, but until the customer has decided on a vehicle, any price, trade, or payments discussed really have no bearing on reality. We must save negotiations for the proper time.

We always commit first, for a reason: To properly set the stage. If we want to kill our deal, we can always ask; "Dakotah, what would you like for a trade allowance?" Some salespeople will ask this question, and they had just as well have stuck their foot in their mouth, because the customer will always throw out a number that is

315

way above what he really had in mind. He figures if you're so new as to have to ask, he may as well go for broke, and hit you at a ridiculously high number. Now, as so often happens in these cases, let's say that he would have gladly accepted $6,000.00 for trade, but now he throws out $8,000.00. He knows it's ridiculous, but since it's now on paper, it becomes what his offer is. That ridiculous number has now become the customer's request, and now he no longer thinks about the six thousand. The salesperson just set themself up to fail!

Remember that customers really seldom have a clue as to reality. Therefore, the customer in this example that would have accepted $6,000.00, but in reality felt his vehicle was worth $4,000.00, is now asking for $8,000.00 and the salesperson just created a monster.

Remember from before, that no matter how new you are, when you write down an offer for a customer, he or she believes that you feel in your own mind that it is reasonable. Even if you just started selling yesterday, the customer still thinks your newness is mainly an act. Therefore, if you write their offer, you do not think it is unreasonable. This is why we commit first, and we *never* ask the customer for his opinion until we first give him ours.

No matter what happens, anything you put on paper for a customer's offer, we must take away from. You must do everything you can, to get the *trade allowance as low as possible, and the cash down and payment as high as possible.*

If you are constructing the offer on the 4-square system, you will be given starting figures to use. If your dealership sends out the first offer on a pre-printed proposal, all you have to do is present the numbers, and see how close to the proposal you can get the customer to agree. At this juncture, you present figures, get a counter offer from the customer, and again, don't write down the counter too quickly. Do some selling, work for all you can get, and take the results to the sales office.

It's not at all complicated, just get to know the procedure, and you'll soon be coasting through this process, having fun with your customers, and making lots of money!

54 TAX DEDUCTIONS – ON LEASES ONLY?

I do not give tax advice, but for years, I have had business clients tell me that they must lease their vehicle so they could write it off against their taxes. Don't believe it! Sometimes, a lease is not the most advantageous for the customer, or the dealer. For a person to lease just for tax purposes isn't smart!

Well, don't buy the theory! The first time I heard this bunk, I called my accountant, and he told me that his fellow bean counters just told clients that because of laziness. Evidently, a lease is an easier deduction to calculate, because it is a fixed amount every month, plus any mileage or fuel deductions. An accountant can calculate your business deduction for a vehicle purchased for business use as well. It just takes more work to correctly calculate this way in order to satisfy the IRS.

Don't forget to mention the business deductions to people who are self-employed, because a lot of them don't realize they may have some tax help here; especially if they are having trouble justifying the payment. A tax savings of fifty dollars a month means you can sell fifty dollars a month more payment! That higher payment being justified, means more vehicle for the customer, and more profit for you.

55 CLOSERS — DON'T MAKE THE DESK WEAK!

This is an area that is seldom addressed! It is overlooked by the desk manager and by the closer, but it is one of the basic, and most important, and most neglected areas of this process of line—close selling!

The desk manager's duty is to be convincing when he or she gives instructions and pencils to the person actually doing the negotiation (closing). The desk must convince the closer as to the fact that what they are being given is the bottom line!

Here, the desk walks a fine-line, as if they give a closer the feeling that there is no more room to negotiate, then the closer may make the last effort, and when the customer says no, the danger is that the closer will just shake hands and say goodbye. Now the customer has been told no, not asked to negotiate further, and that all negotiations are over! The buyer's mindset now changes, the pressure of wanting to make the purchase is off, and the customer asks for their keys.

Now, when the closer returns to the sales office to get their keys, the desk manager goes into cardiac arrest, because the desk was not through negotiating! Now, it will likely be too late for a closer to re-open discussion with the customer, and if there is a chance of making the deal, the desk manager must go out and make a last ditch effort to salvage something!

Remember this rule always; <u>NOBODY WALKS 'TIL THE DESK TALKS!</u>

Closers, here's where you earn the big bucks! Don't ever try to second guess the desk! Just do *your* job, and each time you are given a new pencil, go out and get all you can, make sure the customer will still buy and drive home now, and bring the results to the sales manager.

The manager on the desk must be able to have total confidence in your ability, or you will never hit the big profits! Most anyone can close sales with proper words from the desk, and accepting low gross profits, but that is not the real secret to closing! The thing that sets a master closer aside from the ninety percent of all other closers, is the ability to project to the buyer that the ballistic pencil is the bottom line, and holding firm until the last possible moment!

To look a buyer in the eye, and hold firm without wavering, to the point that the customer is about to give up and leave; and then being able to sense the exact moment to suggest the possibility of a compromise! That's what closing is all about! Until a closer has the confidence and fortitude to be able to control these situations, he or she is still not at their peak! The desk must be able to have complete confidence that a closer will never give up and get weak on them. This is when the big gross profits are made.

Now a lot of you closers who think you're so good at what you do, give some thought as to whether you may be making lower grosses than may be possible if the desk had more confidence in your ability!

Sales managers would do well to realize what may be happening on your end as well! Do you oftentimes roll too easily, and accept a lower gross because your closer convinces you that they're all-in? Are you allowing the closer to make you weak?

Ladies and gentlemen, here is how you work to overcome all of your weaknesses! First of all to the benefit of all, the desk manager and the closers must have an understanding that the customer is *never* allowed to feel that negotiations are over, and until the sales manager hands the customer's keys to the closer and says to let them leave, dealing continues. I have also purposely handed the keys to the closer and just as he was saying goodbye, I came out to meet the customers, sat down and closed it myself. This method really works well if the desk manager has time.

A good desking procedure is to have the least amount of conversation possible between the closer and the desk. The instructions should be given by the desk, and even the exact script to use is often a good idea, especially when the sales manager and closer are getting used to each other. The desk must be convincing, and the closer must be convinced.

A sales manager cannot let the closer know what they are wanting them to achieve. You can't say to the closer; "Now here's what I want you to do, hit 'em with this, and if they won't do it, here's my next move." This will not work! The desk must keep the closer in the dark, and the ideal closer will not want to know where they're at! If a closer knows where they need to be, it will make them weak! Disclosing the entire plan to the closer up front, will achieve the lowest and least profitable results. Closers need to be focused on, and believing in what they are told is needed to make a deal.

When I titled this chapter CLOSERS — DON'T MAKE THE DESK WEAK, I say this from experience! Over my closing career, I had countless occasions to work with new sales managers who were oftentimes intimidated by working with a very experienced closer. When starting to work with the desk, the first thing I always explained was that I would not second guess their figures, and I was there to do what they wanted! This met with appreciative acceptance, as I knew they were expecting resistance from me. I made this gesture, not out of politeness, but in order to protect my income! I made it very clear that I had no intention of ever arguing if the pencil was too hard hitting, but that I did expect a desk manager to hit me hard! By that, I mean that I wanted them to send me out to the customer with every offer going for the moon! I knew that I had the ability to handle it, and the fact is, that many desk managers are easy to intimidate by the salespeople; especially when a new desk comes on board, or is promoted from within.

A strong salesperson will, a lot of times, be afraid of the chance their customers will be insulted by being hit too hard by the closer, and out of fear of this, they set up the desk manager! Remember that the salesperson may be just an average nice person who sometimes to their own detriment is too concerned about the customer's perceived feelings. They allow the customer to control their minds, and they become afraid to even attempt to make a lot of money, for fear of having the customer blow out! Now, the untried and inexperienced desk manager listens to, and believes the salesperson when they're told, "If we try to make a big profit, this guy will get mad and leave!" Now, we have two of the three dealership people convinced, so what chance is there of making a good gross profit? You guessed it! None!

Desk managers, heed this; your job is to stay strong! Do not allow your salespeople or your closers to affect your thinking, or your career will be short lived and miserable. Don't worry about being a nice guy or gal. You're not in your position because you were popular; unless of course upper management is total idiots! You're there because of your strengths, so don't suddenly get weak!

Closers; your job is easier. All you have to do is get the pencil! That's right! Your job is simple. Your sales manager has to do all the work! He or she has to maybe appraise the trade, figure the deal, write the pencil, and give you whatever instructions that are necessary.

I loved closing, because it didn't tax my brain; I could take my smoke breaks, watch my crew, and when a write-up hit the desk (was brought to the sales office), take the pencil from the desk, and go meet the customer, and then get the pencil. Does that sound hard? Easiest job in the world!

Think about it; all a closer has to do is meet the customer, exchange a little small talk (with your salesperson in attendance), show the store's offer to the buyer, and ask them to buy it! Isn't that a piece of cake? Oh sure, we now have to have a dialogue, and go back and forth a few times, see how close to our offer the buyer is willing to go, write it down, and go back to the sales office.

Now the desk takes a look at our counter offer, and they do more calculating, while the closer just looks cool, and they write another offer, and the closer merely has to go back to the buyer and convincingly present the new figures. It's certainly not rocket science, that's why I say it's easy! Sometimes the hardest part I ever had was, keeping the desk strong!

Here's a suggestion for keeping the desk strong; the toughest part of this role-play is the desk is afraid to send the closer out with too strong a pencil, for fear the customer will leave. As a closer, you must let the desk know that you have control over the customer! If the desk feels that you are losing control over the customer, they will tend to get weak, and either make the next offer to the customer too low, or the desk may just roll over and take the last counter from the buyer. In this case, the customer wins and the house loses! Some closers spend more time working the desk, than they do negotiating with the customer.

My best advice to a closer is to make sure to occasionally remind the desk to send you out for more! I have done this all throughout my career, and I oftentimes had to convince the sales manager to make one more attempt. As a closer, you know how much control you have over a customer, and you know if you are at a point where they will just walk out, or if they will sit still for another attempt. Remember, you and your salesperson receive a percentage of every additional dollar that you pick up!

I always tried to influence the desk in only one manner; to stay strong! When I had made several passes, and the desk had a concern over going for a little more profit that would in turn create a bad factory survey from the customer, I had to interject my feelings. If I genuinely believed that I could get a little more movement from the buyer, and still have a strong enough relationship for them to give us a perfect report, I always opted for another pencil. My feeling is that if you go for the maximum profit on each and every deal, your overall income will be higher, and you will have properly done your job.

As a new closer in a store, I always watched for the signs; and if I sensed that the desk was somewhat fearful of the results, I'd just remind them that I had enough control to go out for another pass. After a while, the desk manager will know you well enough that they will ask you, as they always did me, "Is there any more there?" My usual answer was, "Go ahead and pencil me again, and let's find out!"

I know I have beaten this subject almost to death, but this is what separates the master closer from the rest of the herd!

56 LUXURY CAR BUYERS — WORKING THE DEAL BACKWARDS (This still works!)

In this chapter, I am going to give you a method that I used extensively on luxury car buyers. Take these methods for what you can use from them and adapt to your own arsenal of skills.

I created this method when I was closing in a Lincoln-Mercury dealership. We had two sales crews, and this was in the days when Mercury was a very competitive franchise, and Lincoln was known for its quality even more than it is today.

Our dealership was in a nice area, on the main drag, and our biggest competitor in the area was of course, Cadillac. The Cadillac dealership was on a cross street which was not that easy for shoppers from other suburbs to find. Therefore, since we were so easy to spot, we had huge numbers of people just stop and ask directions to Cadillac and then depart.

When I started at this dealership, I saw this was a major problem for us, so I had a meeting with my team to correct this deficiency. We kept some parking areas clear on both of our front entrances, and when customers came in to roll down their window for directions to the Caddy store; we would ask if they had seen the new Lincoln? The loyalty to Cadillac was huge! Some of these people had owned Cadillacs for year after year, and the great majority had never even looked at a Lincoln!

Our pitch was effective! We just invited them to take a couple of minutes to at least see what we had to offer before they left. The salesperson would have them park, but instead of escorting them to the models on the showroom, they, for the most part, took them directly to our Lincoln lot. We moved most of our Lincolns to a separate lot about 150 feet from our showroom. Weather was the determining factor as to the direction they took.

Now, this was how our strategy worked; since I was a chain smoker, I normally was outside near the main showroom entrance, so I could quickly set my cigarette down, and be there to assist my salespeople when a Cadillac pulled in. Being as we only had two sales crews, we were seldom on duty at the same time except on weekends, I usually had one salesperson standing under the showroom awning, and I was near enough to observe and assist in asking the customer to look at our new Lincoln.

When I made the suggestion, my salesperson showed them where to park, and would lead them to the Lincolns. I would step inside and grab a dealer plate, and slowly follow them across the lot. My salesperson would be developing rapport, and generally by the time I caught up with them, they were looking at a Lincoln model that had the most appeal to them.

I would then approach, and since we had already acknowledged each other at a distance when they came in, my salesperson would introduce us, and I would then suggest the test drive. Remember when I said before that the feel of the wheel is half the deal? My next move was to get that handled! I would speak directly to my salesperson, and say, "Artis, please get the keys for this car, so the folks can make a real comparison." My salesperson would turn immediately, and at a fast walk or run, would head for the showroom for keys! Why run? Because invariably the customer would say, "Oh we don't have to drive it, I'm sure it drives well."

Why would they say this? Because they weren't ready to buy, and they didn't want to feel obligated! Keep in mind that these were polite and affluent people. This obligation is why the salesperson would take off immediately, before the customer had the time to object, and even as quick as they would respond, the salesperson was already well on the way! My reply was always; "Oh that's okay folks, we are so proud of our Lincolns that we really want you to see what we truly believe is the best riding luxury car in the world! Even if you don't want to drive it yourselves, at least go for a ride around the block with Artis." The minute the salesperson departs, the obligation is made. They never said no to the ride, because, as I said, these were customers that were affluent and their manners were impeccable! The salesperson came back, and I already had the magnetic dealer plate on the car, and we placed them inside, and off they went. The demo drives were a lot longer than around the block. They were full presentations, and everybody drove!

The next step was when they pulled back on the lot; they were instructed to park in the lucky sold row, right by the front door, where I was still sending up my smoke signals to the car gods. When they got out, I was again there with my, "Isn't that a beautiful car!" They would usually always respond with, "Yes, it really surprised us! We had never considered a Lincoln before!" Then the usual, "We're not ready to buy anything today, we just came out to see the new Cadillac, but now that we've seen this Lincoln, we will really keep it in mind!

Do you think that was the end of their experience? Not at all! We're just starting! My next move was always the same. I would say, "I can understand and appreciate what you're saying, so as long as you're here, why don't we take a few minutes and step inside so we can see what the numbers look like on paper. This way you'll have some figures to compare when you do get ready to buy!" I'd hold the door, and when inside, I'd escort them to an office. The salesperson would then offer refreshments, and once they were eating and/or drinking, and done with their bathroom break, I would instruct the salesperson to do an appraisal slip on their car. This was of course after I had asked if that was the car they would be replacing.

I'd now sit there and develop rapport until my salesperson came back with the appraisal, then he or she would sit down and begin talking about the 3F's, and I would depart for the sales office! This is totally backwards, isn't it? Now, I would get the hit figure (starting offer on the trade), and I'd then head back to the customer with my scratch paper. With my salesperson sitting alongside, I would casually back into a car deal! I very casually would write down the list price of the car they had selected. Such as, our price is $43,537.00. Then; "Vicky, Marvin, while I was in the sales office, I checked our trade-in record book, and the last time we took in a Cadillac similar to yours, it was stocked-in for eighteen thousand, five hundred dollars; if you were to trade, is that what you'd have in mind?" Just casual conversation. Then they would normally respond with, "Oh no, we'd want a lot more than that!" I'd not my head understandably, and ask; "Just out of curiosity, what were you thinking?" The answer would come back, "We wouldn't take less than twenty-three thousand!" says Vicky. My response; "Wow!" Then a long pause, and I'd ask; "Marvin, Vicky, let me ask you this; if I could somehow give you twenty-three thousand dollars for the Cad, is there any reason why we cannot just go ahead and do it right now?" Boom! —done! Commitment! Then I'd write the offer, have them sign it, and ask my salesperson to complete the customer statement (credit application) and bring it to the sales office when it was done. I'd take their keys, and go to the office with a commitment to buy and drive home now!

Statistics had always shown that a Lincoln-Mercury dealership gets about five percent of the total business, and about the same percentage of people that consider even looking at them in the first place.

These scenarios I just covered were always exactly the same. Having a salesperson posted by the entrance just drew in the direction seeking Cadillac owners. This turned out to be perfect, for you could almost hear the wife saying, "Gene, you're lost; just pull over there and ask that salesman standing by the entrance. Then we won't have to drive around all day!"

The same joke from me coming along saying, "They closed up?" They couldn't compete with us!" The laughter, "But seriously folks," and my invitation to at least look at the new Lincoln. The walk to the inventory, my coming over and meeting the people, to sending the salesperson for the key, to the ride around the block, the return and invitation to leave with figures, the initial hit figure from me, and then to the commitment to buy, the negotiation process, and then agreement and delivery!

Every single one the same as I have written it! We had a high volume dealership, and using this method, my sales crew sold eighty-five percent of all the Lincolns and Grand Marquis that the dealership delivered! 85%! Don't be afraid to be creative! We made so much money that we could afford to specialize! I had my crew spend only short demo drives and limited time with all of our products except with Lincolns, Grand Marquis, and used cars. These, they could take whatever time they needed, as that's where the money was!

This was the only time I ever found was an actual advantage to smoke. If I had not been out there chain smoking, and had been sitting around in the sales office or showroom, I never would have discovered this method. Once it worked a couple of times, it became standard operating procedure for my team. We had sales meetings and training on the procedure. All of our product training was from then on focused on the Lincoln! Another advantage of this system was the high quality buyers, and the easy closes just by backing into every sale.

331

If I was not immediately available when one of these scenarios began, I would hear a page for me to come to the sales office. When I'd get there, the sales manager would say, "Gary, Denny has one of your kind of people." Then I'd head for the Lincoln lot!

Develop what works for you, and then perfect it and use it, as I did. These Cadillac owners never had to make a decision to buy a car! All they had to do was look at one thing after another, from car to figures, and they never had the pressure of negotiating! Just a gradual process of questions, until the final one, which was, "Would you buy it and drive it home now?"

I use this example not to point out that the Lincoln was a better car — It was the fact that when people drive any vehicle, unless they do not like it, the excitement of the demo drive creates buyers! The feel of the wheel is half the deal! Test drives create enthusiasm and an impulsive response in the customer's mind to own it now!

57 WHEN YOUR BLUFF IS CALLED – REASONS TO CONTINUE NEGOTIATING

After the customer drives away is a poor time to think about what you could have done differently.

I'm going to just throw out some selections for you to play with, reconstruct to fit your personality, and some that are borderline truthful. When you hear car salespeople pitching their products, the average buyer just usually feels that if your mouth is open, you're lying. Therefore, the old time lies about illness in the family and the really personal woes don't cut it in today's marketplace.

If you're going to tell a story, then make it a real reason for your customer to buy from you right now, and the reason must be of a real benefit to your buyer. They will not buy one for the Gipper!

These statements are some I have used that were absolutely true at various times, and some that I have been told by my desk manager and passed along to my customer as fact, because I always put complete faith in the desk when I'm closing. After all, would my boss lie to me?

Here we go:

- "Folks, the reason we are trying so hard to earn your business tonight, is that today is the final day in a twenty-one day factory contest. The winning dealer goes on a tour of the factory, and my manager said that our dealer is just a few cars behind. We can see where the other dealers in his competition group rank on the computer, and since we are the last one to close due to the time zone, our owner still has a chance to pull it out!"

- "Mr. and Mrs. Buyer, please don't feel that we are being pushy. The reason my boss is trying so hard to make you a deal is he was just promoted, and he'd shoot me if he knew I was telling you this, but he's really so new at his current position. He didn't mean to insult you with his offer, he's just afraid of making a mistake and looking bad in front of his boss. If he does well, and that doesn't mean in profit, but strictly in the number of cars he sells, he will keep the job. His trial period will only be thirty days, so bear with me and we'll get you a great deal. Now, let me ask you this...........」

- "Folks, we're in luck! This is going to work out perfect! Our used car manager is unavailable, and I sneaked out and called a wholesaler friend of mine to see what your car should be worth in actual money. I told him I wanted to get his opinion, as he does a huge business and he knows exactly what most every car is worth and what it will sell for both at the auto auction and to a retail purchaser. I didn't tell my sales manager what I found out, because it wouldn't be in your favor. My manager would be embarrassed to call a wholesaler for advice and I sure don't want to feel like I'm cheating the dealership, but he wouldn't listen anyway. When I was in the sales office, the other manager told him he should call a wholesale buyer for a bid, but he just said he knows what he's doing and to 'butt out,' so who am I to interfere? Besides, I work for you folks, which is how it should be! Let me ask you this; my friend told me the actual cash value of your car is $8,500.00, but since my manager doesn't know that; if I can get you ten thousand dollars for it, would we have a deal?" Now here, you can either wait for their answer, or as I so often like to do, is before they can answer, I immediately interrupt myself with, "As I say, no promises, but I'll do everything I can to make it happen for you. Will ten thousand dollars work?" Notice how I will interrupt myself and repeat the exact same close to double emphasize it!

- "Folks we need just a few more sales, and to show you how important you are to us, my boss is going absolutely crazy on your trade allowance! Our factory incentive level is about to change. Every time we sell one of this model, we earn another $200.00 from the factory. We are just so close to the next level where we start earning $300.00 per car. The beauty of this is that the increase is retroactive! This means that your sale may be the one that tips the scales! If this is the case, it means that your purchase will make my boss several thousand dollars more from the factory. Because of this, I'm trying to time my entrance into the sales office so that your sale is the one that hits our bonus land. Therefore, my question to you is; if, and I do mean if; I can get my boss to give you an extra two thousand dollars for your trade, can we do it?"

- "Folks, we are really in a good position right now, and your purchase couldn't come at a better time! We just got a new factory sales rep, and in order for him to have a good start with the dealers in his territory, he has what we call a bonus inventory! He just told my boss that for every one of these 'hard to get' XYZ models, and you know how scarce they are;

but for every one we sell today, our rep has promised to get us another one exactly like it! This is like my dealer getting a free car; of course we still have to pay for it. As you know, we are almost totally out of this model, and word is that all supplies will soon dry up. In fact I heard that many dealers are already adding 'additional dealer markup' stickers up to $2,000.00 on any of these models they can get! We won't do that of course, because my dealer is a real straight shooter, but you're sure here at the right time. Because of this extra 'allocation,' let's take advantage of it. I know it seems like we're a long ways apart, but since my dealer gets a replacement, I'm sure he will make a deal on the one you're buying as if it was just any other car. This means you can get a choice model for a very small dealer profit. As hard as these cars are going to be to get, what do you think will happen to your future value? You can probably drive it for several years and get most every dollar you paid back! Don't you think? What if I could…"

- Use this when you have told the buyer that you are at the bottom line and there is *no more room*, and they call your bluff and get ready to leave — You always need to be able to restart negotiations, but you must have a logical reason or you'll look like any other liar! Once you bluff and get called; you need a brilliant idea! Anytime I get called, I adopt the hang-dog expression and say, "Well I appreciate your trying folks," and I stand up with them and suddenly the light bulb appears over my head and I say; "Wait a minute! I have an idea. Sit down a minute folks. Now I have an idea, and I just think it's wild enough to work. Exactly how far apart are we?" Regardless of what they come up with, I must now get to an exact number, and I ask them to work with me. Once I have their final number, I tell them that, "I'm going to make one last effort, and if it works you'll have a deal. Keep your fingers crossed!" Now I come back with, "Congratulations, you own it!" I explain to the customer that, "*My idea* that I couldn't discuss was because I didn't even know if my manager would even consider it, but what I did was to get him to take (whatever dollar amount we had to increase the trade allowance by) and add that dollar figure to a different vehicle in our inventory in order to balance it out."

There are many reasons you can use, such as on a used car, "This one has been here a little longer, that this other one that you folks didn't like, so my used car manager just added this amount to the other car and reduced this one by the same amount to help us out. He did this because he's going to sell the other one to the auction anyway, so it will just be part of a large sale and won't even be noticed. He did this for me because I help him out on occasion, and he's a great guy!"

On new cars; "We still had some unallocated factory incentive money left over that we get to use however we see fit, so my manager was nice enough to use that money to help us out."

You can also use the used vehicle inventory adjustments like a lot of used car managers do, like lower one by a thousand, and add a hundred dollars each to ten other vehicles in inventory. Any reason you use must make reasonable sense to the buyer, but you'd better have a reason for doing this for them that makes sense. It *can't* be because they're such nice people! Nobody buys that crap, so don't try to peddle it. You need to give people a reason that ends up being a mutual benefit. We benefit at this moment in their purchasing from us, and we are passing some or all of this benefit on to them. No dealer is going to just give someone something out of the goodness of his heart! Even if he did, the customer would not believe it, so don't try. Just give the buyer a good, sound, logical reason why we can suddenly meet his terms where we couldn't before, and by doing so, we both win!

Reasons for doing special offers, increasing trade allowances, and lowering prices are all easily explained in the fact that our previous offers were all to make the most profit we could. People understand this, and that's all just part of negotiations. We naturally want to sell for more, and they want to buy for less. It's just when you bluff your bottom line" and if your bluff fails, you now need a legitimate and believable reason to reopen negotiations.

I always act as though the numbers I am presenting are unbelievably good for the buyer. You must do this! You cannot present your second best numbers to a customer. You cannot go out and say, "Folks, let's take a look at management's offer, and if you don't like it, just make them a counter offer!" That would be insane wouldn't it? Yet a lot of salespeople do this out of weakness and fear!

When your customer objects and wants to make a counter offer; slow yourself down! Do not be so quick to start playing the game. Present your offer as though it is gospel! When your customer objects, act surprised — not shocked and phony, just legitimately surprised. Then have a discussion and keep selling your proposal. I usually say something to the effect of; "Well, at XYZ Motors, we try to do things differently. Our owner has never liked the fact that negotiations are sometimes so difficult. He feels that if he can make a fair profit and have happy customers, that people will keep coming back time and time again because they like the way they are treated. For that reason, the managers really try hard to make a very fair offer right up front. What is there about this offer that you disagree with, and how would it have to change to work for you?"

In our desire to look ahead in time to visualize the outcome of our negotiations, we tend to trial close too early and too often, and that helps give us a grand reputation! You've worked very hard to get the buyer inside and on paper, now slow down and make the sale. When you tell someone that this is your bottom line, you had better be convincing! Look them in the eye, and take your best shot. Then shut up and keep smiling and making eye contact. *Don't* look down! What are you thinking? They'll think you're lying! Don't talk to their kids, just sit there, keep silent, and keep smiling! Don't you dare to say "Look it over, and I'll be right back." *NO, NO, NO.* Some closers will do this, and it's stupid! I don't care if you need a potty break! Go in your pants! Remember at this point, *when asking a closing question, the first one who talks loses!* Never forget it. So now when your customer says no, and your smile heads straight to your lap, whatcha gonna do? You're going to act surprised, just mildly surprised, and ask why. I used to just look a little surprised, wrinkle my brow slightly, and just quietly ask, "Why?" Then listen intently and discuss the entire offer before trying to defend it.

Seldom will you find a customer objecting to an entire offer; just part of it. If they object to the trade allowance, is it because they really care about the amount, or is it because the payment is too high and they know that there are only two ways to lower the payment; more cash down and more trade allowance. Which one do you think they are wanting? Of course the cash down comes out of their pocket, the trade allowance comes out of your manager's. Don't be too quick to defend what may not even be a real objection to anything. A lot of people just feel it is proper procedure to object to any offer from a car dealer. I have often found that a mere discussion after an objection to reaffirm my manager's offer is all that was necessary.

Some so called assistant buyers, mavens, second basemen, third basemen, and any other *protectors of the buyer*, just object to whatever you say or do in hopes of getting you to go running back to the sales manager for a better deal! Don't be worried when you get an objection. When I get a customer to roll over for the first pencil, I always worry about their sanity, their credit rating, or where they escaped from. Yes, you often will get an acceptance to your first offer if you present it properly. Just don't be so surprised you say, "Are you sure?" Ha!

One can think of absolute lists of reasons we can toss out as to why after telling a buyer we are at our bottom line that we can continue to negotiate. Just make sure to be fast on your feet with your "I have an idea" plan, but you must first acknowledge the fact that your best deal has been rejected and your negotiations are concluded. Only after such cessation of further negotiating and preparations to see the customer to the door, *can you have an idea.*

58 SELL FROM THE OTHER GUY'S STOCK!

Do not limit yourself to what you have on your lot; expand your opportunities. Over the years I have made a lot of money by just expanding my opportunities. Take the customer who really likes you, but you don't have anything this person wants to buy. You have great rapport and you both realize that if you had the right car he would buy from you. You now let this customer know that if he finds something elsewhere that he likes, that you may be able to help him.

I cannot count the times over the years that I have made sales from other dealer's inventory. I'll give you one example that comes to mind. Two female ferry boat skippers from Alaska had come to Portland so one of them could buy a car. They were close friends and this was their vacation; one of them was planning to buy a car and they would enjoy their vacation in the lower 48 and then ship the car back to Anchorage.

I was sitting on the small showroom on our used car lot when these ladies came in. My salesman showed them through our inventory but they left without buying. Since we were on *auto row*, they went down the line walking from store to store. About two hours later the same ladies appeared walking back the way they came on the other side of the street. I sent my salesman out to head them off and take another run at helping them. He returned, saying they had been to ten dealerships and only found one car she liked, but they told my salesman that they were treated rudely so they left. They were on the way up the street to catch a cab to the other side of Portland to resume their search.

I then dispatched my salesman to pick them up in a car and ask them if she would be interested in buying the car she had liked if *we could sell it to her.* He came back with them, and I called the used car manager down the street and asked him how much I could buy the car for. He gave me a price; I sent my salesman to get it, and he then took the ladies for a test drive and we sold it. The salesman at the other dealership had ruined his chances by talking down to these ladies. Asking all the wrong questions and implying that he felt they couldn't afford to buy a car, and just made a total ass of himself. Well, she not only bought that car from me, but she went into the bathroom and took off her money belt and started stacking up the hundred dollar bills in piles. Then, to top it off, the other lady said; "Since you treated us so well and I like that car over there, and even though I didn't plan to buy one this trip, I'll take it." Out came another bulging money belt and she paid the asking price without question.

I immediately sent a purchase order and a check to the dealer down the street so I could send them home with the titles, and I told the used car manager about the two sales and how his salesman had need of some education in the art of qualifying. When I told him how much profit we made on our two sales, he said it was more than they made the entire weekend! I mention this as a viable tool for expanding your horizons.

If people like you, then you'd better let them know that you can assist them in finding certain models if you don't have what they want. Clear it with your management, but don't be afraid to at least make every effort to increase your opportunities. Also, your used car manager can make some calls to see what he can find for you.

A very important thing to remember is that many salespeople make unpardonable mistakes with customers and people will walk away from vehicles that they would otherwise gladly purchase, all because of insensitive and ignorant salespeople. I stress this fact because it has meant a ton of extra income for me and for my salespeople.

59 A FINAL WORD TO CLOSERS

By now you have an understanding of how important this closing job really is! You, the closer are responsible for a lot more than just your own income. You control the sale from the moment you are introduced to the customer. If you blow it, it is doubtful if anyone will be able to step in behind you and save the deal. Once you enter the picture you are the last person the customer intends to work with and your salesperson is dependent on you to make them money. Others who benefit *directly* from your abilities are the new and used car managers, desk managers, service and parts departments, detail personnel, mechanics, the dealer, and the list goes on.

So, you see that you have a lot more at stake than just your own success. I do not say this to over-emphasize the importance of the closer's position, but rather to show you how much of an effect you really have. This is why you're paid the big bucks!

You also need to dress for success! Dress as well as you can! Look like a manager!

You are your team's mentor, their godfather, not their drinking buddy that goes out partying with them after work and keeping them from the quality time their families need! It is only through you that they can prosper. Always share your techniques and your secrets of closing; push them hard and don't allow them to be late, and hold their feet to the fire, even if you think they'll resent you! You must *create winners*! If your people aren't making all the money they can, it's your fault!

Remember; when you are promoted to closer, you no longer can afford to be lazy! Your job now is to make your people successful! If this sounds like a tremendous amount of work, it sure as hell is! It is probably one of the most grueling and yet the most rewarding positions I can think of; but only if you take it serious and give it your all!

I won't wish you luck, because you no longer need it! Make your own!

GLOSSARY OF TERMS

3 on the tree — Old 3-speed column shift.

4 on the floor — Standard 4-speed.

5,6 — Slang used by loan company as a code to remind the loan officer to use furniture (**Sticks**) for collateral on down payment loan. Like the kids' counting chant; 5, 6, pick up sticks. Pick up sticks on a UCC collateral form.

Advance the clock — This used to happen a lot in Northern states when Canadian residents came to the United States to buy cars. The tariff was much lower on vehicles going into Canada with 750 or more miles, so dealers just put the cars on the hoist in drive with the engine running, and waited for the desired mileage to hit; then the Canadian customer came in for delivery.

ACV — Actual cash value – what the vehicle really goes in the books for. Wholesale; not what book value says.

A.G. — Attorney General.

App — Credit application.

Available sales manager (page) — When this page goes out, the desk needs a closer to go in on a deal, and if not a page for the salesperson's closer by name, it probably means to send a closer behind another closer who's having trouble. It's like yelling "hey Rube" at a circus.

Back end profit — The profit created by the finance manager (**business manager**); sources include finance, insurance, extended warranties, etc.

Back of book — Generally a reference to a vehicle that has a value less than the used car guide's "suggested wholesale value."

BDC — Business development center (phone room).

Beater — Auction piece – not worth taking in trade.

Bird dog — Someone who sends in a customer and generally receives a reward.

Book – book out — Book is what the used car guide in the area says the wholesale and retail values are. I.e. wholesale book may be $20,000, but the true value (**ACV**) may be $16,000.

Bubble — Used when we let a customer leave with an idea that he will get a deal much better than we actually can do. When he returns, we have to "burst his bubble" and get him to accept reality!

Bullpen — Where fresh trades are placed to await for clearance of funds, contracts and titles.

Bump — An increase in payment or price.

Buried — A customer who owes much more on his trade-in than it's worth. If they're really out of line, we say, "They have to 'dig up' to be buried!"

Business manager — Title used to professionalize and disguise the finance manager. Finance is a word not allowed in the sales transaction. Instead we use "carry a balance" or similar word whenever possible.

Butternose the trade — Leave the trade-in out of the picture because the customer owes too much to get out of it; with the idea of letting it go back to the bank as a repossession.

Buy rate — The interest rate the bank charges the dealership. The dealer may then increase this rate to the customer and receive the difference as profit. Normally the dealer may raise this rate up to three percent over the buy rate; if the customer holds still for it.

Cherry — Perfect car – hardly broken in.

Cherry picker — Salesperson who sits back and waits for "select" ups and only takes one when it looks ideal; such as the elderly couple in a several year-old car.

Chisler — A customer who negotiates beyond reason for every last dollar.

Chute — Another term for the auto auction.

Clock — Odometer reading.

Close — To negotiate a deal until the customer buys it. The deal is done (closed).

Closer — The assistant manager or sales manager who negotiates for the "house."

C-note — One hundred dollars.

Co-jock — Cosigner or co-maker.

Credit bandit — Customer with really bad credit.

Curbing — Salesperson is selling his personal vehicle to a dealer's customer.

Dealer trade — Where dealers swap new, untitled vehicles to assist one another. Each dealer pays the other's exact invoice amount.

Demo — Demonstrator or demonstration. A "**demo**" drive, or if a manager is supplied a company car as a perc, he or she has a "**demo**."

Desk — Person in charge of the deal (sales manager).

Downer — Same as **sewered**.

Downstroke — Amount of cash available for the down payment.

Eyeball — A vehicle with a beautiful appearance – a showpiece.

F & I — Finance and insurance.

F & I guy — Person who handles finance and insurance.

Finance reserve — Potential profit made by raising the interest rate the customer will pay over the dealer's "**buy rate.**" This difference is paid to the dealer in stages, as the finance interest is earned while the rest is held in reserve by the bank in case the contract becomes prepaid, in which case the dealer's participation ends.

Flake — Someone with bad credit.

Fleet (sarcastic) — *Full List (price) Each and Every Time!*

Fleet department — Generally just one person who works with business accounts; or *anyone they can get.*

Flip — Another word for **turn** or turn-over.

Float — When a dealer sells a vehicle and gets paid for it by cash or on a finance contract, but does not pay it off at the bank that handles his flooring "**floorplan.**" This is a dangerous practice and generally indicates a big problem at that dealership.

Floor check — Inventory checks of a dealer's "**floorplan**" done by the bank at random to make certain that any unaccounted for vehicles are paid off to keep a dealer "in trust." If a dealer has sold vehicles that he has not paid for, he is "**floating**" and may likely be immediately shut down.

Floorplan — New and used vehicles that are available for sale on a dealer's lot and that his bank advances the money for him to operate with. The bank holds the titles for collateral. Most dealers need this line of credit in order to stock enough product to keep them in business.

Floor whore — A salesperson who spends all their time "grabbing ups" and who never follows up or prospects for business.

Fluff & buff — Detail of a vehicle. Clean and wax.

Four square — Basic structure of initial offer.

FNG — F*#king new guy.

A **Franklin** — A $100 dollar bill.

Front end profit — The profit made on the selling of the vehicle and added accessories sold by the sales department.

Geesel — One thousand dollars.

Geitas — Money.

Get ready — Place where sold vehicles are cleaned and "prepped" for delivery.

Going for the throat — After a trial close (see **testing the water**); if the buyer seems receptive, then life a wolf, we tear out the jugular!

Got the blinders on — Customer's excitement where they can only see the good parts; like blinders on the sides of their eyes.

A **Grant** — A $50 dollar bill.

Grape — Person who is easy to "pick their pocket."

Gray market car — Brought in to the United States outside of regular importing channels, i.e. factory, to avoid tax and tariffs. These are difficult to license! This happened primarily with Mercedes and other expensive imports years ago.

Grinder — Standard transmission.

Gross — The gross profit on which you receive a commission.

Guts — Vehicle's interior. Interior fabric choice; leather or cloth.

Gypsy — An ethnic group or wholesaler, generally from Romania. Entire families (tribes) work in teams; all in the wholesale car business. Almost a generic term.

Hammer the check — When the salesman is sent to the customer's bank to get cash for the down payment check. Done mostly when the manager feels the customer may **"come out of the ether,"** and when he does he may stop payment on the amount to try and negotiate further.

Heat & ice — Heater; from the days where manufacturers built cars for the Southern states without heaters and for the Northern states without air conditioning to keep costs down.

Hit — A trial close.

Hit figure — The starting offer on the trade allowance (low).

Hold check — The customer writes a check that the dealer holds for an advance date for deposit when the funds will be covered.

Holdback — An amount added into a dealer's invoice to indicate a higher "cost." This **holdback** is then automatically deposited into the dealer's account (by the manufacturer) the minute an **RDR** (retail delivery report) is entered in the computer.

A Hole in the roof — Moon roof or sunroof.

Home run — Huge profit – all there was!

Hunskee — One hundred dollars.

Ice — Air conditioning.

Ink — get the ink — Signed contract.

Invoice — The amount a dealer pays the manufacturer for the vehicle, but not necessarily the true cost. Dealer incentives plus holdback will still come back to the dealer.

Jack (Jack-off) — Someone wasting your time.

Jonesin' — High on drugs or adrenalin.

Keeper — In reference to a trade-in that the used car manager will keep on the lot for retail sale.

Kick the trade — Try to work a deal without the trade-in, because he either wants too much or he's buried. Note: Convince him to buy now and sell the trade himself.

Kiss the paper — Dealer guaranteeing the finance contract to the bank. If the customer defaults, the dealer pays off.

Knock — A decrease in value, payment or price.

Lay down — One who "flops over" on the first "**pencil**" and buys whatever we present to him.

Lessee — Person who leases.

Lessor — Lease company.

Liner — Salesperson who is "on the line" (selling).

Loaded — A vehicle with most all equipment/options.

Lookie-Loo — Someone who just always seems to "just be looking" and can't decide.

Lot attendant (porter) — All-around "gopher" to shuttle vehicles; basically used by the sales manager to do all the "grunt" jobs around the sales department; wash cars for delivery, run errands, pick up lunch, etc.

Lot lizard — Lot attendant. Referred to as a "porter" in many stores.

Maven — Yiddish term to describe their custom of bringing along an advisor for negotiating and moral support (third base coach).

Mooch — A detestable individual who keeps negotiating for trivial amounts.

Mouse House — The old term for the finance company who made "down payment" loans to buyers. The words "mouse 'em" meant to procure the money required by the bank by having the customer "secretly" borrow it. Collateral for the loan was often their furniture and belongings (**sticks**). Also called the **trap**, as in mousetrap.

Mr. Brown (page) — Pages like this were often a signal to the sales staff that a call was coming in on a special number. This was a number only used for ads such as; "Call Mr. Brown for a free credit check." Customers calling for **Mr. Brown** would be answered only by certain people who specialized in credit challenged customers.

Mr. and Mrs. Gross — A couple driving in who look like they will be easy and solid buyers, and who will produce a large gross profit.

M.S.O. – Manufacturers statement of origin — The vehicle's "birth certificate."

Mullet — A low on the food chain buyer – bad credit.

Music — Stereo.

Net-net — The dealer's true cost of a vehicle; invoice minus **"holdback,"** minus factory incentives.

Nickel — Five hundred dollars.

Note — Seldom used anymore, but was a promissory note used when a check was not available, and redemption by the customer had to be made before payments began. Also references a check.

Odo — Odometer reading.

One legger — Person whose spouse is not there, but will be involved in the buying decision.

Open floor — Situation where salespeople are free to come in to work when they are off shift. Those scheduled need to be there, but the sales are "open" to other salesmen as well.

Pack — An amount added to the invoice or cost of a vehicle on which the dealer will not pay a commission. Example: If a vehicle cost is $20,000.00 and there is a pack of $600.00, it means that the salesperson will be paid on profits over $20,600.00. There is zero commission paid on the first $600.00 of profit.

Qualify — To ask enough questions to determine a customer's needs and wants, and to ascertain what it will take to sell him a vehicle.

Pencil — The offer from the "desk" to the buyer.

Pickie — A pickup payment to be made before the regular payments begin; generally secured by a **"hold check"** and used for additional down payment.

Pink slip — The title to the vehicle. The term often used by managers in other states, but originated in California, as that was the color of their titles. Managers in other states adopted it to "sound cool." As in, "get the pink."

Plain Jane — Stripped car – see Sally Rand.

Potlot — Used car lot with cheap "**beater**" cars.

Pounder — Big **swat**, a large profit. Better than average gross profit.

Pulling my chain — See Jack.

Queege — Small dollar amount.

Rattle can — A spray can with either paint or clear lacquer to improve the appearance of a car or cover up mistakes, flaws and damage.

RDR — Retail delivery report. Note: Sent to the manufacturer. Triggers the warranty (new only).

Reader — A check or promissory note.

Recourse — Done when the dealer has so much potential profit in a sale that he guarantees the bank the customer will make the payments, or the dealer will pay off the contract after the bank repossess the vehicle and returns it to the dealer. **Recourse** can be partial (certain amount of payments) or full; the entire length of the contract. This was used mainly by the really "fast track" operators where the bank would fund anything the dealer wrote. Such high volume operations didn't have time to discuss each contract; they just "rolled" anything; called "**kissing the paper.**"

Red guts — Red interior.

Reg (registration) — A document to show where the vehicle is licensed and titled. Includes address, county and state.

Ring — Auto auction.

Roach — Bad car.

Roll — Delivery of a vehicle.

Rolled around by a two-bitter — Shopped to other dealers for higher bid by a wholesaler.

Roof — Sunroof or moon roof.

Rotation — Term for method of taking **ups**. Rotation means taking customers in turn, and rotating to the back of the sales line.

Rubber — Tires.

Sally Rand — A very basic auto – no extras, no add-ons. Note: Sally Rand was an early burlesque dancer and actress who had been accused of dancing nude; thus the other term, **stripper**.

Scratch a reader — Write a check.

Sewered — Down in the dumps. Bad attitude.

Sheep — Customer who is all too willing to follow to the slaughter.

Shop — Service department.

Shut — Slang to **close**, or complete the sale.

Shutter — Closer.

Skate — **Skater** — A salesperson who jumps in front of another salesperson.

Slammer — A closer.

Sled — A car of marginal value.

Slider — Power moon or sun roof.

Snakes — Anything that is not completely understood or properly explained that could go wrong if discovered by the customer.

S.O.T. or **sold out of trust** — Where a dealer has sold a vehicle and not paid it off on his **floorplan**. This is also called "running a float" and is a very serious problem that will have a bank shut down the operation.

Special finance — A separate department in the dealership whose people only deal with credit challenged customers. They specialize and become an indispensable asset to a dealer whose regular finance managers don't want to endure the enormous work necessary to babysit these lengthy transactions.

Spin the clock — Roll back the odometer to decrease the indicated mileage (illegal). Many odometers could not easily be set back, so they spun them ahead to go all the way around and back to zero.

Straight sell — Where the salesperson works the entire transaction with instructions from the manager. If additional help to close the sale is required, the manager goes out as a courtesy.

Sticks — Furniture – sometimes used for collateral when customer obtains financing for their down payment.

Still in the crate — The old "woody" station wagon.

Straw purchase — Person buying the vehicle for someone else; mostly because of the actual recipient's credit.

Stripper — Stripped model – no extra equipment.

Strokes — Monthly payments (make the strokes).

Switch — Where it is necessary to lead or force the customer to select a vehicle different from the one he initially wanted to purchase.

System — We all have a system, but in the car business it refers to the liner-closer (system house) operations.

Swat — Same as **pounder**. Big gross profit.

Tags — Current registration and expiration.

Taillights — The old saying is that "the deal is never done until you see taillights." The last thing you see as the customer drives over the curb!

Technician — Auto mechanic.

Testing the water — Attempting a huge profit offer, but doing so lightly to take the buyer's temperature. Like sticking only your big toe in the bathtub.

T.O. — **Turn** or turn over, as in hand off the customer to another salesperson or **T.O.** to the manager.

Trade — Car being traded in.

Trade allowance — The figure shown as the amount deducted for the trade-in from the agreed upon purchase price.

Trap — Finance Company (see **Mouse House**).

Trial close — See **testing the water.**

Tunes — Radio.

Turd — See "Beater."

Turn — To "turn over" the customer to another salesperson.

Two-bitter — Old term for a wholesaler from years back who would pick up a car from one lot and go to other dealers to see if he could sell it for at least two bits (twenty five dollars) profit.

Under the ether — Customer is excited about purchasing the new vehicle; like having the anesthesiologist applying the "feel good" medicine.

Up — Customer – (up to bat).

Up money — In reference to a vehicle that is calculated to bring more than suggested "**book**" value.

Upside-down — When a customer owes more on his trade than its' actual cash value (**ACV**).

Warranty clerk (or accessories manager or chemicals manager) — This term changes dramatically, but it is a person who your customers will meet prior to your introducing them to the finance or business manager. This person may spend a couple of minutes discussing the purchase, but their "job" is to *sell* undercoating, paint sealant, and all other accessories on a vehicle.

Write-up — Offer.

W.T. (wretched turd) — Bad trade.

48469138R00207

Made in the USA
Lexington, KY
02 January 2016